THE OTHER
SCHINDLERS

I felt the Jews were being destroyed
I had to help. There was no choice.

Oskar Schindler, 1956

You are a shining light amidst the darkness of the Holocaust;
your stunning bravery is a testament to all humanity.

HE Dror Zeigerman, Israeli Ambassador in London, when presenting
Henk Huffener with his Righteous Among the Nations Medal
3 February 1999

THE OTHER SCHINDLERS

WHY SOME PEOPLE CHOSE TO SAVE JEWS IN THE HOLOCAUST

AGNES GRUNWALD-SPIER

First published 2010
This new edition published 2011

The History Press
The Mill, Brimscombe Port
Stroud, Gloucestershire, GL5 2QG
www.thehistorypress.co.uk

British Library Cataloguing in Publication Data.
A catalogue record for this book is available from the British Library.

ISBN 978 0 7524 5967 7

Typesetting and origination by The History Press
Printed in Malta.

CONTENTS

FOREWORD

It gives me great pleasure to write these few words about Agnes Grunwald-Spier's book about the rescuers. No one can read these pages without a renewed sense of admiration for those who risked their lives to save Jewish lives. Both the stories themselves, and the motives of the rescuers, are examined in this powerful, thought-provoking book, the product of many years of research and effort.

Each story is precious. Each story throws more light into the dark recesses of those evil times. Each story can inspire by its strength of moral purpose.

Agnes Grunwald-Spier makes reference to an important, unavoidable gap in the recognition of righteous deeds. There were many hundreds, even thousands of acts of rescue that failed, mostly through betrayal by a neighbour or a local collaborator, of which no testimony survives: individuals, and even whole families, murdered because they were caught saving Jews. Usually at the very moment of discovery the would-be rescuers and those they were seeking to save were murdered by a savage occupation authority for whom attempting to rescue a Jew was a crime punishable by death. Records of German-occupied Poland show how widespread these reprisal killings were.

Where the names are not recorded, the historian cannot piece together a narrative, and no honour can be bestowed; Agnes Grunwald-Spier rightly calls this a 'tragic fact'.

But this is not in any way a negative book. Its stories are inspiring ones. There is great suffering in these pages, and also great nobility. Agnes Grunwald-Spier has written a book that can serve as a vista of hope for mankind, a modern-day manual for a code of conduct that contrasts with, and can redeem, the selfish, negative, destructive impulses that are still with us today in far too many areas of the globe.

Sir Martin Gilbert
10 March 2010

ACKNOWLEDGEMENTS

A 'thank you' seems inadequate to the large group of informants whose life stories have made this book possible. However, I am most grateful to them for their patience and time and also the information on which this book is based. I started my research in 1999 and so in many cases we have had contact over several years and developed a warm friendship. This book tells their extraordinary stories and I could not have written it without them. Sadly, some of my original informants have died since I initially consulted them but often other members of their family have taken over the role:

John Paul Abranches of California, for information on his father Dr Aristides de Sousa Mendes, a rescuer in Bordeaux. John Paul died in February 2009, but his nephew Sebastian Mendes has provided additional information.

Olympia Barczynska of Leeds, for information on her uncle Jozef Barczynski, a rescuer in Poland.

Judge Moshe Bejski for information on Oskar Schindler, who was himself on Schindler's list and Gabriele Nissim from Italy, for information on Bejski himself and Yad Vashem. Judge Bejski died in 2008.

Primavera Boman-Behram of London and New York, for information on her mother Hilde Holger, and Dr Margit Granz of Graz University for information on her rescuer Charles Petras and exile in India during the Second World War.

Bertha Bracey's relatives and friends – Alma Cureton, Brenda Bailey, Joan Bamford and Pat Webb – for information on the rescuer Bertha.

The late 11th Duke of Devonshire (1920–2004) for information on his father's attitude to Jews.

Miriam Dunner of London, for information on her rescuers Jelle and Elizabeth
van Dyk in the Netherlands. Miriam died unexpectedly in 2006.

Betty and David Eppel of Jerusalem, for information on Betty's rescuers Josephine and Victor Guicherd in France. David died in 2008.

Charles and April Fawcett of London, for information on Charles' work as a rescuer in Marseilles. Charles died in February 2008.
Otto Fleming of Sheffield, for information on Mitzi Saidler, a rescuer in Vienna, and Dr Ho's visas to Shanghai. Otto died in 2007. His widow, Dorothy Fleming, a member of the Kindertransport, has provided additional information.

Milton Gendel of Rome, for information on the Costaguti family who were rescuers in Rome.

Lea Goodman of London, for information on Richard Strauch and other rescuers in Poland.

Rose Marie Guilfoyle of Brussels, for visiting Robert Maistriau to hear about his role as a rescuer and also telling me about Gisele Reich's rescue, both in Belgium.

Gerda Haas of Freiburg, for information on rescuers and for first telling me of Else Pintus' diary about being hidden in Poland.

Agnes Hirschi of Bern, for information on her stepfather Carl Lutz, a rescuer in Budapest.

Manli Ho of San Francisco, for information on her father Dr Feng Shan Ho, a rescuer in Vienna.

Henk Huffener of Guildford, for information on his family's role as rescuers in the Netherlands. Henk died in 2006 but Philip Hardaker provided information on Henk's post-war life.

Margaret Kagan of Huddersfield, for information on her rescuer Vytautas Rinkevicius in Lithuania.

Claire Keen-Thiryn of Belgium, for information on her family's work in the Resistance and as rescuers in Belgium.

Josie Martin-Levy of California, for information on her rescuer Soeur St Cybard in France. Additional help was provided by Daniel

Soupizet of Lesterps, Bernadette Landréa of Confolens and Louis Lacalle, great nephew of Soeur St Cybard.

Ron Mower of Hertfordshire, for information on Hermann Maas, who rescued Martha, his wife, and Paul, his brother-in-law, in Germany. Sadly, Ron died in 2004 and Paul in 2009. I am grateful to Ron and Martha's son Paul for his support.

Henri Obstfeld of London, for information on his rescuers Jacob and Hendrika Klerk in the Netherlands, and Evert Kwaadgras, the archivist of the Grand Lodge of the Dutch Freemasons in The Hague for information on Freemasons.

Benedetta Origo of Sienna, for information on her mother Iris Origo who was a rescuer in Italy, and for telling me to contact Milton Gendel. Frank Auerbach for information on how Iris Origo saved him, and Kate Austin at the Marlborough Galleries for biographical details on Frank Auerbach.

Monica Porter of London, for information on her mother Vali Rácz, a rescuer in Budapest.

Jaap van Proosdij of Pretoria, South Africa, for information about his rescues in the Netherlands.

Maria Sanders of Poole for information on living in the Hague during the war, particularly the 'Hunger Winter' of 1944.

John Schoen of Glamorgan, Wales for information on his parents Joost and Anna, who were rescuers in the Netherlands. John died in 2007. I am grateful to his son Peter Schoen, his nephew Ed van Rijswijk of Amsterdam, and Arleen Kennedy of Massachusetts, whose mother was hidden by the Schoen family, for additional information.

Angela Schluter, for information on her mother Edith Hahn-Beer's story of rescue in Austria.

Doris and Ernest Stiefel of Seattle, for information on Else Pintus and her rescuers in Poland.

Naomi Szinai of London, for information on her rescuers, in particular János Tóth, in Hungary.

Margarita Turkov of Oregon, for information on her paid rescuer Pani Borciñska in Poland.

Henry Walton of Worksop, for information on the rescuers of his parents, Siegmund and Grete Weltinger, in Berlin.

Professor Irena Veisaite of Vilnius, for information on her rescuer Stefanija Ladigiené in Lithuania.

Additionally, there are several other people I'd like to thank here. Three people in particular encouraged me through the long and difficult times between research and publication: Emeritus Professor Aubrey Newman of Leicester University was a kind advisor and also helped with proofreading; Kevin Patrick was a consistent support; and my dear friend Brenda Zinober held my hand through some difficult times. All three were always there for me when I needed their support.

I would also like to thank Sir Martin Gilbert for his support over many years and for kindly writing his generous Foreword when he was so busy with the Chilcot Inquiry.

Thanks go to the staff of the British Library, the Freemasons' Library, the Friends' House Library, the Wiener Library and Yad Vashem for their help, and Phil Jacobs, Tom Keve, Bernadette Landréa and Hamish Ritchie for their translations from Italian, Hungarian, French and German respectively.

This book would never have happened without the input and encouragement of: Robert Smith, who helped me write my book proposal and introduced me to Daniel Crewe, who pointed me in the right direction; my editor at The History Press, Simon Hamlet, and his team of Abbie and Christine, with Hazel, who aided the promotion of the book, who all gave me faith in my work and made publication a very pleasant process; my middle son Ben, who helped in many practical ways, as well as my other two sons Dan and Simon; all three encouraged me when I flagged. Finally, I remember with affection and gratitude my history mistress from Sutton High School, Miss Lucy Clarke (1903–93), who gave me a love of history which has enriched my life.

Inevitably, even with all this help, there will be mistakes and these, I am afraid, are mine alone.

Agnes Grunwald-Spier
Sheffield and London

INTRODUCTION

One morning in Budapest, during the autumn of 1944, an unknown official in charge of deporting Hungarian Jews to Auschwitz sent all the women accompanied by children back to their homes. My mother, Leona Grunwald, was one of those women – and I was a tiny baby in her arms.

I have no means of knowing who that official was and what his motives were for what he did. I cannot know his name or his fate, but it is chilling to think that but for his actions, on arrival at Auschwitz I would have been tossed into the fires with other babies – murdered before I was aware of life. His actions helped both of us to survive the Holocaust.

As George Eliot wrote in the final sentence of Middlemarch:

> For the growing good of the world is partly dependent on unhistoric acts; and that things are not so ill with you and me as they might have been, is half owing to the number who lived faithfully a hidden life, and rest in unvisited tombs.[1]

The actions of the Holocaust rescuers are truly one of the lights in that great darkness – many of the rescuers do lie in 'unvisited graves', unrecognised by Yad Vashem or anybody else. Their bravery will no longer be remembered with the death of those they rescued, merely with the passage of time or even because their rescue attempt failed with tragic results for all concerned. This book attempts to record their courage and understand the motivation of those who had the insight to know what was the right thing to do and the courage to do it, whatever the personal risks.

Stories of the heroism of rescuers have been told by many in the sixty-five years since the true horror of the Nazis' policies became apparent. Even now, however, many still remain untold. There is very little time, as the baby born in July 1944 is now 65; anyone who was an adult witness to the Holocaust will be over 80. Time is running out: for example, Hilde Holger, who responded to my plea for information aged 95, died before I could meet her, but her daughter helped me instead (see p. 167). Additionally, many of those who provided information and stories have not lived to see this book published. Even the children of rescuers and survivors are ageing. It was vital that this task was completed before it was too late and I, as a fortunate survivor, felt an obligation to attempt a small part of it. Encouragement came from the Talmud:

> Rabbi Tarphon said, The day is short, and the work is great, and the labourers are sluggish, and the reward is much, and the Master of the house is urgent. He also used to say, It is not thy duty to complete the work, but neither art thou free to desist from it.[2]

The question may be asked: what is the point of investigating such stories that are now over sixty-five years old? What is their validity in today's world and for us in the twenty-first century? Certainly the story of the rescuers is one of the few optimistic aspects of the Holocaust. My interest in the subject was aroused by my dissertation on Varian Fry for my MA in Holocaust Studies at Sheffield University (1996–98). I had come across Varian Fry accidentally, through seeing a BBC documentary about him in June 1997, and became so interested in what he achieved that after I had completed the MA, I felt that the motivation of rescuers in general was a subject I should like to research further. I wanted to examine what moved rescuers to take enormous risks, risks not only for themselves but also their families, to save someone's life at a time when normal moral standards of democratic life were suspended under the Nazis.

Varian Fry was not the stuff of which heroes are traditionally made. Yet he was for many years the only American recognised as a Righteous

Among the Nations – he chose to involve himself in another continent's woes. He crossed the Atlantic Ocean to become embroiled in Europe's horrors. He was an unassuming man who, after the fall of France in June 1940, offered to go to Vichy France to rescue refugees for the Emergency Rescue Committee (ERC). He only offered to go if nobody else could be found and he went because nobody else was found. He was meant to rescue 200 artists and writers on a list produced by the ERC, using visas obtained by President Roosevelt's wife Eleanor. In the end, he probably saved about 4,000 refugees. On his return to America, after thirteen months, he wrote about his experiences. When the book was finally published in 1945, he explained why he had agreed to go on such a perilous venture:

> After several weeks of fruitless searching for a suitable agent to send to France, the Committee selected me. I had had no experience in refugee work, and none in underground work. But I accepted the assignment because, like the members of the Committee, I believed in the importance of democratic solidarity.[3]

However, he also had other reasons. He wrote about his warm sentiments towards many of the writers and artists whose work had given him pleasure:

> novelists like Franz Werfel and Lion Feuchtwanger; painters like Marc Chagall and Max Ernst; sculptors like Jaques Lipchitz. For some of these men, although I knew them only through their work, I had a deep love; and to them I owed a heavy debt of gratitude for the pleasure they had given me. Now that they were in danger, I felt obliged to help them, if I could; just as they, without knowing it had often in the past helped me.[4]

Fry cited his sympathy for the German and Austrian Socialist Parties, based primarily on their excellent workers' housing projects of the 1920s. 'I had not always agreed with their ideas or their methods, but I knew when I saw those housing projects that their hearts were in the right place.'[5]

But earlier experiences as a journalist were highly influential. Fry had visited Germany in the 1930s and thus had an insight shared by few of his countrymen:

> Finally, I knew from first-hand experience what defeat at the hands of Hitler could mean. In 1935 I visited Germany and tasted the atmosphere of oppression which the Hitler regime had brought. I talked to many anti-Nazis and Jews, shared their anxiety and their sense of helplessness, felt with them the tragic hopelessness of their situation. And while I was in Berlin I witnessed on the Kurfuerstendamm the first great pogrom against the Jews, saw with my own eyes young Nazi toughs gather and smash up Jewish-owned cafés, watched with horror as they dragged Jewish patrons from their seats, drove hysterical, crying women down the street, knocked over an elderly man and kicked him in the face. Now that that same oppression had spread to France, I could not remain idle as long as I had any chance at all of saving even a few of its intended victims.[6]

Although some of this was reported in the *New York Times* on 17 July 1935, with the byline 'Editor describes rioting in Berlin', the most horrific incident was recorded by fellow American Mary Jayne Gold. Mary was a wealthy socialite who met Varian in Marseilles and funded some of his rescue activities:

> At a café, Varian watched a pair of storm troopers approach the table of a Jewish-looking individual. When the poor man reached nervously for his beer, with a quick thrust of his knife one of the storm troopers pinned the man's hand to the wooden table. The victim let out a cry and bent over in pain unable to move. The ruffian shouted something about Jewish blood on German blades, withdrew the knife, and swaggered away. Varian heard him say to his companion, 'this day is a holiday for us.'
>
> Varian told me the story in a low, mumbling voice, as he often spoke when he was deeply moved. I think the mental image of that hand nailed to the table beside the beer mug had something to do with his decision to go.[7]

My study of Varian Fry and his colleagues, such as Charles Fawcett, showed me that rescuers' motives were not as simple as they some-times claimed. Although they sometimes gave a single reason for their actions, in fact the background to their actions was far more complex. It also crystallised a simple and obvious truth which may become dwarfed in the statistics of the victims of the Holocaust – one person can make a difference.

Conversely, it also underlined the tragedy of the Holocaust. If more bystanders had become rescuers, then the millions of victims would actually have survived and flourished. Oskar Schindler saved 1,100 Jews and at the end of Spielberg's film, *Schindler's List*, the descendants of these survivors appeared – they numbered around 6,000. I am no math-ematician, but on the same basis, if the 6 million Jews murdered by the Nazis had survived they would now have 32 million descendants.

Yad Vashem, the Israeli Holocaust museum and Jewish people's living memorial to the Holocaust,[8] has now recognised 23,226 non-Jews as Righteous Among the Nations[9] (see Table 2). It should be noted here that not only these Righteous Among the Nations helped Jews in the war. Belated recognition is now being given to Jews who helped Jews, but many others fought different battles. The Righteous scheme was devised specifically to recognise non-Jewish rescuers, and very strict criteria have to be met. It cannot reward other forms of courage, as in the controversy over Dietrich Bonhoeffer, who Yad Vashem acknowledges as 'a martyr in the struggle against Nazism' but has not yet been proved to have 'specifically helped Jews'.[10]

On 2 February 1996 Varian Fry was named as the first American 'Righteous Among Nations' by Yad Vashem. The American Secretary of State, Warren Christopher, acknowledging the posthumous honour nearly thirty years after Varian's death in 1967, said: 'We owe Varian Fry our deepest gratitude, but we also owe him a promise – a promise never to forget the horrors that he struggled against so heroically, a promise to do whatever is necessary to ensure that such horrors never happen again.'[11]

Walter Meyerhof, who with his parents escaped from France over the Pyrenees with Varian's help, established the Varian Fry Foundation in 1997. Its purpose is to teach schoolchildren the lessons outlined by Warren Christopher and, as Walter explained to me, to demonstrate that 'one person can make a difference'.[12] Walter's father, Otto Meyerhof, shared the 1922 Nobel Prize for Medicine with A.V. Hill, who was later to become Secretary of the Royal Society 1935–45. In 1933 Hill became involved in the Academic Assistance Council (AAC), which helped scholars and scientists from abroad escape the Nazis.

Many rescuers seem surprised that what they did was of interest to anybody else. Modest expressions such as 'what they did was normal or anyone would have done the same' are quite common; loyalty to old friends or good employers are frequent reasons, as is opposition to the Nazis' policies, if not necessarily being the result of wanting to save Jews. Others saw such rescue as an integral part of being in the Resistance or the logical result of their parents' upbringing. Many books have examined the background of rescuers and tried to find patterns of behaviour based on class, education or other similar sociological reasons. Perry London was one of the first to study this topic in the 1960s. He noted three main characteristics of rescuers. He specified a spirit of adventure, a sense of being socially marginal and intense identification with a parent of strong moral character. Such categorisation is unsatisfactory because for every rescuer who falls into the neat boundaries of his category, another one pops up who defies them. The most common reasons noted are religious beliefs or perceiving that it was one's duty to help another who was in trouble. Other reasons are the sanctity of life, obeying one's conscience or shame at not helping a neighbour.

By examining the motivation of several rescuers who may not previously have been written about, it is possible to establish why some bystanders to the Holocaust became rescuers and why so many remained bystanders. An understanding of what influenced their behaviour has relevance today, when the need to support each other in society still exists even if the circumstances are, thankfully, quite different. Naturally, I am aware that whilst the Jews were numerically by far the major target of the Nazis' racial policies, many other groups were targeted for persecution and murder. My concentration on the Jewish Holocaust is not intended to diminish or ignore their suffering.

I was determined from the start to write about rescuers and the rescued whose experiences were not particularly in the public domain.

As a single parent living in Sheffield, I therefore needed to find a way of making contact with people who had not necessarily been approached before. In August 2000 I targeted journals and magazines which would be read by people likely to have personal experiences of the Holocaust, or who might know of others with a story to record, and asked them to publish details of my research. These were:

> *Common Ground* – the Journal of the Council of Christians and Jews (CCJ)
>
> *Jewish Telegraph* – a regional Jewish newspaper published in Glasgow, Leeds, Liverpool and Manchester.
>
> *Menorah* – a magazine for Jewish members of HM forces and small Jewish communities.
>
> *Information* – The Magazine of the Association of Jewish Refugees.

I also attended two major events where I arranged for each delegate to receive a copy of my project details in their conference pack. These were the Oxford Holocaust Conference *Remembering for the Future*, held in July 2000, and the European Council of Jewish Communities Presidents' Conference, held in Barcelona in May 2000. One of the Italian delegates at the latter conference wrote an article for *Shalom*, the journal of the Rome Jewish Community.

Additionally, contact was made with the South African Jewish community through my friend Brenda Zinober, and all the members of the Leeds-based Holocaust Survivors Friendship Association (HSFA) were also circularised.

In 2002 the London Jewish Cultural Centre held an exhibition called 'Visas for Life' about diplomats who between them saved about 250,000 Jews from the Nazis. The opening event gave me an opportunity to meet John Paul Abranches, son of de Sousa Mendes,[13] who lived in California, and Agnes Hirschi, stepdaughter of Carl Lutz,[14] who lives in Switzerland, with whom I had been corresponding for some time.

Other rescue stories were accumulated through the press, in particular *The Jewish Chronicle* and obituaries in *The Times*. Some have been purely as a result of social conversations and sheer coincidence. I attend a lot of meetings and when, in response to enquiries about what I do,

I tell people about my research, quite often they can name someone I should contact. There has certainly been a snowball effect over the last few years. I was surprised at being criticised for stating that these stories were collected at random – I find this odd. Collecting stories about Holocaust rescuers cannot be done in the same way as researching the consumption of fish fingers. Extraordinary stories turn up in the most unlikely ways.

In July 2004 I was in Brussels for a meeting at the EU and wondered if someone bilingual would speak to Robert Maistriau,[15] a rescuer who only spoke French, for me. One of the EU secretaries consented and subsequently in conversation told the driver assigned to us what she had agreed to do for me. He quite spontaneously told her that his mother, Gisele Reich, had been saved from deportation to Auschwitz at the age of 5 in 1941 because the Nazi officer at the transit camp at Malines (Mechelen) felt sorry for her – she was a sickly child who suffered from a lung disease. The driver had never mentioned this to anyone outside his family before and the story would not have come to light but for my request for help and this chance conversation.

My efforts resulted in the creation of a group of about thirty rescuers/rescued from a variety of countries, where I have had personal contact with either the rescuer or the rescued, or their child or other close relative. This has enabled me to pursue the question of motivation directly, by questioning someone extremely close to or actually involved in the events described. Some of these people have also written books about what happened and these have been referred to in the text. Nevertheless, additional specific information has always been obtained by interview (face to face or by telephone), e-mail or letter, and these are all detailed in the footnotes.

The book consists of four parts. The first three contain the narratives of the rescuers and those they rescued. These are categorised by their expressed motivation – religious convictions, humanitarian motives, being a member of the Resistance, feelings of loyalty to the rescued and paid rescuers. The final section discusses the relevance of these events to our lives today and attempts to understand what turns a bystander into a rescuer.

This book is a personal attempt to show the general reader the reality of the Holocaust. This is particularly important now, when the Holocaust is being regularly denied and its scale continually trivialised. Additionally, we are seeing a swing to extreme right-wing politics. When I talk to young people about the Holocaust I ask them to remember four things:

1. Six million innocent Jews were persecuted and murdered through sheer hatred, including 1.5 million children.
2. They were killed in many different ways and places. The Holocaust did not just happen at Auschwitz but included ghettoes, labour camps and special shooting raids.
3. Survivors and their families still suffer the impact of the Holocaust more than sixty-five years on.
4. A simple change of attitude or behaviour could ensure that this will not happen again – a small act of compassion and decency shows you have learnt the lessons of the Holocaust.

This book aims to record the remarkable stories that were entrusted to me. Indeed, many of my informants have died since they contacted me. I hope that I have been able to do justice to their stories and also offer some insight into what made this remarkable group of people turn from being passive bystanders into rescuers during one of the darkest periods in human history.

On 10 March 2010, the Prime Minister Gordon Brown honoured a pledge he made on a visit to Auschwitz in 2009. He recognised twenty-eight British Heroes of the Holocaust who were awarded a silver medal engraved 'in the service of humanity' above clasped hands. I was delighted to be present as, aided by some forceful lobbying by me, Bertha Bracey (see p. 23) and Henk Huffener (see p. 132) were included on the list. Bertha's great niece Pat Webb, with her husband Donn and daughter Delia, received Bertha's medal, and Henk's daughters Clare and Josephine, who I only tracked down on Friday 5 March, received Henk's medal.

As I revised my research for publication during the closing months of 2009, I was awaiting the birth of my first grandchild and inevitably

I thought about my parents and their experiences in the Holocaust. I also wondered about my maternal grandfather, Armin Klein, who refused to leave his native land, and was murdered in Auschwitz around the time of my birth. James Harry Spier (Jamie) was born in London on 1 January 2010 – the great-great-grandchild of Armin and Rosa Klein, and Eugenie and Malkiel Grunwald, and great-grandchild of my beloved parents. Had the unknown official not sent my mother and me back, our line would have ended in 1944. With this in mind, I ask the reader to follow the Biblical exhortation, which Jews everywhere read every year at the Passover meal, telling the story of the flight from Egypt. In the book of Exodus (13:18) it is stated: 'And you shall tell your son on that day ...' If the true horror of the Holocaust and the amazing courage of the persecuted and their rescuers is remembered and re-told to the next generation, is it not possible that people may consider their own views and attitudes, and perhaps create a far better world for everyone?

My father, Philipp Grunwald, was so embittered by his experiences as a forced labourer that he wouldn't bring any more children into the world after the war and he committed suicide in 1955, leaving my mother Leona to bring me up alone. However, I am blessed with three wonderful sons, Daniel (father of James), Ben and Simon, and a lovely daughter-in-law, Michelle. I can only hope that the world in which they bring up their families will never see such horrors again. Perhaps then all the victims of the Nazis – like my grandfather Armin Klein – and all those other millions may not have died in vain?

1

RESCUERS WITH RELIGIOUS MOTIVES

Quakers were amongst the most active group of rescuers which saved Jews in the Holocaust. This was recognised in 1949 by the award of a Nobel Prize for their humanitarian efforts to both the British Friends Service Committee and its American counterpart.[16] The Quakers, so named by Judge Bennet of Derby because they trembled at God's word, have a history of helping social causes and those in need of humanitarian support. They look only to the Almighty for guidance and have no priests or hierarchy of clergy acting as the conduit to God:

> Fundamentally, Quaker worship precluded all hierarchy and transcended principles of political governance. The primary quest was for divine enlightenment, not secular liberty, the overriding belief being that the divine spirit can touch and communicate, ending any separation between the individual and God. Without sermons or sacraments, without clerical intercession, each participant in the silent meeting speaks in his heart to God and, at the same time, to his neighbor. Quaker theology begins and ends as personal experience.[17]

The Quaker religion is different to most, lacking a formal structure; followers take responsibility for themselves. They do not wait to be told what to do or be led by a clergyman; neither do they assume that someone else will deal with a problem.

Bertha Bracey OBE (1893–1989) was a Quaker Englishwoman who had a profound influence in rescuing Jewish children from the

Holocaust in what became the Kindertransport. She was born and brought up in Birmingham where she became a Quaker when she was 19 years old.

> When I joined Friends I was deeply grateful for the joyous discovery of the Quaker business procedure, which at its best combines the virtue of democracy, and is yet theocratic. Our lives as human beings are set in two spiritual dimensions. Upwards toward God, and outward toward the community and the life of our world.[18]

She was the seventh of eight children. All the family were intelligent, but it was only Bertha who received an education because by the time she was born the family had a bit of spare cash. Additionally, all the children except one inherited their father's character. He was very forthright and always knew he was right.[19] No doubt these qualities stood Bertha in good stead in the years ahead.

She attended Birmingham University and spent five years as a teacher. In 1921 she left teaching to go to Vienna to help Quaker relief workers who ran clubs for children suffering from deficiency diseases. Whilst there, her German improved and in 1924 she moved to Nuremberg as a youth worker. From 1926–29 she was based in Berlin. She was subsequently recalled to Friends House in London to do administrative work relating to Quaker centres in Europe. She was to become the central point of a network of help for persecuted Jews coming to Britain.[20]

Because of her time spent living in Germany, Bertha had a very clear view about the situation there. As early as April 1933 she reported: 'For the moment the forces of liberalism have been defeated, and in the March elections fifty-two per cent of the electors voted National Socialist.' She was perhaps more perceptive than many commentators when, within weeks of Hitler's election, she commented on the tragedy of the Jews in Germany based on her own recent visit to Frankfurt for the German Quaker Executive Committee:

> Anti-semitism is a terrible canker which has been spreading its poison for decades in many Central European countries. It came to a head in Germany on April 1st, when Germany dropped back into the cruelty

of the 'Ghetto' psychology of the Middle Ages. The very yellow spots used to indicate Jewish businesses and houses is an old mediaeval symbol. Words are not adequate to tell of the anguish of some of my Jewish friends, particularly of those who have hitherto felt themselves much more German than Jewish; who had in fact almost forgotten their Jewish blood. What cruel fate is this that suddenly snatches them up from German soil and leaves them aghast, hurt and rootless, to find themselves ringed about with unreasoning hatred and calculating cruelty? Jewish doctors, teachers and social workers who have given generously of their skill and devotion suddenly find themselves treated as pariahs cut off from any means of livelihood.[21]

This showed a very full understanding and enormous empathy for the plight of the persecuted Jews. Her close friendship with the Friedrichs influenced her knowledge. Leonhard Friedrich, from Nuremberg, had an English wife called Mary. They had met when he was working in England before 1914 and were married at the Sheffield Friends' Meeting House on 3 August 1922. They were active Quakers and involved in a Quaker relief centre funded by the American Friends Service Committee (AFSC), set up through the intervention of President Hoover, himself a Quaker, who was worried about the impact on Germany of the repara-tions imposed by the Treaty of Versailles. These reparations caused great hardship and malnutrition and President Hoover asked the AFSC to organise a large-scale school feeding scheme and 11,000 centres were opened. This help was badly needed and continued as the hyper-inflation of the 1920s aggravated the situation.[22]

The Friedrichs suffered considerably for their faith and their daughter, Brenda Bailey, has described her mother's response to early anti-Jewish activity:

On 1 April 1933 Hitler ordered a boycott against all Jewish businesses. My mother, Mary Friedrich, decided this was the day on which she would show solidarity with Jewish shopkeepers. We both walked into town. That day it was easy to recognise Jewish stores because they were marked with a yellow circle on a black background, and a brown uniformed SA man stood guarding the entrance. As we tried to go in he would warn us of the boycott, but Mary passed by him, saying she needed to speak to the owner. That evening the cinema showed news-reel film of the boycott, where Mary and I were seen entering shops and the commentator saying that some nameless disloyal people chose to defy the boycott.[23]

This was an extremely courageous act by Mary Friedrich, but further difficulties were to follow. Quakers were sympathetic to the Jews so early on, as, in 1933, many German Quakers lost their jobs because they would not sign the loyalty oath; amongst them was Leonhard Friedrich. A welfare fund was created to help such unemployed Quakers and those still in work contributed.

Bertha was very active in Europe in the 1930s. 'It was Bertha's task to interpret what was happening in Germany to the world outside. So she travelled three or four times a year to listen and to strengthen Quaker links in Germany, Holland, France, Austria, Czechoslovakia, Switzerland, Norway and Sweden.'[24]

Her experiences led her to become involved in the creation of the remarkable Kindertransport enterprise. It became apparent from Germany that desperate parents were willing to send their children away if this would save them from the Nazis. Wilfrid Israel, a member of a wealthy Jewish retail family that owned N. Israel, one of Berlin's oldest and best-respected department stores, was involved in the early planning. His mother was English and that meant that when German Jews were in danger, he was able to exploit both his business and English contacts to help them flee.[25]

Jews seeking to flee could try the Jewish Agency's Palestine Office to get to Palestine, or the newly created umbrella organisation Reich Representation of German Jews (*Reichsvertretung der Deutschen Juden*), finally set up in September 1933 and led by common agreement by Rabbi Leo Baeck. The two largest groups were the Central Committee for Relief and Reconstruction and the *Hilfsverein der Deutschen Juden* (Assistance Organisation for the German Jews). The *Hilfsverein* helped Jews with the procedure of emigration, advice on visas, con-tacting relatives abroad and, if necessary, finding money for tickets and so on. Wilfrid Israel was one of the most prominent members of the *Hilfsverein*.[26] Rabbi Leo Baeck's nephew, Leo Adam, was one of Wilfrid's employees in the store. One of his friends was Frank Foley, whose job as passport control officer was a cover for his real role as MI6 head of station in the German capital. Wilfrid and Frank had been friends since the 1920s when Frank, as a junior consular official, had helped Wilfrid's father, Berthold Israel, obtain a visa to join his wife in London, where their daughter Viva (Wilfrid's sister) was dying. Their friendship was to prove extremely useful for the fleeing German Jews, and Foley himself is now credited with saving 10,000 Jews.[27]

On 15 November 1938 Wilfrid Israel cabled the Council for German Jewry in London and gave them 'details of the problems facing the community, and proposed the immediate rescue of German-Jewish children and young people up to the age of seventeen'. As a result, Prime Minister Neville Chamberlain was approached and, although he was non-committal, the proposals were discussed in the Cabinet the next day. The council decided someone needed to meet Wilfrid Israel, and because it was unsafe for a Jew to travel to Germany, five Quakers agreed to go instead and meet him in Berlin. Ben Greene, who was one of the five, accompanied Bertha Bracey to the meeting with the Home Secretary, Samuel Hoare, on 21 November 1938. 'Greene testified to the plea of the German parents and their readiness to part with their children.'[28]

That very night, in the House of Commons, Samuel Hoare announced that the government had agreed to the admission of the refugee children using Ben Greene's evidence, and the first party of 200 children arrived from Germany on 2 December 1938. Meanwhile, Ben Greene returned from a second visit to Germany and reported that 'the Jewish suicide rate was now so heavy that "the Mainz town authorities have turned off the gas in every Jewish house"'.[29]

Bertha herself noted her efforts more modestly:

After the pogrom in November 1938, I went with Lord Samuel to the Home Secretary, Sir Samuel Hoare, and obtained permission to bring ten thousand 'non-Aryan' children to this country. When concentration camps were being opened up at the end of the European War, I went with Mr Leonard Montefiore to the War Office and persuaded them to put at our disposal 10 large bomber planes, which, with the bomb racks removed, enabled us to bring 300 children from Theresienstadt, Prague, to England.[30]

The UK and its government had no excuse, even in pre-war 1939, for claiming not to know what was happening in Europe. As early as 1936 a book detailing 'the outlawing of half a million human beings: a collection of facts and documents relating to three years' persecution of German Jews, derived chiefly from National Socialist sources, very carefully assembled by a group of investigators', was published by Victor Gollancz. Its introduction was written by the Bishop of Durham, Hensley Henson. He concluded on 12 February 1936:

> As one who has had rather special reasons for holding Germany in high regard, who has an unfeigned admiration for her intellectual achievements, who has often in the past visited with delight her historic cities, and recalled the wonders of her history, I cannot bring myself to believe that the persecution of minorities, and among them specially the Jews, which now stains the national name, can be more than a passing aberration. The publication of this book will, I think, hasten the return of sanity by making yet more vocal and insistent the protest of the civilised conscience itself, that protest which not even the most passionate nationalism can permanently resist or will finally resent.[31]

The Secretary of State for Foreign Affairs had published a Command Paper in 1939 which included several documents listing the horrors occurring in Germany. The introduction refers to the excuse provided by the German government when His Majesty's Ambassador in Berlin made a complaint in 1933 about the 'violence and brutality of the Nazis'. They claimed they regretted the incidents 'but regarded them as unavoidable in the first ardour of revolutionary fervour':

> This plea cannot be put forward to excuse events that occurred five years after the advent to power of the National Socialist Party. It is evident from the published documents, which cover only the period from 1938

onwards, that neither the consolidation of the regime nor the passage of time have in any way mitigated its savagery.[32]

However, even this evidence failed to find overwhelming support. The *Daily Express* commented, 'there is crime and cruelty among the citizens of every nation', and the extreme right-wing weekly *Truth* hinted that it might all be 'a Jewish invention'.[33]

After 1939 Bertha's role changed and she dealt with those refugees that had arrived in the UK and were being interned as enemy aliens. Government policy changed following the fall of France, Belgium and Holland. There was greater fear of invasion and what was called 'fifth column' activity, which led to thousands being interned, and this included both men and women, some of whom were sick. This caused those refugees tremendous personal problems and the refugee bodies combined to create a Central Department for Interned Refugees (CDIR). Bertha Bracey became the chairman and dealt with different government departments to resolve these issues, such as 'the unsuitability of ordinary prisons for internment, the possibility of children joining their mothers as aliens, the provision of married quarters, and the whole business of relief from internment'.[34]

The most important area was the Isle of Man where most aliens were interned – there was a maximum of 10,000 internees during the Second World War. Bertha visited the two women's camps to see for herself the true situation. She found there were only six members of staff dealing with hundreds of internees and suggested they should use volunteers as an interim measure. She also found that those released did not have the money for the journey back to the mainland, and the elderly and infirm, or those who spoke little English, needed help on arrival. Bertha persuaded the CDIR to help out and this resulted in those with special needs receiving financial assistance.

Bertha Bracey was a courageous woman who had an unerring instinct for what needed to be done. She had started her work in Europe as a young woman in the early 1920s: 'Her main challenge was to encourage youth in exploring new attitudes towards international peace and personal responsibilities in the new democratic Weimar republic.'[35] Her faith as a Quaker made her strong and one of her favourite phrases was 'hold on tight'.

The phrase 'hold on tight' might be recalled as a mother's behest to her child or a needed instruction in the early days of the motor car; but Bertha would urge it is also a reminder that there are times in our lives when we need to hold on tight to our faith. And, as we reflect on the dark times she lived through, we know that she spoke from the depths of experience.[36]

Her knowledge of Germany gave her great influence in the early days of Hitler's regime. 'Bertha was one of three or four British Friends who were able to exert pressure through eminent people in church and state both in Britain and Germany in order to secure the release of individuals in political custody.' She was awarded the OBE in 1942 in recognition of her work for refugees, and she was generally recognised as having achieved much in creating the Germany Emergency Committee (GEC) as its secretary from April 1933. On 25 April a Case Committee was appointed, and it reported on 3 May that it had eighteen cases under review. By September 1939 it had 22,000.[37]

Her work with the GEC from April 1933 was summed up:

> Bertha Bracey had borne the chief responsibility for building up the organisation and for directing its work. Her creative vision, her sympathy for the friendless and persecuted, which she invited many others to share, and her wide knowledge of the refugee problem had had an influence far beyond the confines of Friends House and Bloomsbury House, and had brought her the gratitude of large numbers of those she had helped.[38]

Towards the end of her long life – she was 95 when she died – she wrestled with Parkinson's disease, and when it was particularly troublesome she referred to it light-heartedly as 'Mr Parkinson's visiting again'.[39] Her family did not know a great deal about her doings. There is mention in family correspondence of Bertha going to Poland after the Nazi occupation and bringing out mothers and children. Her niece Alma has written:

Bertha was very reticent and *never* talked about her self-imposed commitments. This last episode – re Poland, cannot be verified I don't think – it's sort of word of mouth. Friends certainly backed her and her rescue team but it was all obviously hush hush and the family really knew nothing about her activities ... A brave and far-sighted woman with remarkable organizing ability. She had high standards.[40]

She was an inspiration to many, even towards the end of her life. A letter sent to her, dated 1 April 1988, refers to the words of one of her carers in the nursing home: 'She is wonderful, we are supposed to minister to her but she ministers to us. Whenever I feel a bit low a visit to Bertha bucks me up in no time.'[41]

'Is there anything I can bring you?' asked a visitor of hers in the nursing home during her last days. Bertha roused herself from a partial slumber to the alertness we remember so well. 'Yes,' she responded, 'bring me glad tidings of great joy.'[42]

In July 2001 a sculpture representing the family was installed and dedicated in the courtyard of Friends House in London. It was sculpted by Naomi Blake, one of the victims of the Nazis saved by the Kindertransport. Its plaque reads:

To honour Bertha Bracey (1893–1989)
who gave practical leadership to Quakers in quietly rescuing and re-settling
thousands of Nazi victims and lone children between 1933–1948

Charles Fawcett (1919–2008) was born in Georgia in the USA into a privileged Virginian family, descended from Huguenots on his mother's side and Washington and Jefferson on his father's. He had a difficult start as the family home was burnt down five days after his birth and his mother died when he was 5, followed by his father two years later. He was therefore brought up as an Episcopalian by his mother's sister – Aunt Lily Shumate – in Greenville, a small town in South Carolina. Consequently, he grew up as a Southern gentleman of the old school:

His romanticism, sense of honour, attitude to women, enormous charm, modesty, old-fashioned courtly manners, are all a product of the acceptable face of the old South. His accent remains that of the Virginia gentleman and he has sincerely subscribed to its rigid honour code all his life – the reverse of the narrow bigotry often attributed to the South.[43]

Charles, who lived in Chelsea for many years, told me he was brought up to help people and to be a Good Samaritan. He said his hometown was a place of just one religion, where although there was segregation, black people were well treated because there were no plantations. Charlie recalled that his aunt had two black servants who lived in the family home, and when he came back from school he went to see them before he saw his aunt. Everybody in the sleepy little town had the same ethics and he grew up knowing he had to do the right thing. The people of Greenville 'were really good people who helped each other'.[44]

April Fawcett, Charles' wife, discovered a letter from Charles' mother, Helen Hortense. Helen had married late in life and had four children after the age of 40. She developed breast cancer and was treated in the Mayo Clinic in Baltimore. A month before she died she wrote to her sister Lily entrusting her with the upbringing of her children. In the poignant letter, dated 5 June 1922, she wrote: 'I thank God that I can leave my babies with someone who cares for them and will love them and make them mind too. Please always make them obey you, dear, and when they are grown they will be glad to tell you of your having made them mind.'

I think poor Helen Hortense would have been astounded to learn what a wonderful job her sister Lily made of bringing up Charles. She would have been truly amazed to know how many people he helped during his long and colourful life. It has been suggested that his early experiences influenced the whole of his life:

It is not over fanciful to suggest that the pattern of his entire life – the quest for the most elegant and elevated of women, the immersion in the romance and glamour of Paris, Rome – as well as remote portions of the jungles of the Congo and the Amazon, was fashioned from memories of his unhappy childhood. Always responding to causes of the underdog, deliberately seeking out hardships and dangers – restless and adventurous, he treated the natives of the Sahara with the same courtesy that he showed to the members of the various royal families with whom he became close friends over the years – trusted and admired by one and all.[45]

Charles was a 22-year-old art student in Paris when the Germans invaded France. He had worked his way around Europe using his assorted talents to keep himself; apparently he received tips on his trumpet-playing from Louis Armstrong and learnt wrestling from a professional. He had joined the American Ambulance Corps in 1938; later on in the war his flatmate Bill (William Holland) told him a lot of wounded British troops were being sent to Germany in a few days. Bill was half-German, through his mother who was a German aristocrat, related to the German commander-in-chief of occupied France, which was how he knew what was happening. Bill and Charles 'borrowed' an ambulance from the Ambulance Corps garage, rescued the troops from their hospital and set off for free France. It is alleged that on leaving the hospital Charles told the POWs, 'Gentlemen, consider yourselves liberated.' A British voice shouted, 'You're a Yank.' Charles responded, 'Never confuse a Virginian with a Yankee.'[46]

After several adventures they ended up in Marseilles and Charlie remembered that he knew a Countess Lily Pastré, whose family home was just outside the city. She took the prisoners in but sent Charlie into town where he met up with Varian Fry.[47] Charlie's countess had started an organisation called *Pour que L'Esprit Vive*, which still exists today. It was created during the economic and social crisis of the 1930s to help artists and intellectuals who were often living in precarious conditions. As the war and occupation progressed, she devoted her magnificent home and fortune to sheltering artistic exiles who were mostly Jewish. She protected the harpist Lily Laskine (1893–1988), the pianists Youra Guller (1895–1981) and Monique Haas (1909–87), and the Czech painter Rudolf Kundera (1911–2005) lived with her for three years. She also paid for medical care for the Romanian Jewish pianist Clara Haskil (1895–1960), and in 1942 helped her escape to

Vevey in Switzerland. Since 1963, a prestigious piano prize in Clara Haskil's name has been awarded every two years.[48] It is said that she also housed the Spanish cellist Pablo Casals (1876–1973), who was a Catholic, and the famous black American dancer Josephine Baker, who found fame in France.[49] After the war, Josephine was honoured by the French government with the highest Medal of the Resistance (with officier's rosette) and made a Chevalier of the Legion d'Honneur for her work in the Resistance – which included smuggling secret messages written on her music sheets.[50]

Charlie says he did not know anything about Jews as a young man because he did not come across any until he was a young art student in Paris. One day Jewish students were involved in a fight, and to help them out Charlie kicked a table over. Some considerable time later he met them again, in Marseilles, and they told him about Varian Fry and his work with the refugees. Charlie became impressed with Fry's work and joined his team of workers. He told Fry how shocked he had been at discovering German anti-Semitism. Whilst his story was not as dramatic as Fry's experiences in Berlin in 1936, it obviously shocked him. He had been in a café where Jews had been drinking coffee. When they left, he saw two German officers point to the cups and say, 'Take these away and sterilise them.'[51]

Varian wrote with obvious great affection about Charlie:

> Charlie was a youngster from the South – Georgia, I think – who had been doing 'art' work in Paris before the war. I put that word in quotation marks because as far as I could see Charlie's conception of art consisted of drawings of pretty girls, preferably nude. He had many feminine admirers, and there was always at least one of them in the office as long as he worked for us …
>
> As a doorman, Charlie had one great drawback. He couldn't speak anything but English, and most of the refugees didn't speak any English at all. But his ambulance-driver's uniform awed the over-insistent ones, and his good nature cheered the depressed among them. If few understood what he said, none disliked him. In fact, I think he was probably the most popular member of the staff.[52]

Charlie was an impressive figure in his army greatcoat. Mary Jayne Gold, the young American heiress who bankrolled some other rescues, described her first meeting with him in the Hotel Continental as she made her way down a broad flight of stairs into the hotel lobby late one afternoon:

> up the stairs flapped a large khaki of definite military cut. Inside was a very tall young man with hair of about the same sandy colour as the coat. Another fellow of normal proportions and dress followed him. Instinctively, I retreated a few steps. The tall one introduced himself as Charles Fawcett, then presented his friend, Dick Ball. He glanced around to see if we were out of earshot and made me take a few steps back until I was pressed up against the wall. Leaning beside me as if we were already hiding from the police, he told me he had learned that I had an airplane, so he had come right over. I looked at his well-cut boyish features and curly light hair while he disclosed in a soft Georgia accent that he and his friend wanted to fly to Gibraltar. He was visibly disappointed when I told him that I had left my plane in Paris.[53]

She described him as 'doorman and reception clerk' at the new office on Rue Grignan. He told her that he kept order when people got 'nervous' and then bent over and spoke in a lower tone. 'I'm really the bouncer just in case anybody gets in there that doesn't belong.' He stood up straight 'and drew his magnificent khaki coat together. "See? It sort of impresses people. I've had to cut the brass buttons off – but it still looks official … almost."' Mary said, 'It sure does.'[54]

The situation had to be fluid and Charlie wasn't just a bouncer. In September he and his chum Dick Ball were escorting groups of the younger and more experienced Resistance workers over the low mountains near the coast to the Franco-Spanish border. This became one of the regular escape routes, often led by Lisa and Hans Fittko. According to Varian, at least 100 people were estimated to have escaped that way in the six months that followed.[55]

In December 1940 Charlie left Marseilles whilst Varian was in Vichy trying to help those on his list who were trapped in camps. The area of Vichy France contained 120 concentration camps, containing about 60,000 civilian internees, and between 25–35,000 forced labourers and foreign workers, often in appalling conditions. 'It seemed like the whole of the unoccupied zone was one great, heartless prison.'[56]

Charlie had become aware that the police knew of his work for the French Resistance and for security it was time to move on. Varian later described the preparations for Charlie's departure:

Charlie had been loaded down with secret papers and reports, including some for the British … Since he was a sculptor they had simply put some of the reports in the heads he had modeled, and Charlie had poured in wet plaster to seal them up. One of the most secret reports, listing the Spanish Republican refugees in hiding in France, and urging visas for them, had gone in to the third valve of Charlie's trumpet. Charlie had tightened all the valves with a wrench covered with a cloth and had learned a couple of tunes he could play without ever having to use the third valve, in case any questions were asked. Still other reports had been pasted into the rim of his suitcase.[57]

He made it over the border, but was closely questioned by the French police. Charlie, ever the enterprising art student, saw a prostitute lounging in the railway station and had the idea of drawing a few pornographic sketches which he distributed through his luggage. As the French police searched his possessions they were side-tracked by these sketches and, in their amusement at what they had discovered, failed to look for any other items and waved him through. As he went through Charles was unsure how to behave.

I started thinking what is the best thing to pretend – I think a dog with his tail between his legs – I was ashamed. All I wanted to do was jump in there and click my heels. When I got to the door going towards Spain, I looked back and they were passing it round, roaring with laughter.[58]

Although he arrived at his Barcelona hotel safely, he was arrested later by the Spanish secret police. They took him back into France and handed him over to the Gestapo in Biarritz – Charlie Fawcett, 21-year-old smuggler of secret papers for the Resistance.[59]

Charlie worried, as he sat for hours in a corridor waiting to be interrogated, that the documents he carried could lead to him being executed. Suddenly the door opened and he saw a high-ranking German officer quickly march down the corridor, closely followed by someone who was quite obviously a French informer. Charlie snatched his chance: 'The Germans were so arrogant, that they couldn't even bring themselves to look at the people who were collaborating with them.' He opened the door for the German officer, who of course ignored him. Charlie joined the pair, with his luggage and trumpet; he just tagged behind as though he was part of the group and walked into the street. He walked into the station, boarded a train to Madrid, and the next day he was delivering the papers to the British Embassy military attaché, Colonel William Wyndham Torre – known to his chums as 'Bunny'.[60]

Mary Jayne also reported this story: 'He was arrested in Spain and released probably because, like me, he had an innocent air about him and kept playing several hastily composed airs so charmingly that not even a trained musician would notice that he never pushed the third valve.'[61]

A few days later, while safely in Lisbon waiting for a ship to England, he met one of his wives – Lilian Fawcett. Marriage was one of Charlie's unique methods of rescuing Jewish women incarcerated in camps:

As they were going past the Ritz Hotel, the Nazi HQ in Paris, he met a woman he knew whom he suspected of being a collaborator. She asked him if he was still single, which he thought was a bit odd. When he said he was, she asked him to marry a girl in a camp through a French lawyer. In fact, he married 5 girls in the course of about 10 days from French and Dutch camps. The lawyer was in the underground. Two of the wives were Hungarian, one was Polish and one was Bulgarian.

Charles Fawcett has said of Hitler, some people were glad he never got the atomic bomb. 'I'm glad he never even got the computer,' said Charlie, 'so he could keep track of who was marrying whom. If he had,' said Fawcett, 'the Gestapo would have barged in on my second wedding; and not as "best man" either!'[62]

Gaston Deferre was a young lawyer who was helping Varian Fry in his rescue work. In the 1980s he became Francois Mitterand's Minister of the Interior, but one of his strangest tasks must have been helping to organise the papers that enabled Charlie to marry the six Jewish women in concentration camps. Once they were married to an American, they were automatically entitled to leave France with a US visa. Charlie married six women in three months. After the war, Charlie met someone who had worked in the Lisbon Consulate who wondered at the endless stream of 'Mrs Fawcetts'.[63]

Lilian Fawcett was an opera singer, the daughter of a famous Hungarian conductor Dr Alfred Sendrey. When Charlie saw the poster with her name on it in Lisbon:

> Charles wondered, on a long shot, if it might be one of his many cousins from the South. He went to the theatre the following evening where a beautiful woman with a superb voice sang popular operatic arias. Charles went backstage to 'try his luck'. The beautiful creature took one look at him and gasped with emotion – she was one of the women he had married in order to rescue from the camps, now fully restored to health and with a full head of hair. This resulted in the only honeymoon he had with any of them – consummated on the observation car of a train speeding through the stormy night en route for Oporto.[64]

Charles only met two of 'his wives' in person as they were paper marriages. He met the other one later in Israel when he was the guest of Shimon Peres. However, he did hear that two of them had turned up at the same time in Lisbon and the Ambassador to Portugal's wife, Mrs Herbert Pell, helped Charlie at that time: 'She thought it was very romantic.'[65]

Charles always stressed that it was Varian Fry who inspired him – 'Varian Fry was completely idealistic and courageous – inspired us all'.[66] In April 1991 Varian Fry was honoured by the United States Holocaust Memorial Council and a book of tributes was written by his Marseilles colleagues. Charles Fawcett wrote how Varian had inspired them all, even occasionally encouraging some Gestapo agents to turn a blind eye. The poet Walter Mehring, who had written anti-Nazi poetry and had ten of his books publicly burnt, joined Varian's group and said: 'It gives you hope … courage … just to be with him.'[67] 'I was scared to death half the time. I can truthfully say that I did not do anything out of courage. I did it because I was ashamed to let Fry down.' Charlie always said he was only a gofer; he concluded: 'A brave man is one who realises the danger, fears it, but does not let it prevent him from doing what he has to do. Varian knew. But he did it.'[68] April Fawcett has revealed since Charlie died: 'Varian and Charlie were petrified the whole time they were in Marseilles as it was so incredibly dangerous for them, even though they were not Jewish, and their lives were very much at risk.'[69]

Charles Fawcett was a rescuer who helped people all his life. In 1945 he fought with the French Foreign Legion in Alsace and was awarded the *Croix de Guerre*, he fought with Greek partisans against invading communists 1947–48, in 1956 he helped Hungarian refugees escape into Austria, four years later he was rescuing refugees from the Belgian Congo with a friend who had a plane[70] and in 1979 he went to Afghanistan to help the Afghans fight the Soviet invaders.[71] He was involved there through most of the 1980s and when he died Lord Salisbury wrote to April praising Charles' influence on world events at that time.[72]

Charlie suffered from tuberculosis early in life which caused him to spend considerable time in hospital. He never allowed the disease to stop his courageous adventures which were interwoven with his very full film career. He made 100 plus films over a 25-year period, appearing twice with Sophia Loren; he knew Orson Welles and William Holden, and in Rome, where in the 1960s he was known as the 'Mayor of Via Veneto', he is alleged to have been Hedy Lamarr's lover.[73]

In January 2006 Charles and April were present at the National Holocaust Memorial Day event in Cardiff, where Charlie's courage was honoured and they were introduced to the Prime Minister, Tony Blair, and his wife Cherie (*see plate 3*). Tony Blair also wrote to April when Charlie died, praising his courage and saying what an honour it had been to meet him.[74]

Helen Hortense, Charlie's mother, would have been gratified to know how well her request had been followed. Charlie was certainly brought up to 'mind' and he did so all his life with the world as his concern. When he died in February 2008, aged 92, he had lived a truly full and remarkable life. His personal charm stayed with him to the end and I am proud to have known him.

Carl Lutz (1895–1975) was born on 30 March 1895, the ninth child of Johannes and Ursula Lutz. Christened Karl Friedrich, he called himself Charles when he was in America, and later in Palestine he became Carl. His father owned a sandstone quarry just below where they lived in Walzenhausen, in north-eastern Switzerland. He was brought up as a Methodist. His mother was very devout and an active teacher at the local Sunday school. She was a very strong influence on him all his life. When he found himself in the dilemma of trying to save the Jews of Budapest, he prayed to God and decided God had sent him this mission.[75] Although he brought his stepdaughter Agnes up as a Methodist, she says that he lost faith and became distanced from the religion. It has been stressed that his mother was no religious bigot:

> She insisted that they finish school and learn a trade, so that they would not have to depend on others. Reflecting on the poverty of the Appenzell hill country, she would admonish her offspring that it was more important to help those in need than to always run to prayer meetings. Her pietism was combined with a spirit of social protest against the 'higher ups' who allowed injustices to subvert what had been a democratic way of life.[76]

Johannes died of TB in 1909 when Carl was 14. Carl was not a bookish child and left school aged 15 to become an apprentice in a textile mill in the next village. As a young man of 18, in 1913, Carl Lutz left Switzerland to emigrate to the United States. Four years later, when America mobilised for the First World War, he did not wish to be called up and became a fugitive for three months evading the recruiting agents. 'He wrote later that when he looked into the faces of Budapest Jews nearly thirty years later, he knew what it meant to be trapped.'[77]

From 1918–20 he studied at the Methodist Central Wesleyan College in central Missouri, but he soon became bored with the limited scope of the 'prairie college' and in 1920 he left and joined the staff of the

Swiss legation in Washington DC. He had embarked on his diplomatic career. At 29 he was ready to return to Europe, but fate kept him in America and in 1934 he met his first wife Gertrud. After a traumatic courtship they were married in January 1935, and were due to settle in London when an emergency caused the Swiss Foreign Ministry to send him to Jaffa in Palestine on the very evening of their wedding:

> Curiously, shortly before they parted, at the end of the wedding reception, Ursula slipped a piece of paper into her son's hand. She was now in her eighties, and her handwriting was becoming shaky. She had written a passage from the prophet Isaiah: 'And he shall be a father to the inhabitants of Jerusalem and to the house of Judah.' Perhaps his mother had a presentiment.[78]

Gertrud and Carl loved their time in the Holy Land and travelled extensively in their first year there. However, in 1936 trouble erupted and in Arab Jaffa, where they lived, they were often taken for Jews. One day they were both trapped in their apartment whilst they watched an unarmed Jewish worker being lynched by an Arab crowd. They were too frightened to come out to try to save him. They felt traumatised by their failure to save the man and the brutality of the attack: 'During the same period Lutz heard tales of Nazi horrors from newly arrived German Jews. Why was the supposedly enlightened twentieth century falling into such unspeakable brutality? His sympathy swung over to the Jews.'[79]

It was Moshe Krausz, head of the Palestine Office in Budapest and responsible for distributing 'the few legal certificates for Palestine that the JA [Jewish Agency] managed to send to Budapest prior to the German occupation',[80] who initially managed to persuade Vice-Consul Carl Lutz to issue protective documents or *Schutzpass* (*see plate 8*). It was also Krausz who used 7,800 supposed individual exit permits to save 7,800 families – about 40,000 people. These documents were later copied by Raoul Wallenberg for the Swedes, and by other neutral nations for smaller numbers of Jews. In fact, there was no emigration but the idea of issuing protective documents was recognised as a way of saving large numbers of Jews in Budapest.[81] However, it must be remembered that it was Carl Lutz who initiated this policy in Budapest.

As a committed Christian, he really struggled with the situation he found in Budapest. The Hungarian government had initiated its own anti-Semitic legislation even prior to the Nazi invasion in March 1944. Men like my father were recruited for forced labour from March 1942. As early as 1920 the government had introduced Law XXV, which imposed the 'numerus clausus' on the universities which restricted Jews to 6 per cent of the student body. It is mentioned in the obituary of the late Professor Tibor Barna, who came to Manchester in 1937, that 'one of the benefits of a foreign university was the chance to escape the institutionalised anti-Semitism of pre-war Hungary, which imposed a quota on the number of Jews going to university'.[82]

The local Protestants were no help. Laszlo Ravasz was a bishop in the Hungarian Reformed Church and a keen Magyar nationalist. As early as 1938, as a member of the Upper House of Parliament, he had voted in favour of anti-Jewish measures. His sermons were broadcast weekly and always contained an anti-Semitic statement, either referring to Jews as having killed Christ or refusing to accept him as the Messiah:

> Moreover, the bishop broadcast that the Jews were strangers to Hungarian society, and that they dominated the nation's economy and the liberal professions far beyond their true number. There was nothing in all this which was not being said by others. But the radio sermons of Ravasz, which came on the air week after week, year after year, helped to transform ordinary anti-Jewish popular prejudice into theologically and intellectually acceptable anti-semitism.[83]

His influence was both great, as Horthy, the Regent of Hungary, was a member of his parish, and catastrophic:

> Without realizing it, during the fatal pre-war years, Ravasz helped to remove the intellectual barriers against the physical elimination of the Jews. If Ravasz and some of the other church leaders had followed the example of the German Confessing Church and of other religious resistance movements in Nazi-dominated parts of Europe, the record

of Hungarian Christianity and perhaps of the Hungarian nation during World War II might have been different.[84]

In these circumstances the broadcasts made from England by William Temple, the Archbishop of Canterbury, in May 1944, and others in the spring and summer of 1944, to Hungary asking for help and support for the Jews were probably ineffective. The Hungarians were warned they would be treated as war criminals if they indulged in atrocities on the German scale and were encouraged to follow the example of the Danes who helped their 7,000 Jews escape.[85]

Many Protestants welcomed Hitler's appointment as Chancellor as a day of liberation, but the imposition of nationalist policies and the attempt to subordinate the independence of the churches to a centralised Reich church led to tensions which split the German Protestants. The German Confessing Church emerged in 1933 from Dr Martin Niemöller's 'Pastors' Emergency League', which was created precisely to defend orthodox Protestant dogma.[86]

The Catholic Church was divided in its response. Papal Nuntio Angelo Rotta protested to the Hungarian Foreign Minister on 27 April 1944:

> The Holy Father, he said, was very sad because he saw that Hungary, a Christian nation, was going against the teachings of the Gospels. On May 15 he again protested against the deportations, which had just begun. But he could not persuade the Cardinal Primate, Justinian Seredi, who instead wrote a pastoral letter that agreed with anti-Semitic measures and aimed to protect Jewish converts to Christianity from deportation. The letter was suppressed by the government, though it was read out in some churches, belatedly, on July 1.[87]

Carl Lutz is credited with saving 62,000 Jews when he was the Swiss Consul in Budapest. The situation in Budapest threatened his religious faith and traumatised him. When in the late spring of 1944 he realised what was happening to the Jews, the premises on which he had based himself collapsed and the existence of Auschwitz disrupted his concept of life:

The well-ordered and purposeful universe had vanished, and nothing else was taking its place. In Carl Lutz's pietistic/humanistic worldview, every event, insignificant as it might be, had been part of a meaningful puzzle, a movement of history, which would ultimately complete itself at the end of times, when Jesus Christ returned.[88]

In later life Carl Lutz did not write much about his wartime experiences in Budapest, but in 1961 he wrote an article for the leading Swiss journal, the *Neue Zuercher Zeitung*, known as *NZZ*.[89] He described a situation in which he found himself late in 1944:

Five thousand of these unhappy people were standing in line, freezing, shaking, hungry, with tiny packs on their shoulders, stretching their letters out towards me. Never, never shall I forget those despairing horror-stricken faces. Again and again the police had to intervene to prevent my clothes being torn from my back. For these people it was the last glimmer of hope; for us, this screening was the worst form of spiritual torture. We saw the people being lashed with dog-whips and lying in the slime and mud with bloody faces. Whenever we tried to help them we, in our turn, were threatened with rifles. Whenever possible I would drive alongside these people on their way to the concentration camps to try and show them that there was still hope, until my way was blocked by the guards.[90]

However, Lutz's efforts began to unravel to some extent. The Arrow Cross fascists realised that many Jews had forged documents and, late in November 1944, 'the government declared that they would no longer recognise them'. On one occasion they even forced Lutz and his wife to go to a concentration point where Jews were being gathered for a (forced) march, and false papers were separated from genuine ones.[91]

Lest it should be presumed that diplomats were safe from danger, Lutz described the last weeks of the German occupation. He was forced to stay in Budapest as the Hungarian Nazis had promised not to attack the protected Swiss houses as long as he himself stayed in the city. He and his wife were living in the British Legation building on the summit of Buda:

For weeks we had to live in a damp unheated cellar in the middle of winter, often without candles or water, and very little food. We had to endure fierce attacks from the air for hours at a time. We received nineteen direct hits from artillery and aircraft. On one occasion a couple of incendiary bombs set fire to our building, which blazed for two days and nights with us in the cellars underneath. And while it was burning, twenty armed Nazis burst in and robbed us of most of our private possessions.

When they emerged into a Budapest occupied by the Russians, 'it was like a ghost town'. One of the employees of the Swiss Legation was deported to Russia and Carl only escaped being shot by leaping through a window.[92]

His stepdaughter has summed up Carl Lutz's motivation:

The laws of life are stronger than man-made laws. My father was grown up in a Methodist family in the eastern part of Switzerland and he was the second youngest of ten children. His mother, who was a very strong woman with ethics and social engagement, was the main person and example during his whole life.

Later in Budapest, as an engaged Christian could not tolerate the Jews being pursued and killed, he could not tolerate injustice. He was a deeply religious man and felt he had to protect and help these people. He was not born a hero; he was rather shy and introverted. He launched his mission to save the Jews in Budapest out of his religious and moral convictions. He risked his life and career; he ruined his health working and stressing about the fate of the Schutzbrief-holders day and night. My father always considered his time in Budapest and the rescue of innocent Jews as the most important part of his life.[93]

Agnes Hirschi has noted that whilst her father had been bitter about the failure of the Swiss authorities to recognise his wartime activities, he never regretted his actions. 'He was a committed Christian and felt he had been sent to Budapest for a purpose.'[94]

Hermann Maas (1877–1970) was a Heidelberg pastor who helped many Jews escape from Germany during the Holocaust. His actions caused Rabbi Leo Baeck to describe him as 'our most faithful Christian friend through the entire Hitler period'.

Hermann Maas came from a family of Lutheran pastors but as a child his best friends were Jewish boys. He was a young vicar on holiday in Switzerland in the summer of 1903 when he saw a 'group of bearded, gabardined Jews, who talked in a foreign idiom, while walking through the streets of Basel'. He followed them, out of sheer curiosity, and found himself in the Sixth World Zionist Congress and witnessed a turning point of Zionist history. It was the so-called 'Uganda Congress' where the desperate Theodore Herzl urged his followers to accept the British government's offer of land in East Africa. However, Chaim Weizmann led the opposition to this scheme and persuaded the Congress to adhere to the original scheme to claim Palestine as the national homeland. 'Dr Maas still recalls the memorable scene when Herzl, raising his right hand and reciting the immortal words "If I forget thee, O Jerusalem …", admitted defeat by swearing allegiance to Zion.'[95]

Hermann Maas left Basel a convinced Zionist and attended every subsequent Congress he could manage. He became the friend of Jewish intellectuals and in 1933 visited Palestine, where he was entertained by the Weizmanns and met the poet Bialik. In the same year his eldest daughter Brigitte, an artistic weaver by profession, went to Jerusalem, where together with Ahuva Pickard, the daughter of David Yellin, the writer and educator, they opened a weaving shop which she managed until the outbreak of the Second World War, at which time she was deported because of her German nationality.

Hermann was invited to stay in Palestine, but he knew he would have work to do and returned home to Heidelberg where storm troopers harassed him and tried to stop him entering his church. It was only help from influential English friends that enabled him to keep his parish, but he had a very difficult time for the next six years.

He was noted as a visible dissident on the issue of the position of non-Aryan Protestants (Jews who had converted to Christianity) as early as 1935. The two main factions of German Protestantism both decided not to support Jewish converts and 'This renders instances of individual dissent among their clergy all the more memorable'.[96] It was only the Quakers and the Jehovah's Witnesses amongst the 'Free

Churches' who supported these unfortunate souls: 'Baptists endorsed legislation excluding Jews from national society; Mormons posted "Jews not wanted" signs at their church doors; Methodists agreed that Jews were a threat to German society; and Adventists shunned members encumbered by Jewish ancestry.'[97]

In fact, the Jehovah's Witnesses suffered greatly for this policy. They felt unable to conform to Nazi demands because of their beliefs. In July 1933 they were proscribed for refusing to join the Nazi Party and in 1935 for refusing military duty. Jehovah's Witnesses 'refused to give the Hitler salute because their religious beliefs taught them that such a salutation was due only to their God', and this also led them to refuse to bear arms.[98] Their men were taken to concentration camps, marked by their purple triangles, and 5,000, more than a third of their membership, were killed:

> If we look at the behaviour of other minority Christian and secular groups in the Third Reich, we see, on the whole, a fairly speedy and ideological revolution. Some members of small religious groups hailed Hitler as the Messiah and others expunged from their liturgy all references to anything 'Jewish'. Thus hymns and liturgies were amended to omit the words 'Sabbath' and 'Jerusalem'. Others were prepared to hand over to the Nazis the names of any of their members who had Jewish blood.[99]

Their behaviour stands unique amongst German Protestants who deserted Jewish converts:

> As a formerly Jewish physician, who had converted to Protestantism in 1916, put it in 1933: '[My children] have lost the protection that Jewry had always and everywhere provided to its members. They have [received] no protection from the Christian [sic] church, and, I imagine, cannot expect any. They are outlaws as Christians; they are outlawed as Germans. Can one imagine a more cruel fate visited upon the innocent?[100]

Yet this was precisely the fate of Paul Rosenzweig, his mother and sister – shunned by both Christians and Jews. Pastor Maas was one of the few who helped needy non-Aryans with funds supplied by Christians, and one of those he helped was Paul Rosenzweig, now known as Reginald Pringle.

Paul Rosenzweig was born on 18 February 1920 in Altleiningen, in the Rhineland Palatinate. His sister Martha was born in 1927. His mother was born Jewish but she and her children were baptised into the Evangelical Protestant Church.[101] She had brought them up as Christians even though they lived with her father, a practising Jew – Heinrich Rosenzweig. However, 'After 1933 they were all regarded as Jews. The only Jewish family in the locality.'[102]

After Kristallnacht, in November 1938, a mob attacked the home of Paul's Jewish boss and he realised that his turn would soon come.[103] That very evening two burly policemen came to take him away but attempted to reassure him: 'You'll be back home in a day or two. It's only an investigation.'[104] After forty-eight traumatic hours he found himself in Dachau concentration camp. He spent a full three and a half months incarcerated there and was only freed on 23 February 1939, five days after his 19th birthday. He experienced terrible privations and saw awful cruelties perpetrated, which he has recorded in his memoir. On release he had to sign an undertaking not to divulge what he had seen in Dachau. Whilst he had been incarcerated, his sister Martha 'was turned out of school and received no further formal education in Germany'.[105]

Paul's mother and sister were delighted to see him and his mother said:

> I had been released because she, on someone else's advice, advised the authorities that I had all my papers ready to emigrate from Germany. I asked her if she knew something that I didn't know, and she confessed that she had invented this in order to get me home. I wondered how long it would be before somebody wanted to know why I was still here.[106]

As time progressed he realised his mother had been correct – he would have to leave. The family home was 'Aryanised'. The house had been sold over their heads and the new owner, Herr Frank, wanted them out:

Every week without fail, his wife would come to our door, holding her little boy's hand, asking when we were going to clear out. One time I lost my cool and shouted at her 'Soon I hope. Not just out of here, but out of this country too.' The little boy who held his mother's hand, Otwin Frank, is now Mayor of Altleiningen.[107]

He tried to find a way for all three of them to leave. He approached the local Jewish Community Centre, who said that whilst he was not a Jew, they could not offer direct help, but gave him some names and addresses. Two were in Berlin and the third was Hermann Maas in Heidelberg. He wrote to the two in Berlin and made up his mind to go to Heidelberg the next day to find Hermann Maas. He wrote:

I went to his house to meet him for the first time. He had a sad face. His manner was straightforward and I felt here was a man I could trust. We went into his study and once seated he came straight to the point. 'What can I do for you?' he asked. Without reservation I poured out our story to him. When I finished he looked me straight in the eye. The simple words that he spoke are etched in my memory. 'Your worries are over. Your case and your sister's are now in my hands. I shall try to get you out of here as quickly as possible.' It was a wonderful moment. I felt as if the weight of the world had been lifted from my shoulders.[108]

Maas said that England was the best place for them and that he visited London each month to meet Quakers to make arrangements for people like Paul and his sister. However, when Paul asked if his mother could be included, Maas said the priority was children and young people. Maas asked about their financial position and when Paul admitted it was not good, he put 15 DM on the table for him to pick up and said if he needed more whilst waiting to leave just to send him a postcard and specify the amount. 'As I left, he told me he would contact me by post as soon as he had any information. I expressed my heartfelt appreciation and left with the deep impression that I had encountered an angel disguised as a human being.'[109]

True to his word, Pastor Maas told them that Martha would leave on 12 June 1939, from Frankfurt, on one of the Kindertransports. Within a week they heard that she was safely installed with a Mrs Kennedy – a widow in Ayrshire. Meanwhile, Paul had all his papers ready except for the precious exit permit. As he became impatient, he returned to the Jewish Community Centre to seek help. The response of the official left Paul speechless:

> He put a phone call straight through to the Gestapo HQ. 'What are you lot up to?' I heard him say. 'Here's an enemy of the State, a young man whom you are trying to get rid of, who is doing his best to oblige you, and you are keeping him hanging about waiting for his exit permit.' He put the phone down. 'You should have it within the next few days,' he told me. And he was right.[110]

Paul had to leave his mother behind hoping that he would be able to get her out later – but she was deported to Auschwitz in 1942. At the railway station as he left, he saw on the news-stand what he describes as 'a typical Nazi send off. "We are happy to announce the departure from this country of the Jew Rosenzweig. Good riddance! One less mouth to feed."'[111]

One of the truly remarkable and brave things Hermann Maas did was to fix a Mezuzah[112] to the door post of his home, which indicated to all Jews that they would be safe with him. He wrote of that time: 'with full consciousness I at that time wove my own life and fate closely into that of the terrible fate of the Jewish people.'[113] He was remarkably courageous and:

> was outstanding in the way that he made no distinction between baptised and unbaptised, made a point of ostentatiously moving about among the victims of 'Crystal Night' and cheerfully risked arrest and possible death, in order to be able to say a last farewell and words of comfort to his old Jewish friends in full view of the S.S. guards.[114]

Pastor Hermann Maas was part of a network of Christians who, at enormous personal risk, helped those proscribed by the Nazis. The network was led by Heinrich Grüber, who was one of the leaders of the Confessing Church – the part of the German Christian Church that fought Hitler's attempts to subvert their faith. 'Hitler appeared to many inside the Christian church as the saviour of a nation threatened by godless Bolshevism and eroded in its confidence by bad government, international Jewish finance and the will of its former enemies to keep it in subjection.' These Christians were happy to press for the adoption of the Aryan clause in the Church. 'That clause, introduced to exclude from the civil service all of Jewish or partly Jewish descent, could now be used to extrude all Christian ministers having any Jewish blood at all. It was in opposition to this that Dietrich Bonhoeffer first took his stand.'[115]

Pastor Grüber was born of a Dutch mother in the Rhineland and in 1938, when he took the civil servant's oath of allegiance to Hitler – now also demanded of the clergy – he added the reservation 'as long as it does not conflict with the evident will of God'. He gradually found himself involved in helping non-Aryan Christians and after Kristallnacht he became fully committed to this work – eventually employing thirty-five people at his Büro Grüber. Bonhoeffer met George Bell, Bishop of Chichester (1883–1958), in 1933 and came to call him 'Uncle George'. As a result of their friendship and mutual respect, in spite of the twenty-three-year age gap, Bonhoeffer regarded George Bell as one of the two major influences on him, and 'it was to George Bell of Chichester that Bonhoeffer sent the last message of his life as he was led away to the place of execution' on 9 April 1945.[116]

As a result of this relationship, George Bell became a leading influence on British public opinion, and subsequently, in 1937, his sister-in-law Laura Livingstone went to work in Berlin on behalf of non-Aryan Christians and joined Heinrich Grüber's Büro. She wrote about those times and concluded that whilst the November 1938 pogrom – her description of Kristallnacht – had terrible repercussions for Jews:

> Surprisingly, this did a lot of good in forcing the facts on the public abroad, so that overnight opportunities for children and even adults were given for emigration. Some months earlier the Confessional Church, which had been growing increasingly conscious of their position, decided to take action, and appointed Pfarrer (now Probst) Grueber to

organise the care of non-Aryan Christians throughout Germany. Probst Grueber undertook this difficult and dangerous task with the greatest enthusiasm, devoting all his dynamic energies to it with loyal and ready support from other pastors and sympathetic co-operation of the German Quakers.[117]

They worked extremely closely with the Quakers and, according to Brenda Bailey, Pastor Grüber's 'principal partner in Britain was Bertha Bracey'.[118] Hermann Maas was one of his collaborators across Germany. In 1938 he warned a gathering of Confessional Church clergy that 'Christianity in Germany had become quite as much an alien as were the Jews'.

On 19 December 1940 Pastor Grüber was arrested and confined at Sachsenhausen concentration camp for two and a half years. He was fortunate – his deputy, Pastor Sylten, was taken to Dachau in February 1941 where he died in 1942, and seven other members of Grüber's staff also died.[119] Heinrich Grüber survived the war to be a witness at the Eichmann trial in Jerusalem in 1961.[120] Maas too was not forgotten. He was stopped from doing his parish work during the war and could not even visit schools, hospitals or prisons.

In 1944 the Nazis shipped the 67-year-old clergyman, his wife and younger daughter to a labour camp in occupied France. He was liberated by the Americans in 1945 and maintained his devotion to Jewish matters by attending the synagogue in Heidelberg on the High Holidays and even fasting on the Day of Atonement.[121] Both Hermann Maas and Pastor Grüber became actively involved in the early years of the creation of the Council of Christians and Jews (CCJ) and attended the first international conference in Oxford in 1946, whose report was called 'Freedom, Justice and Responsibility'. There were 150 participants from all five continents and it is recorded: 'Among them were two Christian pastors from Germany, Probst. Grüber from Berlin and Hermann Maas from Heidelberg. Writing of their presence many years later one of the Jewish participants described it as "profoundly impressive – one might say traumatic".'[122]

The CCJ had grown out of the British Council of Christians and Jews, which in turn had been born out of co-operation between

Christians and Jews in Britain to help the victims of Nazi persecution.[123] It was altogether appropriate that these two courageous men should have been part of this innovative group, with their old friend Rabbi Leo Baeck now settled in London. In 1947 Maas wrote to Martha, expressing his delight in the success of her and Paul's emigration to England. He ended the letter:

> What a pity I was not able to drive with you through London on the roof of the buses or wander along the Thames with you. How much there would have been to tell each other. All your guidances under the word: 'People intended to make it bad, but God made it good.' And He has sent every one of you, you too dear child, good people. Thus you have now found your dear mother in your motherly woman and friend. Give her the profound thanks from a German who never stopped for a second to hate the Hitler madness.[124]

Hermann Maas was the first German invited to visit the new State of Israel in 1949, and in 1953 a small grove of trees was planted at Mount Gilboa in his honour which particularly pleased him.[125] Hermann died in September 1970.

Martha herself was present with her brother Paul and her husband Ron Mower when the Hermann Maas Foundation was launched in Heidelberg in 1988 by four private individuals. She wished to express her feelings about him by saying, 'I have travelled to Heidelberg to honour this man who was our friend when we so badly needed a friend.'[126]

The foundation's constitution specifies its aim 'to foster Christian-Jewish co-operation on a broad international base'. One method was to grant a German theology student the opportunity to study at a university in Israel. Dr Meister, one of the founders, described Maas as 'an admirable person with great charisma'.[127]

It was subsequently decided that with the support of the Hermann Maas Foundation, the Hermann Maas Medal would be awarded every four years in Gengenbach, Maas' birthplace. The recipients were to be individuals who had distinguished themselves in the promotion of understanding between Christians and Germans.

In 1995, in Heidelberg's twin city Rehovot in Israel, a street was named after Hermann Maas.

Sadly, Ron Mower, my main informant, died in 2004, and Martha's brother Paul, whose unpublished memoir proved invaluable, died in September 2009. However, I have had contact with his son Paul, who was pleased to hear that their story is being told.

Hermann was always modest about himself, and would no doubt be shocked by the level of attention and the honours he has received post-humously. When Alfred Werner asked him for additional biographical information in 1948, he sent it with a note which roughly translates as 'Am I really worthy of so much effort?'

Valérie Rácz (1911–97), known as Vali, was a Catholic woman whose career as a singer had always been intertwined with Jews. She was also an actress and made twenty films between 1936 and 1956 and simply oozed glamour. She was known as the 'Hungarian Marlene Dietrich'. Her father, Ferenc Rácz, was headmaster of a village school but had a peasant background, and her mother, Gizella Sohonyay, was a member of the old Hungarian gentry. They had moved to Gölle, a farming village in south-west Hungary, after their marriage in 1910.

Ferenc had run away from his family when he was 14. He was the youngest of twelve children and the only one who did not want a peasant's life. He was taken in by a parish priest in another village who began to educate him, and eventually his parents relented and agreed to pay the priest to look after him and continue his education. When they moved to Gölle he became both teacher and cantor. 'He was very religious, and this may have been at least partly due to the fact that it was the Church, in the form of his erstwhile priest-mentor, which had provided him with an escape route from the peasant life, and the alternative he so desperately sought.'[128]

Vali's career as a singer was very influenced by Jews. As a young woman she was a skilled pianist but it was her singing voice which captivated people. Soon after her graduation she was asked to entertain a guest in her parents' home. He was Géza Wéhner, who was a professor at the Franz Liszt Music Academy in Budapest, and also chief organist at Budapest's vast Dohány Street synagogue. She

so impressed him that he invited her to audition at the Budapest
Music Academy, and in September 1932 she left her home village to
embark on her remarkable career. Géza Wéhner was the first of many
influential Jewish figures who played a decisive role in shaping Vali's
career. Another Jew who had a strong influence was Paul Ábrahám, a
successful composer of operettas and film scores. It was through him
that she got her first big break – singing at the famous Budapest haunt
of the jet set: the Negrescó café. This led to a two-year stint at the
famous Budapest revue theatre – the Terézkörúti. Here she was one
of the few non-Jewish performers and worked with some of the most
talented artists of the day. This period must have been formative in her
attitude towards Jews.[129]

The famous Jewish couturier Sándor Gergely offered to design a
dress for her early in her career, on condition that if she liked it she
would have all her stage dresses made at his salon. She accepted and the
resulting dress was a sensation because it was so unlike other singers'
normal outfits. Gergely took her under his wing and 'dressed her as if
she were one of his models, in creations as stunning and flattering as
anything to be found in Paris'. These dresses were the source of remi-
niscences for decades.[130]

Gergely was more perceptive than most of his co-religionists over
the introduction, in 1941, of the Third Jewish Law:

> he didn't share the naive optimism of most other Hungarian Jews, who
> convinced themselves that things were bearable, that they wouldn't get
> worse, and that if they only sat tight, they could weather the storm
> of Nazism. Gergely felt instinctively that things could, and would get
> worse. Since 1940 there had been a series of laws and decrees concern-
> ing the Jewish labour service, which was for the majority of the men
> conscripted into it, tantamount to a death sentence. In late 1942 he
> received his labour service call-up papers. He closed down his salon
> and gave Vali a parting gift of a black velvet dress he had just finished.
> Soon afterwards he poisoned himself.[131]

His death was not only a terrible personal blow to Vali, but also another
example of how desperate things were for Budapest's Jews, even though

many still failed to realise it. They had been lulled into a false sense of security by the refusal of the new Prime Minister, Miklós Kállay, to implement many of the Nazis' demands and his refusal to make the Jews wear the yellow star. Inevitably, this situation could not last and it was discovered that Kállay was trying to negotiate a separate peace with the Allies at the same time as announcing in a speech in May 1943: 'Hungary will never deviate from those precepts of humanity which, in the course of its history, it has always maintained in racial and religious questions.' It was then only a matter of time before the Nazis determined to control 'this Jewish-influenced State', and this happened in March 1944. [132]

Vali's greatest success was ironically during the war, when she was a pin-up for the Hungarian troops fighting on the Eastern Front. Additionally, she became resident singer at the Hangli Kiosk. This was a famous Budapest nightspot overlooking the Danube and was owned by the Rónay brothers – father and uncle of the food critic Egon Rónay. [133]

In May 1944 Vali was phoned by an old friend, Bandi Schreiber, in whose hotel she had found great success as a chanteuse in the summers of 1940 and 1941. Bandi was Jewish but had a Christian wife. He described to her the panic in the city of Budapest as news of mass deportations of Jews from rural areas reached the city. Desperate attempts were being made to get forged identity papers:

> But public opinion had been poisoned by the years of rabid and systematic propaganda by the extreme-Right minority in Hungary. And now Jews were being shunned by their Gentile friends and neighbours, and those living with false Christian papers were being denounced. Humane Gentiles trying to help them were branded as traitors. [134]

Bandi wanted Vali to hide his cousin and his wife who had been denounced and were desperate for somewhere to hide. Vali knew of the risks and said she would have to think about it for a day or so. She consulted her former lover and now close confidant and friend, Paul Barabás, a writer of film scripts and an ardent anti-Nazi. It was he who devised a plan of hiding the Jews in the back half of an enormous wardrobe, by building a false partition in the middle and creating a secret compartment, for when there was a Nazi raid. The rest of the time they were hidden in the basement.

The Mandels were a quiet middle-aged couple. As soon as they arrived, Vali discussed certain essential precautions with them – they could go outside to the garden for fresh air only after dark; they must stay away from the front windows; and in the event of friends or visitors coming to the house, they were to remain silently in the basement until the visitors were gone. No one must discover their presence.

The Mandels were Orthodox, and their unswerving faith saved them from despondency. Despite their vast religious and cultural differences, Vali and the Mandels understood each other very well. She made things as comfortable as possible for them in one of the basement rooms, where, each Friday evening, they lit candles and celebrated Sabbath.[135] They were soon joined by a friend of Vali's, Margit Herzog, and her 14-year-old daughter Marietta. On one occasion poor Marietta had to hide behind a huge bookcase for hours whilst the Gestapo searched the house (*see plate 12*). The Herzogs were a large and extremely wealthy family, and Margit's husband Dezső had already suffered dreadfully during eighteen months of forced labour on the Eastern Front. The family home in Budapest was on Andrássy Avenue, the grandest address in the city, and they owned farms and vineyards which produced some of Hungary's most famous wine. Margit's eldest brother Sándor had proposed to Vali, but although she was very fond of him, she declined his offer.[136]

The Herzogs were among the first people Vali thought of when the Germans occupied the country. No one in the family had thought of taking steps to forestall the dangers of a Nazi takeover. Like many other Jews, wealthy and otherwise, they wanted to believe that, despite the passing political traumas, the traditionally tolerant aristocratic leadership of Hungary would in the end protect them. Also, they were strongly bound to their land and their fortune. They simply couldn't abandon it. It was to be a fatal mistake.[137]

Margit's brother Imre was a decorated hero of the First World War. He had lost an arm on the Russian front in 1915 but his valiant reputation allowed him to go unmolested around Budapest, even in the post-occupation regime. He was known as 'One-armed Imre', but his freedom was short-lived and, like the holders of the Iron Cross in Germany, his pride in his immunity as a hero was not to provide protection for long. One of the first acts of the Szálasi government, which came to power on 15 October 1944, was to revoke all exemptions for Jews, even war heroes, and 'One-armed Imre' had to go into hiding.[138]

Vali's daughter, Monica Porter, has written of rescuers such as her mother:

> They simply did what they felt they had to do and as far as they were concerned, it wasn't about 'heroism' at all … As she well knew, the penalty for harbouring a Jew was summary execution. But how could she not help when, out on the streets, the city's Jews were being rounded up, deported, tortured or shot?[139]

Nevertheless, Vali's motivation was complex. She was a sophisticated woman who had been involved in show business all her adult life. In Budapest that theatrical world was full of Jews and therefore she had known and worked with Jews for just as long, and had loved some of them. When they were threatened she could do nothing but help them. She had been brought up to be a Catholic and her father was extremely devout. Her parents had sent her to a convent for her schooling from the age of 10. There she learnt three skills: 'an iron discipline, a dedication of purpose and self-restraint – which not only helped to secure her later success as a singer and actress, but helped to save her life'.[140] Her daughter also credits her professional and romantic involvement with Paul Barabás, her lover since 1938, as a major influence. Barabás was working for the Resistance and devised the wardrobe hiding place for his precious 'Valikó'. He was able to facilitate the arrangements and without him she might not have been so comparatively successful in hiding her Jewish 'guests'.[141] The house that Vali was living in when she hid the Jews – No 47d Budakeszi Avenue – eventually became the embassy of the government of Columbia.[142]

These courageous activities brought her anxieties and dangers. She came under suspicion and was arrested by the Gestapo and imprisoned and interrogated for two weeks, but she was released without giving anything away. After the Russians had liberated Budapest, a group of Jewish partisans accused her of collaboration and sentenced her to death. It is said that a Red Army colonel, with whom she had been having an affair, intervened and saved her, hours before she was due to be shot. [143]

All the people she hid survived the war and some emigrated to Israel. Vali married a writer, Peter Halász, in 1946. A son, Valér, was born in 1950 and a daughter, Mónika, in 1952. When the 1956 Hungarian revolution failed, the family of four escaped to the USA. They came to London in 1970 and in 1975 Vali and her husband moved to Munich, where she died in February 1997.

Vali was recognised as a Righteous Among the Nations in 1991. When Monica was in Jerusalem with her mother, they met up with some of the residents of the life-saving wardrobe and generations of a family who would not have existed but for Vali's courage. [144] She said of her wartime activities: 'I just did what I had to do'. There is now a website dedicated to her: www.valiracz.com. [145] Her daughter, Monica Porter, a freelance journalist, now lives in London, and her partner is Nick Winton, son of Nicholas Winton, who rescued 669 Jewish children from Czechoslovakia in 1939.

Soeur St Cybard (1885–1968). Josie Martin was born as Josephine Levy in Alsace-Lorraine in 1938, where her family had lived for generations. Following the fall of France, the little family fled to a village in Vichy France where they were accepted and Josie went to nursery school. However, by 1944 there were Nazi sweeps taking place. That was bad enough, but the greater danger was from the French police: the real super Gestapo who were forever trying to show the German Nazis how loyal they were by betraying Frenchmen who were helping Jews. [146]

They fled to a nearby farm to hide and a farmer and his wife, who were family friends, offered to adopt 5-year-old Josie, but her parents could not bring themselves to do it. Then they heard that a nun, Soeur St Cybard, was running a girls' school about 50km away. They made contact with her and she agreed to take Josie. It was a day school and she was to be the only boarder. Josie stayed for seven months, under the cover name of Josie L'Or, and her parents' parting words to her were never to reveal her true name. She was in the convent until the liberation of Paris in August 1944, when she was reunited with her parents who had been hiding elsewhere in the countryside.[147]

Ten years ago Josie recalled:

> The nun was a no-nonsense person and a woman of great importance in the small village. She was very political and very involved in helping the villagers. For example, she was the one who would write to the front and ask about missing sons. In some ways she was almost like a social worker. I developed tremendous admiration for this woman, who was strong, important, and very different from the typical French farm woman of the region. Even I felt a sense of importance in being 'her' child.[148]

It was fortunate that no one knew that the girl the nun initially chose to look after Josie was a Nazi collaborator. They did not like each other:

> She didn't know that I was Jewish. That was lucky, because she turned out to be a Nazi collaborator – a fact that my parents did not know until afterward. So much for their effort to put me in a safe place! Of course the nun didn't know about this woman's Nazi connection either. By the time she realised it, she couldn't do anything because of her own vulnerability.[149]

The nun was a remarkable woman. Josie has written:

> I can only surmise that Soeur St Cybard was a pious and sincere human being who practised her religious beliefs well beyond the dictates of her immediate superiors. She had been serving as director/headmistress of a girls' school in Angoulême before being assigned to the backwaters of Lesterps. In that capacity she apparently engaged in some clandestine underground activities to assist the French Resistance. By the early Forties it seems she was in personal danger and therefore was sent into the interior, both for her own safety and perhaps to have her out of the way. We all know not all Catholics were willing to take risks nor make waves.[150]

Although Josie never saw her rescuer again, the Soeur was very active until her death in 1968. She was born Marie-Elizabeth Lacalle on 14 January 1885 at Marsous, in the south, close to Lourdes and the border with Spain. She became a nun at the very early age of 14, taking the name Soeur St Cybard in 1899. She became a devoted teacher starting in 1901 at Abzac in the Gironde. In 1918 she was at the Saint-André Institute in Angoulême, and she stayed until 1942 when she was appointed headmistress of the St Bernadette School in Lesterps, where she remained until 1958. It was during this period that she cared for Josie:

> At Lesterps she does not content herself with simply running the school; she devotes herself totally to the local community. On Thursdays and Sunday afternoons, she travels the countryside like a little sister to the poor being in turn a nurse, counsellor, secretary, therapist: she fights poverty. Indefatigable, she opens a needlework workshop which provides for the making of sacerdotal ornaments and linen for the Church, as well as the making of articles for religious observance in school.
>
> Besides that she organises adult theatre groups composed of pupils' parents and also a choir for the young of the parish; she herself conducts the choir rehearsals for Sunday mass and for religious festivals.[151]

Josie was present when Soeur St Cybard was honoured in Lesterps in 1999 and a tree was planted in her memory. Josie was given honorary citizenship of the village. She was delighted to be there but expressed concerns: 'I was concerned that by honouring me, and through me the deeds of one courageous nun, I would help to whitewash the generally dismal record of French complicity and collaboration with the Nazis in the Second World War.'[152] The visit back to Lesterps enabled her to meet others who had known Soeur St Cybard, and these meetings led her to conclude, 'it's clear she was a very strong and independent woman who saw her role as reaching beyond the strict definitions of what nuns were supposed to do. She was also described as highly intelligent and progressive for her times.'[153] Josie discovered that Soeur St Cybard was remembered with love and affection in the area:

I also wonder if I could have been a rescuer. When I think of that, I'm always struck by how heroic that nun was – not just for the obvious reason of risking her life by taking in the enemy or a perceived enemy. I also think of the upheaval it must have caused for this woman to take in a child![154]

She wonders why her parents did not keep in touch with the nun. She writes that after returning home she was like a stranger:

silent, terribly polite, withdrawn. I have no memory of missing the nun. Did Soeur St Cybard miss me? My parents did not stay in contact with the nun after the war. Were they fearful of my attachment to her? Were they afraid that I had become the good Catholic child as they watched me pray to a mysterious guardian angel?[155]

Nothing is known of Soeur St Cybard's parents, but she had a sister who died many years ago. Her great-nephew, Louis Lacalle, has since been found and he recalls his great-aunt coming to spend holidays with the family. 'In his child memories she was rather stern and wanted them to write exercises during their holidays'.[156] Quite remarkably, until he received my letter of 21 November 2003, kindly translated by Madame Landréa, he was unaware of his aunt's courageous acts and thinks no one else in the family would have known either.[157] He describes the farming family life into which she was born as very hard and says she had four brothers and three sisters:

The daily life of these farmers was just a lot of work for a very low income so that they were hard at work and extremely frugal but at the same time showing solidarity with their community. A mutual assistance was very natural for them when they had to help a parent, a neighbour and so on … when they needed it temporarily.[158]

Louis writes that they had deep-rooted religious convictions expressed in the religious life of the village. 'However hard the necessities of the daily life were, my grandfather would never have forgotten to go to the Sunday religious services or missed any important event in the religious year.'

One translated letter is not a great deal on which to base a theory, but it is all I have. It seems fair to conclude that Soeur St Cybard learnt two things as a child at home: that we are dependent on each other and the importance of a religious life. Bernadette Landréa was extremely excited by the fact that none of the family knew about Soeur St Cybard's courage until my research led me to write to Louis. He was apparently very emotional and honoured when he heard about her deeds. Bernadette wrote to me: 'Isn't it wonderful that a man of about 55 [Louis Lacalle] may have been informed by your thesis about the important life of his great-aunt?'[159]

Josie went to America with her parents in 1947, and as she grew up her mother tended to dismiss their experience: 'Come, let's forget about it … it was nothing.' Compared with the horrors others suffered, she was right, but Josie's trauma was only treated in her thirties and she became 'a psychologist who entered the profession probably to heal herself'.[160] The war and her childhood were intertwined quite inextricably and the war was always present:

Unknowingly, the war had become that against which all other 'terribles' were measured. But at the same time it also established a benchmark of goodness. The war, devastating as it had been, had also been for me, through Soeur St Cybard, an experience of a rare kind of moral conduct against which I would forever compare all other virtue …

I like to think that what Soeur St Cybard did, not only saved me, but endowed me with a rare example of great goodness. The force of that example has persisted into the present. It lives in the handful of rescuers, the few righteous Gentiles who risked everything to save Jews and other fugitives from the Nazis, from the Holocaust.

These examples of 'light piercing the darkness', beacons of morality, anchors of goodness … are something to grasp when nothing else holds.[161]

As recently as 23 November 2009, Josie heard from Yad Vashem, after three years of correspondence, that Soeur St Cybard was to be recognised as Righteous Among the Nations for saving Josie from the Nazis. In response to my query about whether the nun had rescued anyone else, Josie wrote:

I have not seen the citation, but I'm reasonably certain that it is only about her caring for me.

I know there has been a lot of enquiry about her activities during the war. Not much could be unearthed. She was modest, discreet (a necessity for carrying out clandestine work) and she certainly did not view what she did as heroic. Even the story my parents told about why she was demoted to the small village of Lesterps after serving at the much more prestigious St Andre School in Angoulême (supposedly because of being involved in the Resistance) could not be verified.

She did carry out her mission of looking after needy children after the war, e.g. insisting a crippled child who was always kept at home be given a proper education … that kind of thing. This child, now a woman, still lives in Lesterps. Many of her former students spoke of her integrity and courage as well as telling stories of her severity often accompanied by an 'Oh la-la' and a shaking of the fist to accentuate it.

A complex personality. I so wish we'd have kept in touch.[162]

Josie says this success with Yad Vashem is partly due to the efforts of her French publisher, Francois Julien Labruyere, and 'Now her name and courage will not be forgotten'.[163]

Aristides de Sousa Mendes (1885–1954) was also a deeply religious diplomat who rescued thousands of Jews. He was Portuguese Consul-General in Bordeaux from August 1938 until he was summoned back to Lisbon in the June/July of 1940. He helped in excess of 10,000 Jews escape from the Nazis. Like Carl Lutz, he suffered for what he had done, but he was actually charged with an offence by the dictator Salazar, who ruled Portugal from 1933–68. Both Aristides and his wife Angelina died prematurely, in poverty, as a direct result of his courageous and humane actions, and it took his family over fifty years to gain justice for him.

Aristides was a devout Catholic, with Jewish ancestors who converted to Christianity 400 years ago. He was an extremely humanitarian man and was always helping people. His son John Paul Abranches has written:

my father was a very compassionate man, always willing to help someone in need. During his lifetime he would help an unemployed person find a job, or give money to someone without funds. It was customary for my parents to open their kitchen to the needy once a week in our home village when we were there on our annual vacation. When we were living in Belgium, Portuguese students who were attending the university were always welcome in our home on Sunday for a good Portuguese meal, along with singing, dancing and conversation.[164]

In 1940 he found himself as Consul-General in Bordeaux, representing President Salazar, who was claiming Portugal was neutral, but in an unenviable position. England could lay claims to his support as the Anglo-Portuguese alliance was the longest-standing diplomatic union, which went back to the Treaty of Windsor signed in 1374 as a result of negotiations by John of Gaunt, whose daughter Phillipa subsequently married King João I. However, Salazar was also bound by the March 1939 Treaty of Friendship with General Franco. He was concerned that any pro-Axis activity by Spain would drag Portugal closer to Germany, and he worked to avoid this event: 'To curb the pro-Axis leanings of the Spanish dictator, by displays of Iberian solidarity, was Salazar's primary concern. He used diplomacy, supplemented with gifts of wheat and corn. And he promptly adhered to Franco's hands-off policy regarding refugees from Hitler's aggression.'[165]

The dictator dealt with the situation of thousands of refugees attempting to enter Portugal by issuing what came to be known as Circular 14. On 13 November 1939 all Portuguese diplomats received a circular from the Foreign Ministry in Lisbon which 'radically called into question Portugal's centuries-old tradition of hospitality and officially introduced a hitherto unknown element of racial or religious segregation into the question of immigration'.[166]

The circular was very specific about the three categories of people to whom consuls were forbidden to grant passports or visas without referring first to the Foreign Ministry in Lisbon:

– Aliens of undefined nationality, Stateless persons or holders of 'Nansen passports'

- Aliens who in the consul's opinion were unable to provide valid
reasons for entering Portugal
- Jews expelled from their countries and stripped of their nationality

De Sousa Mendes found himself in conflict when he realised that the
government's instructions went against the constitution of Portugal,
which guaranteed the rights of everyone regardless of their religion.
This caused him great inner conflict and stress. He was very vulnerable
with a family of ten children in school; he could not afford to risk his
career and income:

> He was so exhausted and upset he went to bed for three days. On the
> third day, he woke up invigorated, saying he had heard a 'Voice' stating
> that he should go ahead and issue visas to all who requested one, regard-
> less of nationality or religion, and he was going to do this free of charge.
> Asked why he would do this, he stated, 'I would rather be with God
> against man than with man against God'. [167]

He was influenced by a Belgian Rabbi, Chaim Kruger, whose congregation had been in Antwerp, although he originated from Poland.
Rabbi Kruger had uprooted his family of five children in mid-May
and swept them off on a train full of German refugees. When they
reached Bordeaux, Kruger and de Sousa Mendes met by accident and
Aristides immediately invited him to stay in his home overnight. The
Rabbi recounted:

> Our children were then between the ages of two and ten. The Consul-
> General told me he had thirteen children. He told us to make full use
> of all the amenities of his flat but I had to explain that that would be
> impossible. I could not set myself apart from the large community of
> Jews who were milling around near the border. Also his home was full
> of [Christian] statues, which made a terrible impression on our chil-
> dren, who refused to eat a thing. I thanked him for his generosity. Next
> morning we returned to our milling brethren, and afterwards I went
> back to talk to him, to explain that there was one way he could save us –
> by giving us visas to Portugal. [168]

The Rabbi continued his discussion with de Sousa Mendes. They were interrupted by the Vice Consul, who overheard the conversation and 'warned him not to fall into my net. All his efforts were to no avail. Mr Mendes told me that I and my family would receive visas.' However, de Sousa Mendes' request for permission to grant these visas was refused by Lisbon on 13 June, along with those of thirty other people:

> Sousa Mendes promised his friend he would do everything in his power to get him the precious visas that would allow him to leave France with his family. The Rabbi then said something that had a radical effect on Sousa Mendes: 'It's not just me that needs help, but all my fellow Jews who are in danger of their lives.'[169]

But Aristides was already in difficulties with the authorities, having been approached by an elderly Austrian professor by the name of Arnold Wiznitzer and having granted him a visa. Unfortunately for him, Aristides had written to Lisbon on 27 November and 6 December 1939 asking for permission to grant the visa.[170] When his actions were subsequently queried by Lisbon he said: 'He [Wiznitzer] informed me that, were he unable to leave France that very day, he would be interned in a concentration [read detention] camp, leaving his wife and minor son stranded. I considered it a duty of elementary humanity to prevent such an extremity.'[171]

There were other cases as well, including a Dr Laporte, who was a professor from Barcelona trying to get to Bolivia with his family, and by April 1940 de Sousa Mendes was given a stern official reprimand. He wrote to his nephew Cesar in May 1940:

> The ministry is giving me a lot of trouble ... The man [Dr Laporte] and his family would never have been able to leave here if I hadn't done that [given them a visa]. In the end, everything went through quite normally, but the Portuguese Stalin decided to pounce on me like a wild beast. I hope that will be the end of the matter, but I can't rule out another attack. I've no problems with my conscience.[172]

He was, therefore, already struggling to deal with these matters prior to 10 May 1940, as his nephew Cesar Mendes, son of his twin brother, wrote:

Before May 10, 1940, the Portuguese Government granted visas or refused them, but this was slow, and after that when the refugees kept coming, there was no use writing anymore, and it became necessary to wire, but the Government stopped answering, and consequently the work in the Chancellery concerning passports and visas froze. This way the number of the refugees increased frighteningly, leading the situation to a dramatic climax. This is when my Uncle made up his mind to help all the refugees. [173]

With the fall of France imminent, in June desperate refugees flocked to Bordeaux where de Sousa Mendes was housing many of the most desperate in his own home. His nephew described the scene:

the dining room, the drawing room and the Consul's offices were at the disposal of the refugees, dozens of them of both sexes, all ages, and mainly old and sick people. They were coming and going, there were pregnant women who did not feel well, there were people who had seen, powerless to defend themselves, their relatives die on the highways killed by the machine guns firing from planes. They slept on chairs, on the floor, on the rugs; there could never be any control again. Even the Consul's offices were crowded with dozens of refugees who were exhausted, dead tired because they had waited for days and nights on the street, on the stairways and finally in the offices. They could not satisfy their needs, they did not eat nor drink for fear of losing their places in the lines, what happened nevertheless and caused some disturbances [sic]. Consequently, the refugees looked bad, they did not wash themselves, they did not comb their hair, they did not change their clothes and they did not shave. Most of them had nothing but the clothes they were wearing. [174]

It was the pressure of all these desperate people and the failure of Lisbon to understand or care which made Aristides so ill. The three days he took to his bed were 13, 14 and 15 June 1940. Whilst Aristides wrestled with his soul, Angelina coped. 'She became the rock, bearing up under the pressure and sustaining her husband as he lay prostrate, rent by anguish. One son, Sebastian, later heard the father speak of a night spent entirely in prayer, together with his wife. It was during those three days that his father's hair turned white, wrote Sebastian.'[175]

But afterwards he was clear about what he would do. He got up, washed, shaved and dressed, and marched into his office and announced to all that he would issue everyone with a visa. He added:

> I cannot allow all you people to die. Many of you are Jews and our con-
> stitution clearly states that neither the religion nor the political beliefs of
> foreigners can be used as a pretext for refusing to allow them to stay in
> Portugal. I've decided to be faithful to that principle, but I shan't resign
> for all that. The only way I can respect my faith as a Christian is to act in
> accordance with the dictates of my conscience.[176]

Thus, on 16 June the work on issuing visas was begun and it continued for three days. A production line was created with passports collected, often by Rabbi Kruger, and de Mendes Sousa signed them all – no questions were asked. The Rabbi's son was astounded by his father's role and noted that in his enthusiasm to save as many people as he could, 'he went out into the street without his black jacket, without his hat and even without his skullcap – something I'd never seen him do before'.[177]

On the night of 19 June, Bordeaux was bombed by German planes and the desperate refugees fled closer to the Spanish border, to Bayonne and Hendaye. De Sousa Mendes left his family and struggled through the crowds to Bayonne where some 25,000 people were besieging the Portuguese Consulate in which the Consul had locked himself. Aristides used his seniority to tell Consul Machado that he would be responsible for issuing visas and began a new 'visa assembly line'. During the next forty-eight hours thousands of visas were issued, but meanwhile, the Consul was reporting this activity to Lisbon and the Portuguese Ambassador in Madrid.

On 22 June Aristides followed the frantic crowd to Hendaye, which is on the French side of the border marked by the river Bidassoa. There, too, he distributed visas for entry into Portugal, often written on odd scraps of paper. However, the border gates were firmly shut and Aristides personally went to speak to the border guards. Eventually he opened the gates to Irun – the town on the Spanish side – himself so people could get on the trains to Portugal. He later spoke of people he could not help committing suicide in front of him. It was this scene that greeted Ambassador Pereira when he arrived at Irun, and that he described in his letter to Prime Minister Salazar.

The visa signing, called by Yehuda Bauer 'The greatest rescue operation carried out by a single person during the Holocaust', continued for three to four days and many famous names were amongst those he saved, including Otto of Hapsburg and his family, who went to Portugal and then on to the USA. Otto himself saved many of his compatriots but he commented: 'I was only doing my duty, whereas what Sousa Mendes accomplished was an admirable action.'[178]

Nevertheless, he was recalled to Lisbon and disgraced. Some time after his return to Lisbon he again met Rabbi Kruger, who asked him:

'My friend, why did you give up your career to help us Jews?' My father answered, 'If so many Jews have to suffer because of one Catholic (meaning Hitler) then it is all right for one Catholic to suffer for so many Jews, and I welcome the opportunity with love, and I have no regrets.'[179]

When de Sousa Mendes got back to Lisbon there was a hearing about his actions, with fifteen separate charges, on 10 August 1940; the tribunal decided on 29 October 1940 that he should be reduced to a lower rank, which permitted him to carry on working. This was too lenient for Salazar who quite unconstitutionally forced him out of the diplomatic service, causing him financial ruin because his pension was forfeited. He still had his large family to feed and he continued to try to fight the authorities. His pleas for financial aid from the government were ignored and he was only helped by the Jewish community of Lisbon, who gave him a small monthly allowance and fed the family in their soup kitchen. Meanwhile, during 1941, he was struggling to justify his actions as 'the powerful imperatives of human solidarity'.[180] In 1945 he presented a protest to the President of the National Assembly. An English version was sent to me by John Paul, and Aristides defended himself yet again, asking for financial compensation. He concludes:

> The claimant cannot bear the evident and absured [sic] injustice be [he] suffered and solicits that it be brought to a swift end, inasmuch as the Administration has been lauded in Portugal and abroad for an act which manifestly, the government opposed, and for which the credit is due to the country and people whose altruistic and humanitarian sentiments were praised, and justly so, for an incident created by the disobedience of the claimant.
>
> In short, the attitude of the Portuguese government was uncon-stitutional, anti-neutral, and contrary to all humane sentiments – consequently undeniably against the Portuguese Nation.[181]

No response was received. But the validity of his actions was corrobo-rated as a liberated Europe revealed the full horror of the Holocaust and the fate that one brave man had saved so many people from. Angelina died in their poverty in 1948 and Aristides himself in April 1954.

After his death, his children gradually left Portugal to live in different countries, and his heavily mortgaged home at Cabanas de Vriato was sold to pay debts. In 2007 his grandson Antonius told of plans to restore the dilapidated house as a library and a centre for the Aristides de Sousa Mendes Foundation with the support of the Israeli Embassy.

John Paul Abranches wrote to me that Cavaco Silva, Prime Minister of Portugal (1985–95), and President since 2006, told his sister Joana in 1986: 'My dear lady, if any of my ministers disobeyed my orders, they too would be dismissed.'[182]

The following fact emerged during the course of researching de Sousa Mendes: Henrie Zvi Deutsch (1901–2007), a recipient of one of de Sousa Mendes' life-saving visas, explained:

> What is not stated is that these visas were not to individuals but to fami-lies; in our case, both my father and my uncle Paul, Belgian refugees who had settled near Bordeaux, were issued one visa each that rescued

nine individuals. The number of people rescued by Mendes far exceeds 30,000 and remains unknown.[183]

Even after Portugal became a democracy in 1974, Aristides was not recognised by the state. It was only in 1986, following a petition by John Paul, that the then President of Portugal, Mario Soares, rehabilitated and honoured Aristides. He himself had been exiled by the dictator Salazar, so presumably he was more sympathetic to a rebel's cause.

In March 1995 President Mario Soares and his wife hosted a reception for fifty members of the Mendes family, together with supporters from America. Henrie Zvi was the only visa receiver present and noted wryly: 'Unfortunately the goodwill of the former president and first lady have not affected the official stance towards Mendes; the Portuguese prime minister informed Pedro Nuno, one of two sons who helped issue visas, that if his father were to disobey his government's orders today, he would be punished just as severely.'[184]

De Sousa Mendes' Jewish ancestry has often been mentioned as a motive for his rescues. David Shpiro, a researcher at Tel Aviv University, dismissed this theory:

> He saw himself in no way as a Jew. He saw himself as a humane Christian. He was a devout Catholic, and he acted as a devout Catholic. He knew somewhere in his remote background there was someone who was a Jew, but like thousands of others in the Iberian peninsula that didn't make him a Jew. He saw himself as a Christian and a Portuguese patriot.[185]

John Paul Abranches established the International Committee for the Commemoration of Aristides de Sousa Mendes in 1986 with other family members. I met him in London in April 2002 at the London Jewish Cultural Centre at the launch of the exhibition called 'Visas for Life', about diplomats who between them saved about 250,000 Jews from the Nazis. John subsequently sent me considerable personal information on his father. Sadly, he died on 5 February 2009 – the last surviving son of Aristides de Sousa Mendes. His nephew, Sebastian Mendes, an art professor in Washington, told me that he now speaks about his grandfather all over the world and that it was his own father,

Sebastião Miguel Darte de Sousa Mendes, who wrote the first book about his grandfather in 1952.[186] The family had worked valiantly to get Aristides rehabilitated and to tell the world about his actions. John Paul ended a letter to me: 'Whenever I give a talk, I always remind the audience that one day they too will have their "moment of truth". There will be no time to think, only to act. Hopefully, helping your neighbor will be second nature to you.'[187]

Jelle (1912–93) and Elizabeth (1912–92) van Dyk. Miriam Dunner (1941–2006) was born in Rotterdam as Miriam Cohen. Her parents were Arthur and Rosetta, and in 1942, when she was 16 months old, her parents, who went into hiding, left her with a Protestant couple. The couple, who were childless, were Jelle van Dyk, a baker, and his wife Elizabeth. Miriam could not speak yet – children of such an age were easier to place because they could not betray any confidences. They called her Anke.[188]

The van Dyks were in a risky position because they owned a bakery, employing staff who would be aware of Miriam. They said Miriam had been left on the doorstep and they adopted her legally, so she then had two birth certificates. Her father and Jelle were both in the Underground and it was as a result of that contact that Jelle agreed to care for Miriam. It was not easy for them – in 1944 Jelle was caught with false ration cards, in the course of his work for the Underground, and was sent to a camp where he had to stay until the end of the war. Elizabeth then looked after Miriam on her own and they became very close. When the war ended she was 4½ years old. Her parents returned to Rotterdam and Miriam went back to them in September 1945 without warning or explanation. She was merely put in a car and sent off to her parents where she was told she was a Jewish child with different parents and a different name. As a result, in those days before counselling, she was completely traumatised and never really bonded again with her own mother. Miriam described her as a cold, jealous woman who resented the relationship Miriam had with Elizabeth.

Unfortunately, although the van Dyks saved Miriam's life, the traumatic experience of failing to readjust after the war caused Miriam great emotional problems. She was married in 1960 and came to

England. She kept in touch with the van Dyks and Miriam knew that Elizabeth was very ill the last time she visited her, before she died in November 1992. She attended the funeral with her husband but was so overwhelmed with emotion that it made her ill. She spoke to Jelle on the telephone every Sunday until he died months later. It was the end of an era to her and she felt she had lost part of her identity. She has visited her foster brother in America.

Her own parents died within five weeks of each other in November/ December 2000. Her mother had been incapacitated for four years and died first. Her father had always been very wrapped up in his wife and constantly took her side. She remained extremely angry with her parents for the way they treated her. She had seen a British psychologist but he did not understand about 'hidden children'. She later saw a Dutch one and attended a conference with 700 other hidden children which she found helpful. She told me, 'Hidden children feel that no one likes them and are always trying to be good and to be liked'. She explained that she had such a personality. However, she grew up knowing little about the Holocaust until she read the book *Exodus* in the 1960s.

In spite of the trauma Miriam suffered, the van Dyks were extremely good to her and certainly put themselves at risk by taking her in. They could have been betrayed at any time by their employees. They were very religious, particularly her stepmother Elizabeth, who was also very strong, and they really wanted to save her. They were also extremely anti-Nazi. Miriam felt that perhaps they thought they would be able to keep her if her parents did not survive the war. In fact, they subsequently adopted a little boy when the war was over.

Miriam trained in education and later became a remedial teacher. She had five children: four boys and a girl. Sadly, Miriam Dunner died very unexpectedly in 2006, at which time she and her husband had thirty-four grandchildren.[189]

I discovered, after meeting Mrs Dunner in 2001, that the question of the return of such 'hidden' children had been the subject of legislation in the Netherlands. Apparently, the united Dutch resistance groups proposed to the Dutch government in exile in London in 1944 that all Dutch Jewish children who were being hidden from the Nazis should remain with their foster parents after the war. This legislation was implemented in May 1945 and caused tremendous problems. Jewish parents had to defend their claim in front of a committee and had to prove that they were able to bring their children up properly; that they had the financial means to do so; that they had a house; and that they were practising Jews.

I am grateful to Max Arpel Lezer for his article on this issue and subsequent information.[190] In 2002 he was the Chairman of the *Het Ondergedoken Kind* (The Hidden Child Association), which was active in trying to get the law repealed. Max himself was subject to this law and his father had a long fight to get him back. Those parents who were unsuccessful lost their parental rights and, in effect, their children were legally adopted without their agreement.

2

RESCUERS WITH HUMANITARIAN MOTIVES

Józef Robert Barczynski (1900–80) rescued 250 Jews in Poland. He was the eldest of seven children, born in Poland into a family of rich landowners on his mother's side and Polish nobility on his father's. His father, Józef Kazimierz, was a political activist and a member of the Polish Socialist Party who fought for the independence of Poland from Tsarist Russia. He was first arrested in 1901 and imprisoned for four months. In 1906 he was arrested again and sent to Siberia to do forced labour in a coal mine. He was released after two years but had to stay in Siberia, in a town called Kustanay (now Kazakhstan) beyond the Ural mountains. His wife and family were allowed to join him in 1908 and they were only permitted to return to an independent Poland in 1921.[1]

Józef's formative years from 8 to 21 were thus spent in exile, but during his childhood he saw the example of his parents helping those in need. He used to speak of displaced people calling at their home or business asking for help, work or food:

Apparently, frequently, destitute strangers were invited to sit with them for dinner and were treated as equals. (I do not know whether any of these displaced persons were ever of Jewish origins.) My grandfather grew up in a family where Social Democratic political beliefs were adhered to. They believed in the equality of all people. This was a big influence on all the children growing up in the Barczynski home. In addition, from the side of my grandmother, Paulina, there was a strong religious influence. The kinds of principles that the children grew up with were to be found in the Bible. We are to love, not hate. We are to make peace, not war. We are to love our neighbour as ourselves, to care for the oppressed, to extend our hand to the sorrowful. The principles of scriptures as found in Isaiah and Proverbs were not only commended, but Józef would have seen them lived out in his family home.[2]

This example made him a very caring man and 'in Siberia he witnessed his parents caring for strangers when they had no obligation to do so'.[3] Yet he would not have been described as particularly brave. His niece Olympia has said that in her family it was always said that her uncle would not hurt a fly. In fact, he was quite timid and Olympia recalled that as a child, on seeing a cockerel strutting in the yard, he rushed back into the house, wailing to his mother that the cockerel was staring at him.[4]

Józef was aware of the impact of the 1917 Russian Revolution on his parents. When the Red Army came to Kustanay his father's timber businesses were taken from him and he had to work as a night watchman in his own factory. The family lost their home and their servants and had to live like the ordinary workmen. However, Józef's father had foresight and had converted many of his assets into gold coins which he kept hidden. Although Poland regained its independence in 1918, the family were only permitted to return home in 1921, when Józef's father had a small fortune with him. He continued his philanthropic work by sponsoring the University of the People, which was the first Polish university open to the ordinary people. Józef Robert, therefore, 'grew up in a climate where other people less fortunate than themselves were always cared for, and what was owned was for the benefit of others too'.[5]

His experience working in his father's timber works in Siberia enabled him to become a director of a timber and forestry scheme when he returned to Poland. In the late 1930s he was employed by a Czech man called Cezar Andrieu to run a factory in Krakow making timber products, minutes from Oskar Schindler's enamelware factory. Olympia is not aware of how the two men came to work together but presumes it was through business since 'Schindler produced enamel ware and then ammunition. My uncle's factory produced the wooden cases in which the ammunition was packed.'[6]

As a result of his involvement in the 'war effort', Barczynski was able to operate relatively freely. He personally rescued four Jewish families from the Krakow Ghetto. He had a truck fitted with a false bottom, which he drove into the Ghetto regularly. Schindler gave him the money with which he bribed the German guards. He was in the Polish Resistance with his brother and was called a 'White Courier' (in Polish *Biaty Kurier*). He took people out of the occupied territory, even as far as the Pyrenees. Apparently, 'he personally escorted over 250 Jewish people to safety and is credited with saving their lives'.

On one occasion he was arrested and was in a convoy of prisoners being taken to Auschwitz. He managed to escape by asking to go outside to relieve himself. But his brother, Olympia's other uncle, Wladyslaw, was not so fortunate. It appears that he was arrested in Warsaw, having been betrayed by some children. He spent six weeks in Auschwitz as a political prisoner and was questioned, tortured and shot. His family received a telegram on Christmas Eve 1941 describing his fate. Olympia has written: 'I remember frequently hearing of the sorrow they all had on that day, as one of his sisters was just laying the table for the Christmas meal.'[7]

When the Nazis began to persecute the Jews, Józef Barczynski was able to empathise with their plight:

> They were displaced people, like his family once were, in a land taken over by the enemy. He could empathise with them as his family too were plunged into the unknown and lost all they had. He would have had a strong sense of injustice, especially as now many of the Jews he knew and worked with were being arrested and losing all they had. Even more so as the Nazis began their campaign of extermination.[8]

Józef was posthumously recognised as a Righteous Among the Nations as he had refused the honour previously saying that he 'had only fulfilled his duty toward his fellow human beings'. After his death, his widow gave her permission and he was recognised by Yad Vashem on 7 November 1993. His niece Olympia only heard about it by accident when she visited her aunt in 1998, as his rescue of persecuted Jews had never been mentioned before.

The citation, which stresses that his job enabled him to save victims of persecution, both Poles and Jews, from mortal danger, describes his rescue of one Jewish family. Artur and Lola Frim, and their daughter Bronislawa, originally Przemysl, had moved to Lvov at the outbreak of war. When the Nazis occupied the city, they were interned in the Ghetto:

> They remained in the Ghetto, and throughout their stay there, until the autumn of 1942, received help from Józef Barczynski, who had been superficially acquainted with Artur before the war. Prior to the Ghetto's liquidation, Józef succeeded in smuggling out 7-year-old Bronislawa Frim and placing her with a Polish family, passing her off as a niece of his, whose parents had been exiled from the country. In due course, Artur and his wife also escaped from the Ghetto, and Barczynski found them employment in a factory and a place to live – all without requesting material recompense. After the couple had settled in the village where they were employed, Barczynski personally brought Bronislawa to join them. The Frims survived and immigrated to Israel after the war.[9]

Bronislawa continued to correspond with Józef's widow after the war, as is common between the rescued and their rescuers. Olympia used to visit her uncle's widow until she died in 2007.[10]

Achille Belloso Afan and Guilia Afan de Rivera Costaguti. The Costaguti family lived very close to the Ghetto area in Rome. The head of the family was Achille Belloso Afan de Rivera Costaguti and his wife was Guilia Afan de Rivera Costaguti. They had five children. One was Clotilde, who was my main informant, and another was Costanza, who verified the rescuees' story to Yad Vashem's investigator in 2002.[11]

At No 29 Via della Reginella there is a memorial stone high up on the wall commemorating the deportation of Jews from the area on 16 October 1943. At No 27 at that time the Costagutis took in eighteen Jews from four families who were all related by marriage, 'a deed which, under the Nazi occupation, could have cost them their lives'.[12] Apparently the eighteen were well hidden for a couple of months:

In December 1943 fascists forcefully entered the building but luckily no harm was done. Donna Guilia moved her charges, sixteen in all, to the home of one of her servants. However, this hiding place was also discovered by fascists who, through threats of handing her over for deportation, extorted a high sum of 50,000 Liretta from Donna Guilia, who personally objected to the arrest of her charges. Following this incident, they were compelled to abandon this shelter and Donna Guilia arranged for their transfer to various locations under her auspices, where they remained until the liberation of Rome.[13]

These eighteen Jews all survived the war, although they are all dead now. The rescue seems to have been based partly on the proximity of the Costagutis' palace to No 27, which was an all-Jewish house in the old Ghetto area. The rescuers' daughter Costanza, born in 1950, confirmed the rescuee Nicla Fiorentino's story in her testimony to Yad Vashem:

Since the window of the stairwell in that building faced the balcony of their home, her parents placed boards between the window and the balcony and always left a window open so that during the Nazi actions, people could escape to their home. There they could stay or escape through the building to another street where there was no danger.[14]

Costanza also spoke about a Jewish family, originally from Poland, who lived in her parents' property and changed their name to Kellner to elude the Nazis. She also said her parents 'never boasted of their deeds and always stressed that any person would have acted as they did in the same situation'. Nicla Fiorentino stressed that Donna Guilia was a very good woman whose actions put her in personal danger and she expected no recompense or acknowledgement. It is noted that after the war she returned 'all the belongings that she stored in her home, including gold and merchandise, to the owners'. Warm relations were maintained between the rescued and their rescuers after the war. Costanza said that 'When her parents died the Jews closed their shops during the funeral and participated in a prayer service in the church'.[15]

Nicla's two daughters repeated the story but their evidence was hearsay as they were born after the war. However, they added an interesting detail that Donna Guilia had helped their Aunt Renata when she was giving birth to her son Mario in the cellar. Because of the dangerous conditions he was only circumcised eight months later.[16]

The Costagutis' other daughter, Clotilde Capece Galeota, explained: 'What I can tell you now is that everything my mother did was out of humanitarianism. We live just at the border of the Jewish Ghetto so she knew these people and she didn't think twice in helping them without any question and at risk of her safety.'[17]

Milton Gendel, a historian who originally told me about the Costagutis, said: 'Her parents, long-since dead, were right-wing. I doubt that they were generally pro-Jewish. The people they helped were neighbors, and some were early members of the Fascist Party, I've been told.'[18]

In December 2002 Donna Guilia and her husband, both now deceased, were awarded the title of Righteous Among the Nations in Rome, in the presence of their daughter Costanza and several members of the four families who would not have been there but for their rescuers' bravery. It was held at Palazzo Valentino before the Israeli Ambassador and the Chief Rabbi. At the ceremony, Silvano Moffa (President of the Province of Rome) particularly emphasised the role of Donna Guilia, and said: 'with the simplicity and profound dignity, which comes only from the love of one's fellow men for humanity's sake, beyond all rhetoric, stands out like a mother to all those who came to her for help and comfort.' The President concluded:

> They never gave up. After the war, they never spoke of what they had done as an act of heroism but as something that it was right to do; they have taught us to be on the side of the weak and to face the future with confidence, seeking to build a better world with every deed in our daily lives.[19]

It was noted:

> Unfortunately, there were few people in Europe who behaved like the Costagutis and who, beyond the bounds of politics (Achille was a volunteer in the Fascist militia), felt it was their moral duty to follow

their sense of natural justice and did not passively accept racist laws and deportation.[20]

One of those present at the ceremony in 2002, Giovanni Terracina, the son of one of the families rescued, remembered that a year back, when an increase in anti-Semitism was evident, he had jokingly asked Costanza whether her cellars were still available.

Christine (Christl) Denner (1922–92). Edith Hahn-Beer was born in 1914 in Vienna. She became a law student but was forced to abandon her studies, like other Jewish students, in 1938 after the Anschluss. After being a forced labourer in a rural area she was sent back to Vienna, which would have led to deportation. She decided to ignore the Nazis' edicts and although she boarded the train sporting her compulsory yellow star, when she got off at Vienna she was no longer wearing it. She was fortunate that a Nazi woman she knew as Frau Doktor enabled her to visit another Nazi who dealt with racial identity – a Sippenforscher, named Johann Plattner. She had been told to tell him the truth and, sitting at home 'wearing a brown Nazi uniform with a swastika on his arm', he told her exactly how to get Aryan papers – but she needed an Aryan friend's help.[21] He explained that if her friend previously obtained a vacation ration book as proof, she could claim she had been on holiday and say she had lost her papers. She would receive a new set and Edith could then use the original ones and pass as an Aryan. Plattner even told her not to apply for a *Kleiderkarte* – ration book for clothing – as these were distributed from a national list and the authorities would realise there were two people with the same identity. Plattner's role is remarkable as he saw her in his own home and his two young sons, aged 10 and 12, opened the door to her.

His instructions were very specific but she needed to find someone of the same age. Edith had a friend called Christl Denner, who was eight years younger at only 20, but seemed a likely person to ask. The two young women had lived in the same building before the war and the concierge had recommended Edith as a tutor to the two Denner girls. The building was Palais Salvator, an old Hapsburg palace. When the Nazis created the Ghetto, the Hapsburgs were forced to evict any

Jews and Edith's daughter still has the very apologetic letter that was sent to the family[22] and told her the plan:

> Christl did not hesitate for one second. 'Of course you may have my papers,' she said. 'I'll apply for the vacation ration card tomorrow.' And that was it. Do you understand what it would have meant if Christl Denner had been discovered aiding me in this way? She could have been sent to a concentration camp and possibly killed. Remember that. Remember the speed with which she assented, the total absence of doubt or fear.[23]

Yet the fear was there. She knew how dangerous this was because she never told anyone what she had done until after the war – not even her sister Elsa, to whom she was extremely close, for fear of betrayal to the Gestapo. She was right – when she eventually told Elsa after the war she responded: 'How could you do it? How could you put my life in danger like that?' As Edith's daughter commented, Elsa never said what a wonderful thing Christl had done or how proud she was of her sister.

Edith used the papers to go to Munich, far away from Christl because they now both had the same name. She also had to act eight years younger than her real age. There, sewing to pay her rent and working as a Red Cross nurse, she met a German, Werner Vetter, who fell in love with her and wanted to marry her. She felt obliged to tell him she was Jewish but he accepted it and they married in 1943, with Edith giving birth to her daughter Angela in 1944. Ironically, Christl could not marry her childhood sweetheart, Hans Beran, during the war because Edith, holding her name, was already married. It was only after the war, when Edith was able to regain her true identity, that Christl and Hans were able to marry.[24]

At the end of the war Werner was sent to Siberia. Edith, having already completed her law degree before the war, became a criminal and family law judge in Brandenburg. In 2007 a plaque in her honour was unveiled on the new court house there.[25] Her husband returned in 1947 but could not cope with a wife who was a judge rather than the dutiful *hausfrau* he had left behind. They divorced and he returned to his first wife. After living in Israel for many years, it was only when, in 1997 aged 83, she sold her wartime papers through Sotheby's to pay for cataract operations, that her story became well known. In 1999 her account was published in a co-written book *The Nazi Officer's Wife*.

The difference between the two Denner sisters' response belies the theory sometimes put forward that family upbringing creates rescuers, because they reacted so differently to Edith's plight. However, Christl and Edith remained extremely close friends and their friendship lasted until Christl died in December 1992.[26] Christl was recognised by Yad Vashem as a Righteous Among the Nations in 1985 in her married name Christa Beran. Edith died in March 2009 aged 95. A film is to be made of Edith's remarkable story. The irony of the tale is that, apparently, Vetter was married about seven times, but confided to Angela: 'The time I spent with your mother were the happiest two years of my life.'[27]

Josephine and Victor Guicherd.[28] Berthe (Betty) and Jacques Lewkowitz were hidden by the Guicherds for about three years in the tiny village of Dullin in the Savoie mountains in France. Berthe's mother Perla and 2-year-old brother Michel were less fortunate. They were on transportation No 84 which left Valenciennes, their home-town, on 15 September 1942 with 1,054 Jews on board, of whom 264 were children. The train travelled via the Belgian transit camp of Malines to Auschwitz and Betty's mother and brother were never seen again.[29]

Betty's parents were both Polish and her father, Schmuel Lewkowitz, had been trying to get to Lisbon around 1932 when he ran out of money in Valenciennes and stayed there to become a furrier. The family home was also his shop and had entrances to the street at the front and the back. Betty was born on 19 April 1935.

She recalled her mother as a very kind soft person who sang a lot with a lovely voice. Her parents spoke Yiddish to each other but spoke French to the children, even though their French was not good. The family were not observant and she had no recollections of her mother lighting the Sabbath candles on a Friday night or celebrating Passover with a Seder. In fact, her mother was not a good cook.

In June/July 1940, when France fell to the Germans, Betty was 5 and her brother Jacques was 3. Her mother was pregnant and her father arranged for them to flee on a truck. They were very limited in what they could take and Betty had to leave her 'walking/talking' favourite doll behind. There were lots of people on the road going north to Normandy – not just Jews. Their baby brother was born in Donfront. Eventually they returned home and found the house empty. They did not know whether it had been emptied by the Germans or the French, but Betty's father went to a local auction house to refurnish the home.

When Betty was 6 she started going to a local Catholic school and although she was the only Jewish girl in the school, the nuns were very kind to her. She had to wear a yellow star on the left side of her clothes as the Germans specified; children aged 6 and over were included. A nun at the convent sewed hers with poppers so she could take it off inside the school. In spite of this consideration, each day there was a prayer in the convent about the Jews killing Jesus.

In the summer of 1942 her father began to worry about the children, and Betty and Jacques were sent to stay with a young couple in a nearby town. On 7 September it was Jacques' birthday and her parents came to visit with their baby brother, bringing a cake. Betty's father told their mother to stay there with them but she said she would go back with him. On 11 September, at 5.00 p.m., the Gestapo arrived at the home with French police. They knocked at the door and when no one answered a neighbour said there was no one home. Schmuel escaped through the back door but the Gestapo took Perla and the baby. They were never seen again by the family.

Betty and Jacques were saved because in the few days between the birthday and the arrival of the Gestapo, their father had taken them away to another house where their aunt looked after them. He told them they had a new name – Leroy. He was very tough with them and shouted a lot. Later he came to collect them and they travelled a long way; part of the journey was on a barge on the Lescaux river. They had to travel in the coal-hold and Betty did not like the smell, but her father just shouted and pushed her in. During the journey Betty asked her father about her mother. He initially said she would come when they were in Lyons, but subsequently he cried and said she had been taken by the Germans but she would come back after the war.

At the end of September, accompanied by their aunt, they were taken to Dullin by a Monsieur Nicolai. It was another long journey and at the end they had to walk about 3km. They were extremely tired when they arrived at the Guicherds' farm. Apparently, M. Nicolai was a member of the Jewish Underground and saw Victor Guicherd working on his land one day and asked him if he would like to look after some children. Victor said he and his wife were very poor and had no *confort*. Nevertheless, he said he would like to but he would speak to his wife Josephine. The Guicherds had no children of their own and Josephine agreed to take the children. Betty only heard this story late in life.

Betty described her life on the Guicherds' farm as a paradise, and said the three years she spent there were the happiest of her life until she had her own children. She described with enormous pleasure the chickens and cows and the mountains. There was no running water or bathroom and the children never had to wash except on Sunday when they had a bath before going to church. She enjoyed going to church and prayed to the statue of the Virgin Mary to bring her mother back. She also enjoyed going to school, where she was taught by nuns who she was sure knew they were Jewish but never said anything. She also learnt to play the piano because she liked hearing the nuns play the organ.

She had a wonderful relationship with Victor, who was very wise and knowledgeable about country matters and the seasons. He taught her about birds, the flowers and trees, the weather and stars. He had his breakfast in the fields and she used to take it to him in a basket, and whilst he ate he taught her about country life. They had eleven or twelve cows, who each had a name, and she helped with them after school. She learnt how to make butter, cream and goats' cheese. Josephine had been in service before her marriage and was an excellent cook, so she taught Betty how to do it.

In the video Betty describes the three Christmases they spent with the Guicherds, and watching everyone go to Midnight Mass. All the villagers carried lights to go to the church and it looked like a Bruegel painting.

There was also another Jewish family hidden in the village, which was more of a hamlet with only ninety villagers. There were some collaborators but most people hated the Germans and accepted they were Jewish, although because of bombing, as in England, many non-Jewish children were evacuated to the country.

The Guicherds had taken enormous risks in looking after these children. The infamous Klaus Barbie was based at Lyons and personally supervised the deportation of forty-one Jewish children, aged between 3 and 14, to Auschwitz. They had been hidden in a large country house in Izieu, only 3 miles from Dullin. Collaborators had told his agents that Jewish children were hiding in Izieu, in Dullin and in the other Savoie mountain villages, and he had set out to find them. For five days, while a German armoured personnel carrier patrolled the footpaths, and the soldiers knocked on the doors at Dullin, Victor Guicherd concealed Betty and Jacques in a hollow table of the kind French *paysans* use to store bread and flour (*see plate 22*).[30]

Some years ago I visited Barbie's HQ in Lyons, which is now a museum to the Resistance. It was very quiet with few visitors and I found the atmosphere heavy with dread, knowing that members of the Resistance had been tortured to death – I could not finish the tour and escaped outside. So the Guicherds knew they were running dreadful risks, but when asked why they did it in subsequent years they always responded: 'Why do you ask?' In answer to my question on their motivation, Betty wrote:

This, of course, is the question of questions. There was no ulterior motive – financial, religious or egocentric – of which we are aware. It may have been an altruism that really cannot be defined in normal human terms – the Guicherds certainly didn't want and couldn't put it into words – 'why do you ask?' they said.

We think they, M. Guicherd, in particular, fell in love with Betty as the daughter they did not have and decided to defy the Germans and French collaborators to keep her alive. They knew that they were running risks – Barbie had rounded up Jewish children a few miles away in Izieu – and were well aware that they would be shot if their activities were discovered. We think that even in such terrible times remarkable people emerge to show us that humanity and the Just, no matter how few, are more than mere trees, planted in Yad Vashem, but the seeds and blossom of our future.[31]

This view is corroborated by the letter Victor wrote around 1980–81 when Yad Vashem was endeavouring to honour him. He explained he was unable to go to Paris because Josephine was disabled and his own age precluded such a journey. He continued:

> You ask me for a testimony on behalf of the Jews during the years of Occupation. I helped as much as I could those who were in distress and, as I have already told you, I consider that as natural as simple human solidarity.
>
> You are asking me for memories; those I prefer are those that concern the two children, Berthe and Jacques, who were confined to our trust for three years. It is their aunt who brought them to us when their mother had been deported with her baby. We did our best to educate them, to give them instruction and in one word – to love them.
>
> We were very sad to have to give them back to their father and since we have always been in touch with them.
>
> Today Jacques is a doctor in Paris, married and the father of three children; Berthe went to Israel, lives in Jerusalem. Is married to a journalist, Mr Eppel, and is the mother of two children.
>
> Their affection is the best reward for what we have done for them.[32]

Betty described how the joy of liberation was tempered by the sorrow of leaving the Guicherds, with whom they had been so happy. Victor heard about the end of the war on the radio, to which he used to listen in his cellar. The church bells were ringing and everyone was very happy, but in August their father came for them. They no longer knew their father, he was a stranger to them, and they did not want to go back with him. Josephine made them a packed lunch for the train and Victor walked with them to the station. Everyone was crying.

Their aunt looked after them for a year and took Betty to the cinema to see the films of the liberation of the camps. After a year she was sent to a boarding school in their old hometown but her father never visited her. She was the only Jewish girl in the school and hated giving her name. Her father remarried when she was 14 and she told me that the immediate post-war years were the worst of her life.[33] Betty's father died in 1989 aged 86.

Only many years after the war did the Eppels discover the true extent of the Guicherds' courage:

> ... sitting at the same table in which he had hidden the children, when we asked Victor Guicherd if Betty or Jacques had been any trouble did he tell us his secret. No, neither of the children had been any trouble – but 'les autres ...'
>
> There were others? 'Oh, yes, there was Oxenberg, Nikolai, and Barr.' The harvest 'labourers' at his table had, in fact, been Jews trying to escape across the mountains into Switzerland.[34]

Betty wrote regularly to the Guicherds all through this period and in 1951, when she was 16, she visited them whilst she was staying at a Jewish holiday camp. She went to Israel in 1964. She stayed in touch and visited them regularly. Victor died on 12 March 1988 at the age of 90; Josephine had died in 1984.[35]

Betty told me that Victor had a long correspondence with Yad Vashem but was not willing to have the medal of the Righteous Among the Nations. Although he was honoured by Israel, he never received it.[36] However, he made Betty a gift of the large metal key to the barn where she and her brother Jacques used to play and hide. It hangs on the wall of her home in Jerusalem, a tangible memento of a truly remarkable couple.

Since I conducted my research a website, www.hiddenroots.org, has been created for both Betty and David's family histories. Sadly, David died on 31 March 2006. Betty recently visited the village again with her grandchildren and found that the bread box they used to hide in was still there and offered to buy it. The current owner refused to sell it to her as he was giving it to her. Betty's problem now is to get it to Jerusalem.[37]

Dr Feng Shan Ho (1901–97) was at the Chinese Embassy in Vienna at the time of the Anschluss in March 1938. He witnessed Hitler's triumphant parade through Vienna and later, with the diplomatic corps, met him. Dr Ho recalled: 'He was a short little man. He had a ridiculous moustache. He was an unspeakable martinet.'[38] He subsequently told his daughter how appalled he had been by the fanatical welcome he witnessed the Austrians give Hitler.[39] Immediately following the arrival of the Nazis, vicious persecution made many of the 185,000 Austrian Jews desperate to leave their native land, but no country was willing to accept them. In May 1938 the Chinese Embassy became a consulate and Dr Ho was appointed Consul-General at the age of 37.[40] The Evian Conference in July 1938 confirmed the Jews' appalling situation.

Dr Ho was so perturbed by the Jews' circumstances that he personally decided to issue visas to Shanghai. These visas were not actually required by the authorities for entry into China, but the Nazi authorities required such proof of emigration to give permission to leave Austria. Additionally, possession of such visas meant that some Jews detained in camps such as Dachau and Buchenwald were released to return safely to their families; and countries such as Italy and Britain were prepared to grant transit visas with such proof of a final destination.

Dr Ho was extremely sympathetic to the plight of the Jews. He later wrote in his memoirs:

> Since the annexation of Austria by Germany, the persecution of the Jews by Hitler's 'devils' became increasingly fierce. The fate of Austrian Jews was tragic, persecution a daily occurrence. There were American religious and charitable organisations which were urgently trying to save the Jews. I secretly kept in close contact with these organisations. I spared no effort in using any means possible. Innumerable Jews were thus saved.[41]

Dr Ho knew that many people would not wish to go to China, but his visas simply gave them an escape route from Nazi Europe. By September 1938 knowledge of the availability of the Chinese visas was widespread and queues were forming at the Chinese Consulate. Many Jews waited for days, like Hans Kraus, whose wife Gerda recalled:

> There were long, long lines in front of the Consulate and while people were waiting, the Gestapo were outside harassing them and beating them up. There were so many people that Hans stood in line for many days, wondering when he would be able to get in. One day, when he lined up again, he saw the Chinese Consul General's car about to enter the Consulate. He saw that the car window was open, so he thrust his visa application paper through the open car window. Apparently, the Consul General received it because he then got a call and received the visas.[42]

The difficulties of evading the Nazis have been confirmed by two Viennese escapees. Charles Peter Carter was only 17 when he was 'thrown down the stairs at school a week after the Anschluss, when being a Jew in Vienna meant, among other things, experiencing the transformation of people's attitudes from friendliness to hostility'. He decided to leave and relatives in London acted as guarantors for his visa which was granted. However:

> Collecting the visa was an altogether different matter as it meant running the gauntlet of Nazi thugs surrounding the British Embassy; achieved with the assistance of Peter's English tutor who fended off aggressive taunts by replying that she was English and Peter was her nephew![43]

Otto Fleming also corroborated the difficulties. In 1938 he was thrown out of the University of Vienna just before he was due to sit his final medical examinations, and thus, having no qualifications, no country wanted to take him. Hearing that the Chinese Consulate was issuing visas to Shanghai, he bought a steamer ticket there and then approached the British Consulate requesting a tourist visa for Palestine, en route for Shanghai.[44] This was granted without difficulties but Otto stayed in Palestine and never reached Shanghai. He never actually obtained the Chinese visa, but knowing it would be easy led Otto to leave. He confirmed the dangers of being seen in the streets of Vienna at this time and told me that women rather than men tended to go out more because they often were less Jewish-looking and less likely to be harassed by the Nazis.[45]

Dr Ho personally intervened for his friends the Rosenbergs on the very morning after Kristallnacht, when he called at their home to say goodbye. He had issued them with visas for Shanghai but the Gestapo had called at the house to take Mr Rosenberg to a labour camp. His courageous intervention[46] led to the release of Mr Rosenberg and the family left Vienna safely.[47] Dr Ho's behaviour caused considerable concern amongst the authorities, as the Nationalist Chinese government continued to maintain good diplomatic relations with Nazi Germany, and Chiang Kai-shek, China's ruler, admired the Nazis.

Not surprisingly, the Chinese Ambassador in Berlin, Chen Jie, who was Consul-General Ho's direct superior, was adamantly opposed to the issuing of visas to Jewish refugees. He wanted to maintain good diplomatic relations with Germany and did not want to contravene Hitler's policy against Jews. Having learned that the Chinese Consulate in Vienna was issuing large numbers of visas to Jews, Ambassador Chen called Ho by telephone and ordered him to desist. Ho tried to deflect him by saying that 'the Foreign Ministry's orders' were to maintain a 'liberal policy' in this regard. On hearing this, Chen snapped: 'If that is so, I will take care of the Foreign Ministry end, you just follow my orders!'[48]

But Dr Ho continued with his 'liberal policy', issuing visas at a rate of about 500 a month for two years. It is estimated that he saved in excess of 12,000 Jews but it is not possible to know the real number. It is known that on 18 October 1938 he issued visa No 1681 to Mrs Lustig and visa No 1787 to Mr Lustig. They used them to escape to Shanghai in January 1939 and their daughter Lotte, now 76, still has them. She concludes that these numbers prove Dr Ho issued at least 106 visas that day.[49]

Aware of the dangers in Vienna, Dr Ho sent his wife and 11-year-old son to America for safety. In the spring of 1938 the Nazis confiscated the Chinese Consulate's building. Dr Ho's government refused his request for funds to relocate the Consulate. He therefore moved the Consulate to smaller premises, meeting all the costs himself. He was censured by his bosses on 8 April 1939, and in May 1940 he was transferred from Vienna. He alone seemed willing to help the desperate Austrian Jews. When asked why, he replied: 'I thought it only natural to feel compassion and to want to help. From the standpoint of humanity, that is the way it should be.'[50]

After he left Vienna he returned to China, where he was involved in the war effort against the Japanese. In 1947 he became Ambassador to Egypt and other Middle Eastern countries for nine years. His daughter Manli was born in Cairo. After the civil war, he sided with the Chinese Nationalists in Taiwan and was their Ambassador in Mexico, Bolivia and Colombia. He retired in 1973 but the Chinese Nationalist government in Taiwan 'launched a public vendetta to publicly discredit him' and he was denied his pension after forty years' service. Manli has written that the reasons for this attack have never been revealed, and thirty years later his name had not been cleared.[51] He lived to be 96 and died on 28 September 1997, having written his autobiography, Forty Years of My Diplomatic Life, in Chinese in 1990. On 7 July 2000 he was recognised as a Righteous Among the Nations by Israel but, as Dr Paldiel commented on Dr Ho's nomination: 'I find it sad that Mr Ho was nominated only after he passed away in 1997. We could have put these questions to him, which would have made it easier … But also we could have thanked him in person.'[52]

Normally Righteous have to have put themselves at risk and have received no payment. In the case of diplomats, Yad Vashem has to be clear that the diplomat was disobeying his government's instructions before an award can be made. Manli Ho believes it was her father's poverty-stricken childhood that influenced his behaviour towards the Austrian Jews. She does not regard him as having been a religious man. She considers that it was education that influenced him most – both in the Western liberal arts and traditional Chinese Confucian ethics. Added to this was the influence of growing up during a transitional period in Chinese history, when the ancient East met the new West. She therefore believes he tried to live his life according to 'the best in Confucian and Judeo-Christian values'.[53]

Manli also confirms her father's pride in being Chinese and how he brought her and her brother up to value their Chinese heritage, naming them after Confucian principles. She also feels that he was influenced by the times into which he was born. He was part of 'a generation of Chinese who felt that China had been humiliated and persecuted by 100 years of foreign imperialism. His generation was determined not to allow that humiliation to continue. In that sense my father was very sensitive to persecution and to bullying of any peoples.'[54]

Ho was born on 10 September 1901, in a rural part of Hunan Province. At the age of 7 he was not only poor but fatherless as well. The Norwegian Lutheran Mission in China not only helped him and his family, it educated him as well, and for that he was grateful all his life.[55] He wrote in his autobiography:

> At the schools that I attended, from the schools of the [Norwegian] Lutherans, to the College of Yale-in-China ... The emphasis in their education was to build individual character; that is to learn the Judeo–Christian values of self-sacrifice in giving unto others, and of service to society.[56]

When his daughter turned 20, the Chinese legal age of majority, Dr Ho wrote to her saying 'that after having raised and educated me, he hoped that I would live my life as a "useful" human being. I don't think I could have asked for a better role model.' Rabbi Moshe Linchner spoke at an event to honour Dr Ho in Jerusalem on 19 February 2004, in the presence of Manli, the Chinese Ambassador and some of the survivors and their children. He said:

> He sacrificed his career and endangered his life to save thousands of Jews who otherwise would have perished at the hands of the Nazis. It takes tremendous courage and integrity to stand up against a cruel foreign country like Nazi Germany. It takes even more courage to stand up to one's superiors and own country. Dr Ho did this because it was the right thing to do.[57]

He did not believe in telling everyone what he had done and his daughter quotes an ancient Chinese proverb: 'Good deeds performed to be seen by others are not truly good.'[58] Dr Ho expressed his philosophy of life in a poem he wrote for his wife Shauyun on New Year's day 1947:

The gifts Heaven bestows are not by chance,
The convictions of heroes not lightly formed.
Today I summon all spirit and strength,
Urging my steed forward ten thousand miles.[59]

In September 2007 Manli took her father's ashes back to China, ten years after his death, as he had always wished to be laid to rest in his native land. He was buried in his hometown of Yiyang in Hunan Province in the beautiful Hui-longshan Park. The city of Yiyang scheduled a commemorative event on 28 September 2007 in honor of his 'homecoming'. Manli wrote on that occasion:

It has taken me 10 years of research and documentation to piece together the history of my father's humanitarian efforts. During his lifetime, he neither sought nor received recognition for his deeds. In fact, he rarely spoke of his tenure as the Chinese Consul General in Vienna from 1938 to 1940. It was only by chance, after his death in 1997, that his helping thousands of Austrian Jews escape the Holocaust came to light. But, having to piece together this puzzle nearly 70 years later means that we may never know the full extent of my father's humanitarian efforts …

I was often asked why a Chinese diplomat would save Jews in Austria when others would not. My response has been: 'If you knew my father, you wouldn't have to ask.' This is usually followed by: 'But weren't you surprised to discover this facet of your father?' No, I was not surprised because what my father did was completely in character.[60]

Manli has said, 'I am often asked why he did it', and she explains:

My father strove to live his life according to the best in Confucian and Judeo-Christian values. If helping those in distress is natural to a human being, then why should it warrant particular praise or mention? For his reasons in helping Jewish refugees, my father simply said: 'I thought it only natural to feel compassion and to want to help. From the standpoint of humanity, that is the way it should be' … And although my father is gone, I feel as though he lives on through the survivors.[61]

Two cousins in Lithuania, Irena Veisaite and Margaret Kagan (see p. 107), were rescued separately by Roman Catholics who were true humanitarians. Jews had been in Lithuania since the fourteenth century. In 1939 Jews made up one-third of the urban population and yet during the Holocaust more than 90 per cent of Lithuania's 240,000 Jews were killed, mostly by Lithuanians on Nazi orders.[62]

Stefanija Ladigiené (1902–67). Irena Veisaite was born in 1928 in Kovno and was protected by several Lithuanian families. Her last place of hiding was provided by Stefanija Ladigiené in Vilnius, whom she called her second mother. She was the widow of a general, Kazimieras Ladyga, who had been shot by the Russians. She was a very good woman – intelligent and well educated, who had worked as a journalist and was involved in the Resistance. Irena was sent to her in March 1944 by a couple who had rescued her from the Kaunas Ghetto. Stefanija told Irena she had taken her in to compensate for the injustice that had been done to Jews by her compatriots. Irena was overwhelmed by Stefanija's kindness to her as when she first arrived she was very pale and hungry. 'Food was very scarce – she gave her more pasta than her own children – later she kissed her and Irena cried because it was such a long time since someone had kissed her and been kind to her.'[63]

Irena Veisaite was rescued for purely humanitarian reasons:

Stefanija Ladigiené's sole motive in accepting me was her profound humanity, love to her next. A deeply believing Catholic, she became my second mother. In those hard occupation and post-war years, she shared her last bite of bread with me. She did not have a separate flat, and the SS headquarters were located in the same building. If I had been caught, Stefanija Ladigiené would have been killed in Paneriai with her children. However, her act, I would say heroism, was so natural as if there could be no other way. This gave me an unusual feeling of security at that time.[64]

Irena arrived at Stefanija's home after a series of unfortunate adventures but, as she originally wrote to me, she 'was saved by several Lithuanian

Christian families'.[65] She had a very pleasant childhood in a large middle-class family. In 1938 her parents divorced and just before the war in 1941 her mother was in hospital. Her mother was arrested while there and sent to prison. Irena then described how as a young girl of 13 she was sent to the Kaunas (Kovno) Ghetto with her parents and Aunty Polla Ginsburg, where she stayed for two and a half years.

In 1942 friends of her parents from Belgium, Ona and Juozas Strimaitis, managed to get a message to her that they were looking for her and wanted to help her go into hiding. The wife had worked with her father. They encouraged her to escape from the Ghetto. It was a difficult decision, but she did it. She left the Ghetto with a working brigade, with her yellow star just pinned on for easy removal later. At the particular moment that she left the column of Jews, she could have been shot at any moment. However, she was two hours late to the meeting point and there was no one there. She therefore went to the Strimaitis' home and spoke to the caretaker. She was extremely scared because he could have betrayed them all. They gave her false documents and a passport and it was decided she should go to Vilnius where nobody knew her. One of the documents she was given said she was the daughter of a director of a *gymnasium*.[66]

On 7 November 1943, aged 15, Irena travelled to Vilnius on a very crowded train. She was to have stayed with a dentist who was Mr Strimaitis' sister, but the family were very nervous so she was moved to a surgeon, the brother of Ona Strimaitis, Pranas Bagdonavicius, who knew her family as well. He told people she was from the country. She was registered at his address and went to church. She spoke good Lithuanian, unlike many Jews who were used to speaking Yiddish, and spoke it with an accent. All was well until some friends came round with a book on Van Gogh and she said how much she liked his work. Perhaps this was unexpected from a country girl and people began to suspect she was Jewish. Her host's fiancée heard the rumours so Irena had to be moved on.

By 1944 she was put with a woman who had a daughter of a similar age, whose husband had been deported. The woman was unkind to her and warned her not to touch her daughter's food. She also made unpleasant remarks about Jews. A kind neighbour found her some work in an orphanage for children under 2 years old. The director, Dr Izidorius Rudaitis, was told she was half-Jewish and she worked as a domestic help. She had only been there a week when the Gestapo arrived. She went to the toilet and decided to stay put to protect her rescuers. The Gestapo had come looking for Jewish children they had been told were in the orphanage. The director denied it and winked at Irena. The Gestapo went away and she felt much safer. However, two months later the Gestapo came back, to the house she was staying at. Her woman rescuer told her to leave immediately by the back door as they came through the front door. She went back to the dentist where she stayed for one day.

It was after all these traumatic experiences that in March 1944 Irena was finally sent to Stefanija. She had six children but only three were living with her at the time. Irena arrived late in the afternoon and Stefanija told her own children to treat Irena like a sister from the country. Although she was a very devout Catholic, and was very tolerant, she was a strict mother to her children.[67]

After Lithuania was liberated by the Russians on 13 July 1944, Irena stayed with the family and started going to school. On 14 March 1946 Stefanija was arrested, tried by a KGB three-man board and sent to Siberia. She was only allowed to return in 1956 after Stalin's death. In 1967 she died in Irena's arms. She was only one of many tens of thousands of Lithuanians who were exiled to Siberia. Historians have calculated that between 1940 and 1952 up to one-third of the Lithuanian population was lost to massacre, war casualties, deportations, executions and immigration.[68]

Irena stayed in Vilnius and is now a Professor of Philology, World and German Literature at its university. In 2001 she led a seminar at the Stockholm International Forum on Holocaust Education and in answer to a question on the motivation of teachers; she replied:

As a Nazi Holocaust survivor myself, I would like to say, that the terrible experience we went through should motivate us not only to concentrate on our own suffering, but be open and especially sensitive to the suffering of our fellow man and do everything to prevent a new Holocaust in the future. It is a question of the survival of mankind in general.[69]

Professor Veisaite was also the founding chair of the Open Society Foundation of Lithuania. It was founded in 1990 with the aim of fostering democracy in the former Soviet Republic, and she chaired it from 1993 to 2000. Lithuania is trying to examine the truths of the past and Irena has said this is not a Jewish project. She added:

> It is a question for all of us in common. Of course it has not been an easy process, but it is very important equally for Jews and Lithuanians. We are trying to create a civil society, and in this effort it is crucial for Lithuania to understand what happened here. Because as long as you are hiding the truth, as long as you fail to come to terms with your past, you can't build your future.[70]

The Lithuanians are accepting their role in the Holocaust and accordingly, in 1995, the new President of Lithuania, Algirdas Brazauskas, appeared in the Knesset in Israel to deliver a formal apology for Lithuanian collaboration with the Nazis. Meanwhile, Veisaite was active with various projects. She participated in the creation of the House of Memory which ran an essay competition for the whole country called 'Jews: Neighbors of my Grandparents and Great-Grandparents', which encouraged children to interview their elders and several volumes of winning entries have been published. She initiated the creation of the Centre for Stateless Cultures at Vilnius University. She also helped to initiate a travelling exhibition: 'Jewish Life in Lithuania'. She is anxious to promote tolerance and an understanding of beliefs and practices different to one's own but with complete non-acceptance of intolerance.[71]

Irena wrote about Stefanija's family in 1997: 'My relations with the whole family remained extremely close up to the present. I feel that her children are my brothers and sisters, and their children – my nephews and nieces.'

Irena has concluded:

> Unfortunately, to kill thousands of people only a few men with machine guns are needed, and they do not risk anything except their souls. Saving of just one man involved exceptional devotion, undescribable courage of

many people, and they were risking not only their lives, but also those of their children.[72]

Iris Origo DBE (1902–88) was a writer with an American father and Anglo-Irish mother. She grew up in Italy after her father's death when she was 8. He had expressed the wish that she be brought up in Italy or France – 'free from all this national feeling which makes people so unhappy. Bring her up somewhere where she does not belong, then she can't have it.'[73] She was educated in Florence, where she later met an Italian aristocrat, Marchese Antonio Origo, whom she married on 4 March 1924. They settled on a neglected Tuscan estate, La Foce, which they restored and maintained under German occupation.[74] Mussolini had come to power in 1922 and the Origos benefited from his policies to keep people on the land rather than moving to the towns.

When Italy entered the war as an ally of Germany, Iris worked with the Italian Red Cross in Rome dealing with British POWs until she became pregnant in 1942 and returned to La Foce. She was in a very difficult position because her own country was at war with her adopted country and she was married to an Italian. Her husband Antonio, who in the early years approved of Mussolini's agricultural policies, took some time to understand what fascism really meant. Iris, initially uncertain, came to detest it long before he did. As a writer, Iris recorded her wartime experiences in her adopted country in diaries which were published after the war. They provide a valuable insight into how life changed around her.

Writing of the pre-war period 1935–40, Iris was aware of the changes occurring in Europe, even in her isolation at La Foce, and describes the impact of the radio at that time: 'Previously, non-combatants had been, for the most part, only aware of what the press of their own country told them, or what they saw with their own eyes. Now, we were all constantly exposed to these confusing, overwhelming waves, from friends and enemies alike.'[75]

In this period she wrote of her shock at a telephone call she received from a woman acquaintance in the immediate pre-war period. 'She and I had been asked to send a nominal invitation to an old Czechoslovak professor and his wife, which would enable them to get a transit visa through Italy and thus escape from Prague and rejoin their sons in England.' Her acquaintance was complaining about having been asked to get involved and complaining that this 'might have got us into trouble'. Iris tried to explain that the professor and his wife were old and ill and this was their only chance to rejoin their sons. The woman was quite unmoved: 'I have no sympathy with such people. Why didn't they get out months ago, when their sons ran away?' Iris managed to ring off. A few minutes later the woman rang back demanding to know what Iris was going to do about it, and warning Iris that Italy was not neutral and she could get her husband into trouble. 'Why, it's the sort of thing one would hardly do for a member of one's own family!'

Iris was very upset and she wrote:

> Swallowing my anger — which was sharper for being mixed with a mean little twinge of uneasiness — I hedged, and then, having rung off, sat on the edge of the bed, trembling. The ugly trivial conversation seemed to have a dispro-portionate importance: it seemed to symbolise all the cowardly, self-protective, arrogant cruelty of the world — our world.[76]

Fortunately, Iris Origo did not allow this acquaintance to influence her. In the late 1930s, with 'the Juggernaut approach of war', she still visited England regularly. She wrote that through her close friend Lilian Bowes Lyon (1895–1949), cousin of the late Queen Mother, and some Quaker friends she 'was able to share the efforts of some people who, already then, were devoting their energies to enabling a few Jewish scholars, old people and children, to make their escape from Germany before it was too late'.[77] The children came on the Kindertransport and most never saw their parents again. Iris sponsored six Jewish children and paid for them to go to Bunce Court School in Kent, run for Jewish refugee children. Quakers were instrumental in the running of the school. When one boy from Berlin left in 1947 aged 16, he stated his intention of becoming a painter and eventually became a pupil of David Bomberg. His name was Frank Helmet Auerbach.

Bunce Court had evolved from a German progressive boarding school called Herrlingen, sited in the Schwabian Jura mountain region, created and run by a remarkable Jewish woman called Anna Essinger. In 1933 she realised she and the school had no future under Hitler and, aged 54, she moved it to England with the help of the Quakers, bringing seventy pupils with her.[78] Eventually it housed many children whose parents were exterminated in the concentration camps. Walter Block wrote of Bunce Court:

> The school gave me a sound foundation for my working and family life and I am forever mindful and thankful that the actions of concerned individuals and organisations, including Quakers, made it possible for so many of us 'Kinder' to survive; to lead constructive lives and give something back to our host country.[79]

I asked Frank Auerbach how a Christian woman in Italy had rescued a little Jewish boy from Berlin. He told me it came about through his uncle Jakob Auerbach who was a lawyer. Uncle Jakob's partner, called Altenberg, had retired to Italy and had already sent his own children to England. In Italy he got to know Iris Origo and heard that she wanted to sponsor six Jewish children to go to safety in England. He suggested his niece and nephew, Ilse and Heinz Altenberg, and Frank Auerbach, his partner's son. Frank has described how they three children, all under 8 years old, travelled from Hamburg accompanied by the Altenbergs' nanny on the SS *George Washington* on 7 April 1939, arriving on the same day in Southampton and going straight to Bunce Court. The nanny returned to Germany.[80]

A biography on Frank Auerbach fleshed out the story. Charlotte, his mother, was artistic and was married to Max Auerbach, a patent lawyer. He was born in 1931 and recalled a childhood of parental strain and worry, partly because of the economic situation – Austrian and German banks were collapsing – and also because of the rise of the brownshirts. As Auerbach learnt to toddle, the Nazis were marching down Berlin's streets and the persecution of the Jews began:

> People like Auerbach's parents, the liberal, educated German Jews of the professional classes, men and women in whose family traditions stetl and pogrom were vague memories at most, could not imagine the Final

Solution; it still lay incubating, like a dragon's egg, in the minds of Hitler and Himmler.[81]

Frank's parents' anxiety hung over the small child and turned into what he called 'frantic coddling': 'I remember velvet knickerbocker suits and no freedom. I couldn't run in the park near the house. I couldn't step outside the door on my own, of course, and my mother would begin to worry if my father was half an hour late home.'

By 1937 they felt the 6-year-old would be in real danger if he stayed in Germany. 'But his father would not go; presumably, like many other Jews, he hoped that Nazism would soften, that its racial policy would be diluted by cultural and economic necessity, and that resolute adults might still breathe the air that would choke a little boy.'

Iris Origo offered an escape route by turning her concerns about Jewish children into actions. It was fortuitous for Auerbach that his family's tentacles reached to her as she knew none of the six children whose escape she financed.[82] I have not been able to find out about the other three children, but Iris Origo's autobiographical writings are littered with references about what she thought was happening to Jews and others. Her daughter has spoken about her mother's humanity. This is demonstrated by her insight into the difficulties of the Jewish parents whose children had the chance to leave:

> I have never been able to forget the description given to me by one of the Quaker workers in Germany of the agony of mind of the parents obliged to make a choice, when they were told (as was sometimes neces-sary) that only one child from each family could go. Should it be the most brilliant or the most vulnerable? The one most fitted, or least likely, to survive? Which, if it were one's own child, would one choose?[83]

Reading this reminded me of the story of Lore Cahn (*née* Grünberger), who was 14 when her parents put her on the Kindertransport to go to England. At the last moment her father couldn't bear to let her go – he had been holding her hands through the window as the train began to move and he just pulled her out of the train through the window. She had a terrible time, being sent to Theresienstadt in 1941 with her parents; she was then separated from them and sent to Auschwitz. She was finally liberated in Bergen-Belsen. Her mother had been murdered but her father survived.[84]

The parents' choice was diabolical and showed enormous courage, and as Louise London has written:

> We remember the touching photographs and newsreel footage of unaccompanied Jewish children arriving on the Kindertransports [by July 1939, 7,700 had arrived, compared with 1,850 admitted into Holland, 800 into France, 700 into Belgium and 250 into Sweden]. There are no such photographs of the Jewish parents left behind in Nazi Europe … The Jews excluded from entry to the United Kingdom are not part of the British experience, because Britain never saw them.[85]

Iris also ended up providing refuge to many Italian refugee children. Early in 1943 the first group of seven children arrived at La Foce from families in Genoa whose homes had been destroyed. Another little group of six girls arrived from Turin in February and Iris wrote in her diary:

> Children such as these, all over Europe, have had to leave their own homes and families, and are arriving – bewildered but hopeful – among strangers. There is something terribly moving in this exodus – something, too, so deeply wrong in a world where such a thing is not only possible but necessary, that it is difficult not to feel personally responsible. For the present we can try to salve our consciences by giving them food, shelter and love. But that is not enough. Nothing can ever really be enough.[86]

How right she was and how universal was the uprooting of families and bewildered children by the war – even those evacuated in their own countries, let alone those sent to another country by the Kindertransport.

At La Foce they were pretty well self-supporting, and this included the twenty-three children. After Mussolini fell in 1943, and following the surrender of the Badoglio government to the Allies that September, the Germans were still occupying much of Italy. The community really pulled together, 'as the old barriers of tradition and class were broken down and we were held together by the same difficulties, fears expectations and hopes':

> Together we planned how to hide the oil, the hams and cheeses, so that the Germans could not find them; together we found shelter for the fugitives who knocked at our door – whether Italians, Allies or Jews, soldiers or civilians.[87]

Very late the same year, on 15 December, Iris noted:

> Two other fugitives turn up – an old Jew from Siena and his son. Both of them, clad in the most unsuitable of town clothes and thin shoes, are shivering with cold and terror. The father, the owner of an antique shop, produces from an inner pocket, drawing me aside, a little carved ivory Renaissance figure which he wishes to exchange for food and warm clothing. We supply the latter, and suggest that he should keep the figure for future needs. He and his son wish to walk through the German lines to Naples – and to all our dissuasions (since it is clear that the old man, who suffers from heart-disease, will die upon the way) they only reply – 'We have no choice. We must.' After a rest and some food they start up the hill in the snow, the old man groaning a little as he leans on his son's shoulder.[88]

That Christmas, her diary records that the Pope's Christmas Eve homily sounded fairly despairing as little goodwill abounded, but she commented that in her own village she felt there was 'a bond of deep understanding born of common trouble, anxieties and hopes such as I have never felt before. And in the attitude of the farmers to all the homeless passers-by (whether Italian soldiers or British prisoners, whether Gentile or Jew) there is a spontaneous, unfailing charity and hospitality.'[89]

I first heard about Iris Origo from an article in *The Times* on 25 July 2002, about the music festival her daughters, Benedetta and Donata, were running at La Foce to celebrate the centenary of their mother's birth. I e-mailed the address given and have had great help from

Benedetta. Like many relatives of rescuers, she had known little of her mother's activities during the war. She told me:

> Yes, my mother – and many others like her, in Italy at that time – helped Jews on the run … Also, I found out only after her death that she was among some people (from London, I think) who financed the escape to England of some children from Jewish families in Germany. Among these was the child Frank Auerbach, later to become a famous artist.[90]

Subsequently, Benedetta wrote that she could not tell me much more but:

> beyond this, my family in Italy gave help to any person who appeared in distress or need during the war years, as a matter of course, whether they were Jewish or not … And so did many Italians – who, as a whole, are not antisemitic, contrary to fascist appearances.
>
> As to motivation, I am sure it was pure humanity and fellow feeling that brought not only my mother but countless others in this country to help, hide, feed, save Jewish people during the war. There are so many single stories that are moving – and stories that often deal with very simple people.[91]

A couple of days later she reiterated her mother's humanity in another e-mail:

> Though my mother had strong religious feelings – that is, she was constantly searching for some kind of religious certainty – she was not particularly observant. She was brought up vaguely Anglican, then converted to Catholicism in her sixties – but was never completely convinced. Anyway, her motives for helping others were humanitarian and based on compassion, more than anything else.[92]

Max Rubino, an art expert, wrote an article in *La Stampa* on 20 October 1990 about Frank Auerbach, and commented on Iris Origo's help towards him. This was the first that Benedetta knew of her mother's impact on Frank Auerbach's life. He concluded that due to her unsentimental nature Iris had never contacted the Auerbachs. I felt this had gone on too long and, having had considerable contact with her eldest daughter Benedetta over a long period, I sent her a copy of his letter and gave him her address.

A biography of Iris Origo described her concern for the refugee local children she cared for at La Foce. Their mothers came to visit them and were overwhelmed by what they saw:

> The food the children were given was good and olive oil was added to the diets of the more malnourished. Fannina Fè is now in her late seventies. She was a helper working at the school – her entire family worked for the Origos – when the refugees arrived. She remembers the way Iris appeared every day, tasted their food and brought across new toys …
>
> Fannina remembers, 'I once asked her why she did all this for us. She replied that "if you have too much, you never really want the things that life gives you".'[93]

Iris was made a DBE in 1977 and died in 1988. Without her charitable and compassionate nature the little 8-year-old boy in Berlin might have become one of the 1.5 million Jewish children murdered by the Nazis. Auerbach's long creative career as an artist, which still continues as he approaches 80, would never have occurred. This fact cannot but lead us to ponder what those 1.5 million children might have achieved had they not been destroyed because no one came forward to save them.

Vytautas Rinkevicius (1906–88). Irena Viesaite's cousin, Margaret Kagan, was born in Kovno, Lithuania, on 12 July 1924. She was hidden for several months in a factory by Vytautas Rinkevicius, a Roman Catholic. Margaret was born Margarita Stromaité; her parents were Jurgis Stromas and Eugenia Stromiene.

Lithuania was independent until the Russians invaded on 15 June 1940, to be followed a year later by the German invasion of 22 June 1941. This unleashed anti-Jewish attacks from the Lithuanians themselves, who held the Jews responsible for the year of Soviet occupation. On 27 June they rounded up fifty Jewish men and beat them to death in the Lietukis garage on Vytautas Prospect. Margaret's father was one of these men. A few days later, Lithuanian partisans raided their house and took their valuables. In August Kovno's Jews were ordered to the Ghetto being created in the suburbs. At the same time, Jews were being rounded up and killed. Margaret, her mother and her brother Alik (born 1931) were all safe but thousands were killed, including her aunt and her son.[94] By August 1941 all the Jews in Kovno were in the Ghetto, created in the old Jewish quarter of Vilijampole.[95]

Margaret was still in the Ghetto with her mother, grandmother and 11-year-old brother Alik when, in October 1943, conditions worsened and her friend Chana Bravo offered to find Alik a hiding place so he could be smuggled out to live with a non-Jewish family. He stayed with a couple, Antanas and Marija Macenavicius, who kept him until the end of the war. Also at this time, Margaret had become friendly with Joseph Kagan who was a slave labourer in a foundry. The man in charge of the foundry was Johannes Bruess, whom Joseph had known before, and Johannes agreed that Joseph could build a hiding place in the loft of the factory. The bookkeeper, Vytautas Garkauskas, also agreed, but the 'heart and soul of the scheme, without whom it would have been a non-starter, was the modest factory foreman Vytautas Rinkevicius'.[96]

Margaret was extremely sceptical when Joseph first asked her to join him and his mother in his hiding place. She agreed to inspect the site and wangled a day's work at the factory where she met Vytautas:

> The man we were approaching was tall and lean, wore blue coveralls and a beret, looked alert, yet reassuringly relaxed. He wore heavy rimmed spectacles and their thick lenses seemed to set him apart from our ugly world. From behind these lenses his eyes exuded calm, hope and confidence. When I got back to my mother in the Ghetto that evening, I found it difficult to explain just why this man had made such a monumental impression on me; but I did manage to convey my deep-felt confidence in Vytautas' integrity and goodwill.[97]

Margaret and Joseph got married in the Ghetto before they left. When I asked Margaret about her marriage she said it was a civil ceremony conducted by Avraham Tory (1909–2002), a young lawyer who was appointed secretary of the Kovno Jewish Council set up by the Nazis. He subsequently became well known when his meticulous diaries covering 1941–44 were published as *Surviving the Holocaust: The Kovno Ghetto Diary*. He was one of the few Holocaust diary writers who survived to publish his work after the war.[98] Apparently the Jewish Council was authorised to carry out civil marriage ceremonies because religious ceremonies were banned.[99]

Eventually, in November 1943, the three of them went to the hideout where they hid for 300 days. Meanwhile, her brother Alik found someone to hide his mother but it was becoming much harder to leave the Ghetto. In July 1944 she was deported to Stutthof concentration camp where she perished in November.[100]

The trio continued hiding in the factory and each day Vytautas came to bring them food and tell them when they could move around. He also dealt with their personal waste. They had to be quiet during the day when the factory was operational and were therefore only active during the hours of 6 p.m. to 6 a.m. Margaret describes the difficulty of obtaining water and how they poured water through a towel into a bucket to cut down the noise.[101]

Vytautas was a wonderful support throughout the difficulties of living that half-life:

> How he managed to remain so calm (unrattled) and supportive throughout these nine mouths will forever remain a mystery to me. We Jews were under sentence of death and in this 'no choice-ein breira' situation would, not unnaturally, have to accept risk and deprivation in an effort to save our own skins. Yet there was Vytautas, risking not only his own life, but also his family's – voluntarily (out of his own free will), without any financial incentive or hope for reward, simply in order to save our lives.[102]

One difficulty was his wife, Elia, whom he had tried to protect by not telling her what he was doing:

> Apparently she had noticed that Vytautas now seemed preoccupied and absent minded more often than before; besides, valuable food items

started going missing out of her pantry. This led her to start suspecting
Vytautas of being involved with another woman. It was only when faced
with this suspicion that Vytautas confessed to hiding us.[103]

Once she knew, she proved to be extremely supportive, but understandably worried whether as parents they were right to risk their own
child's life. Margaret describes Elia as a generous and kind-hearted
woman. However, because of these reservations poor Vytautas could
not share his worries about the project with his wife or the Kagans.[104]
These difficulties were exemplified the day the bookkeeper, Mr
Garkauskas, was arrested and the Kagans and Vytautas did not know
whether or not it was related to the Kagans. Fortunately, the next day
'an exceptionally agitated Vytautas came to tell us that Mr Garkauskas
had managed to smuggle a letter out of jail to tell us that his arrest was
unconnected with us'. But their relief was short-lived when they heard
the truth:

> Sadly, he had been denounced by a neighbour for harbouring a Jewish
> child and the inevitability of tragic consequences marred our own relief
> at not having come to the end of our road. As it happened, G. managed
> to escape death, the child did not. To reconcile our double-edged emo-
> tions of horror and relief was hard.[105]

Vytautas continued his care for them and even arranged a brief 'holiday'
with some Lithuanian friends for Joseph's mother when the claus-
trophobic conditions became too much for her.[106] As German defeat
became more likely in the summer of 1944 there were concerns that the
retreating Nazis would blow up the factories. Vytautas arranged with
Alik's foster family for Joseph and his mother to go to them. Margaret
was to follow a few days later but had to stay in the loft because of her
Jewish appearance. Vilijampole was liberated by the Russians on 31 July
1944. The Ghetto was set on fire by the Germans as they left and the
surviving inhabitants met a horrible end. Finally, Vytautas installed the
three of them in his own home which seemed like a palace after all their
privations. After finding a flat to rent they tried to come to terms with
what had happened to Europe and its Jews.

In January 1945 they set off to try to find Joseph's father who had gone to England before the war. The subsequent Cold War years prevented contact but Margaret saw Vytautas in 1964 and recalls: 'Words failed us both at this indescribable moment, but our emotions mingled in a long silent embrace.' In 1972 Margaret and Joseph met Vytautas in Moscow, with his daughter Vitalija, and the couple who hid Alik. The rescuers all died before Lithuania gained its independence: Marija and Antanas in 1979 and 1980 respectively, and Elia Rinkevicius in 1981. Vytautas died in 1988. Both couples were recognised as Righteous Among the Nations in 1976.[107]

In 1989 Vitalija was able to visit London with her husband, and at the House of Lords – in the presence of Dr Kahle, Chaplain of Westminster Cathedral, family and friends – the Chief Rabbi, Dr Jakobovits, made a moving speech and presented the medal of a Righteous Among the Nations to Vitalija.

Vitalija's words were few but memorable. Naturally she was happy and grateful for this honour to her parents and thanked everyone; but above all she wanted to convey what she felt sure her father would have said on this occasion: 'I am no hero, I have done nothing out of the ordinary; nothing other than any normal human being would have done.'[108]

When Margaret's husband died in January 1995, Tam Dalyell wrote an obituary in which he referred to Vytautas. He wrote that Kagan had told him that 'one day he noticed that Rinkevicius was angry when he saw a boy being beaten up and he decided on the spot that he could trust him and confided his plan of hiding his fiancée's family behind a wall in the factory'. Dalyell reminded his readers that the penalty for helping Jews was summary execution for the offender and his family.[109]

When I asked Margaret what she thought about his motivation, she wrote to me: 'simple human decency – cannot really explain'.[110] Sadly Margaret Kagan died peacefully in Huddersfield on 31 March 2011.

Jaap van Proosdij (1921–2011) was only 21 when, in 1942, he helped rescue about 250 Dutch Jews. His Resistance group was so successful that they almost rendered genuine baptismal certificates useless because:

> The possession of a baptismal certificate often gave protection during a razzia, and some Christian churches were prepared to assist in providing such documents. Later we printed letterheads of fictitious churches. As the Germans had great respect for rubber stamps we invented a real beauty from an imaginary non-existing 'Dutch Ecumenical Council of Churches', with a cross and several Latin words. All our certificates were embellished with that stamp.[111]

Everything was fine until 'One day the Jewish Council phoned and said it had genuine Church certificates in its possession, but these had been refused by the SS because they did not have this particular stamp on them'.[112] From then on they had to put their fake stamp on all genuine documents to ensure their acceptance by the SS. Unfortunately, Jaap told me the stamp was lost some years ago and cannot be reproduced here.[113]

Jaap was born in 1921, the second of five children, to an independently minded advocate in Amsterdam and he too eventually became a lawyer. He describes his mother as having a strong personality but his father as being the main influence. 'He loved his profession, had a very independent spirit and cared for his clients more than his fees.'[114] As a young man he knew nothing about Jews, having attended both a Protestant school and university. The law firm he joined in 1942 was called Van Krimpen & Kotting. The Sephardi Jewish community had approached the firm to get some sort of protection from persecution for its members. Dutch Jews were being deported regularly from Amsterdam and whilst the firm started the work acting legally, eventually it became clear to Jaap and his colleagues that the only effective way to save Jews from the Nazis was to prove that they were not Jewish, and accordingly they began acting illegally.

The Germans had invaded the Netherlands on 10 May 1940. After vicious air bombardment the country capitulated on 14 May, Queen Wilhelmina and the government having fled to London. A civilian German administrator, the Austrian Artur Seyss-Inquart, was installed on 18 May 1940 and independent Dutch control ended.[115] There were 140,000 Jews in Holland at this time, of whom 30,000 were refugees from Germany and Austria, and the majority – 80,000

– lived in Amsterdam. Seventy-five per cent of these Jews were murdered by the Nazis and a major tool was the *Joodsche Raad* (Jewish Council), created under duress on 12 February 1941, ostensibly to prevent disturbances between Jews and Dutch Nazis. On 9 May 1942 the wearing of the yellow star was made compulsory.[116]

Jaap has explained that Holland had very detailed population records. 'It had a meticulous population register which traced most people back to the time of Napoleon' and they therefore realised the only chance of success was to prove to the German authorities that people were not Jewish. In one particular case, Jaap even managed to convince them that a man who was chairman of his synagogue was not even remotely Jewish.[117]

This work was based on the fact that:

> If you were single and could prove that you had two non-Jewish grandparents, then you were considered a non-Jew. In the case where a Jew was married to a non-Jew, proof of two non-Jewish grandparents was also required. If a Jew was married to another Jew, it was then necessary to have three non-Jewish grandparents. All the cases Kotting and I dealt with were illegitimate and we had to forge documents and falsify papers.[118]

Jaap had been asked to help Dr Hans Georg Calmeyer, the civil administrator during the occupation of the Netherlands, who dealt with racial classification. Calmeyer ultimately decided whether someone was Jewish or not. His decision determined who was sent to the Dutch transit camp Westerbork and then on to labour or death camps.

Before he got involved, Jaap made several visits to The Hague to meet the officials who were dealing with this vital documentation:

> I travelled daily to The Hague for three weeks and made copies of official rubber stamps and the handwriting of the officials, studied the internal procedures and befriended the staff. My partner, Mr Kotting, persuaded the Dutch secretary in Calmeyer's office to accept a monthly payment equal to her official salary. From then onwards we had access to

all Calmeyer's other files as well. All this information was very valuable for what we were to do later with other applications.[119]

Jaap was plausible because he was young, blonde and innocent-looking. Calmeyer approved of Jaap initially because he prepared a list of people who he felt were not worth saving. This impressed Calmeyer who believed in Jaap's '"honest and loyal" work, and he trusted me as a professional, honest and trustworthy person from that time until the end of the War. (Little did he know that the names we gave him were of people who no longer existed.)'[120] After the war, Calmeyer refused to accept he had been misled by Jaap. 'But van Proosdij was always honest and had no part in those lies,' he claimed.[121]

In 1942 the SS started urging Calmeyer to hasten the process of classification and fill a weekly deportation train holding 1,000 people. This policy was relentlessly pursued, reducing the Netherlands' population of 140,000 Jews to 40,000 by September 1944, when the Arnhem allied offensive destroyed the railway lines. Jaap van Proosdij recalls one horrific occasion when, in desperation to fill their weekly Tuesday 'quota', the SS rounded up every man, woman and child – whether patient, medical staff or visitor – in the Jewish psychiatric hospital at Apeldoorn, and herded all 1,500 of them into the death train.[122]

Looking back, Jaap admitted they used an excellent forger and 'faked marriage certificates, entered false birth certificates in church registers, and forged baptismal certificates and counterfeit papers attesting to secret adoptions which showed that the person had not been born Jewish'.[123] This was all done at great personal risk; had he and the rest of the team been discovered at any time, they would have been executed. One particular girl whom he saved from Westerbork grew up to become a paediatrician and visited him in South Africa in the 1960s. He said it was a very emotional time and they talked well into the night about what had happened. He commented that it was the first time he had felt safe to talk about what he had done.[124]

Even before the war was over, Jaap was planning how to restore Jewish property to its owners. He set up a committee which, in effect, drafted the legislation and subsequently handled many cases. 'We handled a lot of those cases – you should have seen how irritated the

top lawyers got with me, this cheeky young upstart who had specialised in these laws.'[125] Restitution work became his speciality until he
emigrated in 1951. In South Africa he had to re-qualify and then had
what he describes as 'a low key practice'.[126]

With the war over, Jaap married his sister's best friend in 1947. In
1951 they emigrated to South Africa – a country which in due course
became a pariah state because of its racial policy. He notes:

> Nothing can compare to the pure evil of the Nazis, who organised the
> scientific murder of millions of Jews. In South Africa it was oppression,
> not annihilation. But the frightening connection is that in both cases
> there was a total intolerance and lack of respect for another race – which
> is unacceptable on any level.[127]

Jaap acknowledges the influence of his parents. 'We were brought
up with high ethical standards, which together with your religion, I
believe, contribute to you acting righteously.' He adds: 'Why did most
people not help the Jews? You should ask them. Maybe they were not
in a position to do so, or were too scared. It is possible, of course, that
maybe they just didn't care about their fellow beings.'[128]

Jaap is extremely modest about his achievements and will not be
called a hero: 'I hate the inappropriate word "hero". This is an example
of the debasement of human values which makes common decency
heroism!'[129]

> Why did I do it? Because it was the only normal thing to do. One can't
> sit and watch when people are in mortal danger even when you do
> not know them. While working we got to know more and more Jews
> and many became friends. Yes, it also became more risky. If the land-
> ings at Arnheim in September 1944 (when the German collaborators
> fled) had happened two weeks later, we would have been caught, as we
> found from the papers after the war. But we were saved and that is all I
> can say.[130]

After a long and fruitful life, Jaap regards the work he did saving Dutch
Jews as the time 'when I was most useful':[131]

It is an important thing in my life to feel that I was useful somewhere
… that I did not live just to enjoy myself. Nothing else I ever did was
as important. A friend of mine said to me that the war was the time he
really lived. For me, it was the time I lived the most intensely.[132]

Jaap seems to have a feeling for individuals rather than causes:

I don't know whether I am an humanitarian. I must confess that I don't
get exited by a flood in India or an earthquake in Iran, as tragic as these
events may be. But I will automatically help an individual or family, as
both my parents always did. My father, being an advocate as I was, had a
more general influence on me. As to South Africa, I was never involved,
nor in Holland or here, in any organised politics. I might, however, have
influenced some individuals. Sixty years have passed but sometimes I
think what happened during those train transports to the extermination
camps. All I can do is try to forget.[133]

When asked about his actions he was humble: 'Why did I do it? How
could you not do it? If I see you drowning, I would get you out. Any
decent person with the imagination to do something to help would
have helped. If you did not help, you were not decent.'[134]

On 29 May 2003 Jaap was honoured at Yad Vashem where, in the
Remembrance Hall, he was recognised as a Righteous Among the
Nations. He had travelled with a group of fifty South African Jews on
a solidarity mission and they planted fifty trees in the South African
Memorial Forest 'Golani Junction'. 'Apparently Mr van Proosdij was
overcome by emotion at this ceremony which for him represented the
incarnation of an oppressed people into a sovereign nation.'[135]

Sadly, Jaap van Proosdij died in South Africa on 22 January 2011,
a few months short of his 90th birthday.

John/Jaap Schoen (1923–2007). John Schoen's family provide a
similar example of humanitarianism as they brought up their children
to be kind to everyone and help people. John grew up in Geldermalsen,
about an hour by train from Amsterdam. His father was a supervisor on
the railways and they lived near the station:

My father always helped people, every night we had people come to the house wanting a job and my father gave a lot of people a job on the railways. During the war we had a lot of people coming from towns wanting food, my mother always gave food to these people.[136]

John was born on 26 July 1923. John said his parents were very loving and charitable, but not religious. He said he had a happy family life. John was 21 when in July 1944 his parents were approached by a beautiful young woman from the Dutch Underground. She was aged 20 and John admitted he really fancied her and escorted her back to the station later.[137] She had come from Amsterdam to ask John's parents to look after a little Jewish girl aged about 5. At the time, John's brother Joost, known as Joop, was 10 and his sister Trijntje, known as Tiny, was 15. They all knew Suze was Jewish and that keeping her was very risky. However, she looked more Indonesian than Jewish. If the Nazis had found out about Suze, the whole family could have been sent to a camp, but they agreed to keep her.[138]

John told me that when Suze's family were rounded up by the Nazis, she must have been at a neighbour's home because she escaped. John also said the family members were all sent to Auschwitz and gassed. He says that understandably she was very disturbed when she first arrived at their home and cried a great deal: 'At first Suze woke up during the night to shout for her mother and father, and was also wetting the bed, but being so young, she accepted my mother as her mother. She loved my mother very much, so did my mother.'[139]

John has said that his parents had joined the Underground because they were opposed to the German invasion of Holland, and also because of the Nazis' persecution of the Jews. They were involved in sheltering Allied airmen, using a hidden radio and a printing press to pass on vital information.

In September 1944 parts of the Netherlands had been recaptured by British and Canadian troops and they launched Operation Market Garden which was intended to retrieve the rest of the country. The mission failed and the film *A Bridge Too Far* portrayed the story. As a result, a general railway strike was called to disrupt German transports and 90 per cent of the workers supported the strike. Anyone who par-

ticipated in the strike was in grave danger of being arrested with the
risk of death. Therefore, as John's father still worked for the railways
they had to leave their home and go into hiding in Asperen, a small
town near Geldermalsen. That hiding place housed the print shop
where work was done for the Resistance.[140]

It should be remembered that the strike led to dreadful repercussions: the Germans had to bring in their own railway workers to get
the trains working and therefore decided in October 1944 to forbid
the importing of food into the Netherlands. Food rations were reduced
from 1,400 calories a day in August 1944 to 1,000 calories in December,
and by April 1945 it was down to 500 calories. This winter is known as
the 'Hungry Winter' and people were so desperate for food that they
were eating tulip bulbs.[141] Ria Sanders, who was born in 1926 and
lived in The Hague, sent me her recollections of that time. She told me
that people ate sugar beet which was normally considered cattle food,
and tulip bulbs which were quite nice sliced and fried like onions, but
when the power stopped they couldn't cook even if they had food. She
said all rabbits, cats and dogs disappeared at that time.[142]

Whilst the Schoens were staying in the printing shop, they were
nearly betrayed by a Nazi infiltrator, who they thought was also in the
Resistance, and asked them to do some printing. A little while later
the house was raided by three men with guns who forced their way in
asking for a boy of 20. His father said there was no such boy there. Jaap
was hiding in one of the two attics, shivering with fear and cold in his
pyjamas. Apparently, the 'Gestapo did not sense that our little girl, the
only brunette in a blond family, was Jewish'. They asked Suze what was
in the cellar and she said there was nothing but mice. Jaap said:

> My mother Anna Johanna started to laugh, to the annoyance of the
> Gestapo, who told her to put her hands up or they would shoot her. My
> mother said ladies don't do things like that, and refused. We were very
> frightened, but they didn't shoot her. They went away, and we were safe
> for another day.[143]

Apparently they checked the other attic, so Jaap was not discovered.
Jaap recorded that the boy in question was caught eventually, sen-

tenced by a court of two judges and, after digging his own grave, was shot.[144]

The sheer absurdity of the Nazis' methods of control was exemplified by the Dutch being forbidden to grow orange flowers in their garden because they were interpreted as a sign of loyalty to the Dutch queen as head of the House of Orange. John's father allegedly dug up all their marigolds and put them on the compost heap, only for John's mother to rescue and re-plant them. He said: 'She showed great courage throughout the occupation.'[145]

It is significant that John has recorded that all his parents' friends had Jewish girls to hide. Significantly, more Jewish girls were saved all over occupied Europe simply because circumcised Jewish boys were easily identified and were therefore a more risky proposition.[146] John Schoen specifically told me there were no Jewish boys hidden in his village.[147]

John has said his parents had no Jewish friends themselves because their home was not in an area in which any Jews had lived. However, he has commented that most people in Holland 'have always kept the Jews in high esteem. Soon after the Germans went to Holland, we saw the Jews wearing the Jewish cross, but as time went on, we saw less and less of them. We knew they were sent to the gas chambers.'[148]

He has written of becoming aware that Jews were disappearing and seeing them being transported:

One of the trains packed with Jews on their way to a concentration camp stopped at our village station and I will never forget their faces – full of despair.

There was an immediate reaction – all the onlookers on the platform rushed to buy all the food on the snack trolley to hand in through the train windows to the poor souls.[149]

Suze became extremely attached to the Schoens and maintained contact with them even after she moved to America. In 1953 Suze came back for Tiny's wedding,[150] and she visited Anna Schoen in Holland every year until Anna died. Suze married a Jewish policeman, Arnold Brown, in 1956.

John visited Suze in Florida in the mid-1990s and said: 'It was wonderful to see her again, to know that she had had a long and happy life.' She had two daughters, Arleen Rose (1959) and Diane Kitty (1963), but died of lung cancer in May 1999 aged only 60, after suffering for five years. Arnold still maintains contact with John Schoen and has said:

> I met Suze in Connecticut in 1953 and we were married three years later. We used to talk a lot about the war, and she told me about how her family had been taken to the camps, and how she had escaped, sheltered by Jaap and his family.
>
> Even though my wife has died, I still talk to Jaap on the telephone from time to time. It's a kind of bond between us that no amount of time could erase. Without the Schoens, I would never have met and fallen in love with my wife, and I would not have had the wonderful life I was privileged to share with her.[151]

When I spoke to Arnold Brown, he told me that Suze had been moved from place to place by the Underground, and although the time she spent with the Schoens was very happy, she was very traumatised by her experiences. She did not tell her daughters about those times.[152]

John joined the Dutch army in June 1945 and for part of his training was stationed at Wolverhampton Barracks in 1946. At a local dance he met Pamela Cox and they were married in February 1947. In May 1947 he was sent to serve in Indonesia until 1950, when he came back to England to set up home with his wife and worked at the local Co-op. They had three children – Christopher (1952), Peter (1955) and Gerard (1959). In 1966 the family moved to Cardiff and John became manager of the food hall at the David Morgan department store; he worked there until he retired in 1984.[153]

Sadly, John Schoen, my original informant through the CCJ, died on 8 May 2007 aged 83.[154] His son Peter has provided some additional family history, and Peter's cousin Ed van Rijswijk, Tiny's son, has provided remarkable information about Suze's story and the work of the Dutch Resistance. He has traced the family's history back to around 1700. Arleen visited Ed in March 2009 when he told her about the research on her mother's family: Suze's parents were Samuel van der Bijl (born

23 October 1908) and Alida Hamerslag (9 January 1911) whose children were Bernard (16 November 1931), Kitty (3 February 1933) and Suze (14 January 1939). All five of them were born in Amsterdam. The family were arrested at their home there, Ruyshstraat 98 II, on 20 June 1943. About 5,500 people were arrested that day in the city as a result of a big razzia (a round-up of Jews – similar to Aktion).[155] Ed explained:

> In the case of 20th June 1943, a whole section of Amsterdam was sealed off, nobody could get in or out and all the people that lived within that section were taken from their homes. They had to leave their houses with minimal baggage and lock their houses. Housekeys had to be given to the Germans. Later on all the furniture was taken from these houses and most of it disappeared to Germany. The people had to gather in nearby squares and from there were taken to nearby railway-stations in trucks or trams. The people that were [there] on this day, more than 5,500, went directly to the Westerbork Camp.[156]

Westerbork was a Dutch transit camp in the north-east Netherlands. The Dutch Jews were either sent there or to Vught. They were then moved to the Sobibor extermination camp in Poland on 13 July 1943 and killed on 16 July 1943. John thought they had gone to Auschwitz, which is understandable as often the victims' true fates and destinations were not known until after the end of the war, and by then he was in the army. Over 110,000 Dutch Jews were sent either to Auschwitz or Sobibor and some other smaller camps; 75 per cent of these Dutch Jews did not survive.

Suze was saved by a Resistance group called NV-Groep (*Naamloze Vennootschap*) which was based in Amsterdam, also on the Ruyschstraat. It was part of a network of four groups that rescued Jewish children. They were organised by a German Jew called Walter Süsskind, a former employee of Unilever who lost his job because he was Jewish. He was put in charge of a deportation centre which was opposite a kinder-garten and Süsskind devised a scheme for smuggling Jews through the kindergarten. Over eighteen months he saved over 1,000 children and many adults. Unfortunately, he and his family were sent to Auschwitz where he died. It is believed he was perceived as a collaborator due to the relationships he developed with the Nazis to divert their attention from his activities; he was attacked by Dutch Jews in the camp. His life has been celebrated in a film, *Secret Courage*.[157]

The members of NV-Groep had to ask around to find foster families. One of the members, Annemarie van Verschuer, described how much she hated the task: 'I always found it frightening ... I found it more frightening than taking the children from Amsterdam to Heerlen, for you never knew how the people would react. And like a door-to-door salesman you had to persuade people to take in a child.'[158]

There is some confusion in the paperwork as to who brought Suze to Geldermalsen on 19 June 1944. It is believed it was Truus Vermeer. She was a daughter of the Vermeer family based in Brunssum, in the south. Her whole family was involved in the Dutch Resistance and worked closely with the NV-Groep.

The NV-Groep were particularly involved with moving children. They moved them from Amsterdam to Brunssum and its environs, where they were hidden with families. Later they were moved to other areas such as Betuwe (Geldermalsen area) and the Achterhoek (Nijverdal area). Ed has not been able to establish what happened to Suze from June 1943 to June 1944, but he assumes she was in hiding with another family. Arleen told me that Tiny told her (via Skype) that the first family did not want to keep Suze because she wet the bed. Apparently, Tiny's father said he did not care because Tiny, at 15, still wet the bed.[159] The NV-Groep supported families hiding Jewish children with money and food cards and this involved visiting the families. It was Truus Vermeer who did this for Suze and she also checked that Suze was being treated properly.

After July 1945, Suze spent six months with another family in Geldermalsen and then she stayed with an aunt. She was then moved to her Aunt Klara Hamerslag – her mother's sister – who had survived the war with her two sons. She remarried, became Klara Aarderwerk, and in 1949 formally adopted Suze. The Netherlands introduced legislation in 1949 that anyone who had not returned from the war was officially declared dead. As a result, there were many marriages and adoptions and other legal issues resolved. In November 1953 the whole family, including Suze, emigrated to the USA.[160]

Arleen Kennedy told me how she had known about her mother being hidden by the Schoens since she was a little girl. She wrote that in 1964, when she was 5, they went to visit Tiny in Holland and she thinks she learnt about it then. She confirmed Suze did not like to talk about the war in detail and she never said exactly what happened to her family. Arleen presumed she did not know. It was Ed's research that gave Arleen and her sons, Craig (1988) and Jason (1990), the information about her family's fate. As a result, Arleen returned to Amsterdam in March 2009 and, during a visit to the Jewish Museum, saw a photo display of rescued Jewish children and recognised a photo of Suze which the museum had not identified. Tiny immediately said: 'that is Suze'.

Arleen concluded: 'I love Tiny and her whole family so much. They are amazing, kind, loving people. I am grateful to have them in my life.'[161]

3

RESCUERS WITH OTHER MOTIVES

Oskar Schindler (1908–74), who became known across the world through Stephen Spielberg's 1994 film, did not live to see his surname become a generic term for non-Jewish rescuers in the Holocaust. Other rescuers are referred to as Schindlers of various types: Varian Fry was described as the 'Artists' Schindler';[1] Henk Huffener was called 'Surrey's own Oscar Schindler';[2] Chiune Sugihara was described as 'Japan's Schindler';[3] Dr Ho was called the 'Oskar Schindler of China';[4] and the British Ambassador to Lisbon in 1940, Sir Ronald Hugh Campbell, has been called the 'British Schindler'.[5]

However, Oskar's complex personality and motives exemplify many of the aspects of all rescuers and therefore a study of his role as a rescuer is necessary before other rescuers' motives are discussed.

At the end of the war, Oskar Schindler wrote about his efforts to move his factory, together with his 1,000 Jewish employees, from Krakow to Brinlitz in the Sudetenland. Hoffman, the owner of the factory, objected and as a good Nazi tried every possible way of stopping the transfer. 'He went to the Gestapo, to the Landrat, to the district governor, urging that Schindler not be allowed to fill the area with his Jews, who are liable to bring smallpox, attract the attention of enemy bombers etc.' But Schindler succeeded in getting permission from SS Headquarters:

> It is impossible for a person from the outside to imagine how hard I
> had to work before I succeeded in carrying out my decision to transfer
> the Jews, before I saw the 1,000 people lodged in their new place. The

general confusion which reigned at that period, the bureaucracy, the envy and the malevolence of various people brought me at times to the brink of despair. I was sustained, however, by a burning desire to save the Jews, some of whom had become close, loyal friends of mine during the preceding 5–6 years, from the crematoriums of Auschwitz or some other place, after I had succeeded in protecting them for so many years, and at the cost of so much personal effort, from the clutches of the S.S.[6]

Oskar Schindler was not a religious person but he was humane. Victor Dortheimer, No 385 on Schindler's list, one of the Jews who got to know Oskar best, said he knew Schindler would look after him from the first time he met him: 'It wasn't anything he said – it was just that he was polite to me, and spoke to me like I was a normal human being. None of the other Germans treated me like a human being.'[7] Victor believed Schindler's motives for helping the Jews were his sense of adventure and morality: 'He was always a little bit drunk and always with a beautiful woman. He was a gentleman gangster, but I think when he saw what was happening to the Jews he knew he had to help us.'

Victor was a decorator and was chosen to decorate SS Commandant Amon Goethe's villa, and was then seconded to paint in Schindler's factory. He got to know Schindler as they sat drinking vodka in Oskar's flat. They exchanged confidences and Victor asked him for favours for his co-workers. Victor described him as a skilful wheeler-dealer. 'He made a fortune which he spent on protecting us, his Jews. If the Germans had found out, he would have been shot.'[8]

In 1995 Victor Dortheimer was the subject of a television documentary in which Schindler's actions were described. He had saved, among others, two women from Auschwitz who had Victor's surname – one was his wife Helena and the other was his brother's wife – they were Nos 28 and 29 on the list. Victor said the factory was a huge deception. It did not produce anything:

We did not produce even one cartridge. The company acted as a camouflage to protect us. What is more, Schindler allowed us to listen to BBC on the car radio in the garage. We knew what was happening on the front even earlier than our German guards. If they had caught us, we would have been shot.[9]

Another perspective was offered by Herbert Steinhouse, a Canadian journalist, who knew Oskar in the immediate post-war period in Germany. He had met a neighbour of the Schindlers from Svitavy,[10] Schindler's hometown, whose father had been the local Rabbi. He told Steinhouse:

> This fellow said that as a man who was a Sudetenland Fascist, was a member of the Henlein party which was later absorbed into the Greater Germany's Nazi party, Schindler apparently had been a true believer in everything but one. That was the racial policy. He had been friendly with several of the Sudetenland Jews. He'd speak with his neighbor and the neighbor's father, the Rabbi. They'd talk about the sophisticated Yiddish literature in Poland and Czechoslovakia, about the folk tales and the mythology and the anecdotes and the ancient Jewish traditions of the villages of eastern Poland, or Moldova.[11]

Herbert kept a record of meetings in Munich in 1948 with Oskar and Emilie Schindler. The subsequent article was only published in 1994. He speculated on Schindler's motives, noting that Ifo Zwicker, whom Schindler had also saved, knew him from their hometown: 'As a Zwittau citizen I never would have considered him capable of all these wonderful deeds. Before the war, you know, everyone here called him Gauner (swindler or sharper).'[12] Oskar himself used a specific German word to describe himself – 'maßlos' – which means literally 'without moderation or restraint, but it has the additional connotation of the presence of an irresistable inner force that drives a person beyond what is considered acceptable behavior'.[13]

Schindler was a good judge of character – he chose a future Israeli Supreme Court judge to produce forged documents. Moshe Bejski described Schindler 'warts and all':

> Schindler was a drunkard, Schindler was a womanizer. His relations with his wife were rather bad. Each time he had not one but several girl-friends. After the war, he was quite unable to run a normal business …

You had to take him as he was. Schindler was a very complex person. Schindler was a good human being. He was against evil. He acted spontaneously. He was adventurous, someone who takes risks, but I am not sure he enjoyed taking them. He did things because people asked him to do them. He loved children. He saw all the children and grandchildren of those he had rescued as his own family. He was very, very sensitive. If Schindler had been a normal man, he would not have done what he did. Everything he did put him in danger ...

One day in the late 1960s I asked Schindler why he did all this. His answer was very simple: 'I knew the people who worked for me. When you know people, you have to behave towards them like human beings ...' That was Schindler.[14]

The psychotherapist Luitgard Wundheiler wrote a long article about Schindler's moral development during the Holocaust in 1986, long before Spielberg's film. She herself is of interest because her father was a judge in Germany. In 1936, in common with all German civil servants, he was asked to join the Nazi Party by signing a loyalty oath. He discussed the issue with his 14-year-old daughter Luitgard, and explained the possible consequences which included his death. In fact, although he did not sign and was dismissed as a judge, he got a job as a court messenger for the duration of the war and they survived living in poverty. Fifty years later her article discussed how Schindler changed from being an impulsive and opportunistic helper, to a compassionate person and finally a principled altruist, and also from a man whose concern was limited to people he knew, to many he did not know.[15]

She refers to Oskar's self-knowledge of his impulsiveness, again in response to Bejski, who asked: 'Why did you do what you did, why did you risk your life for us?' Schindler replied:

If you would cross the street, and there was a dog in danger of being run over by a car, wouldn't you try to help?' This reply is revealing. Schindler apparently thought of his rescue actions as direct and human responses to the sight of suffering; he thought them so normal that it did not occur to him that they needed an explanation; hence the challenging question at the end: 'wouldn't you try to help?' One almost senses a certain impatience at being asked something so obvious. There is also an endearing innocence in this reply, as if, even after the Holocaust, he still did not realize that most people do not try to help another creature in danger, if by doing so they endanger themselves.[16]

This view is corroborated to some extent by a woman called Ingrid, who was saved by Schindler. She claimed: 'he could not take the suffering. He did not expect it would come to what it did.' Her husband added:

Look, he was a Nazi, but he was working for the Abwehr [military intelligence] and they despised the SS. But you know, he made a lot of money; he could have taken it all. Every cent he made, he put in to save these people. He had nothing at the end.[17]

Some years later, Judge Bejski added: 'Schindler was different for two reasons. His exploits were on a very large scale, and he carried them on for a very long time.'[18] In that long time he was supported by his wife Emilie, who was shrewder about the Nazis than Oskar. She later wrote that she tried to persuade him that the Nazis were planning 'to impose National Socialism by force of arms and ruthless domination ... But my protests to Oskar, repeated over and over again, were of no use. By the time he realized what was happening, the war had already claimed most of its victims.'[19]

Schindler had married Emilie in 1928 when they were both very young – he was 20 and she was 21. She was educated in a convent where her best friend was Jewish. The marriage seems to have been unhappy from the start – perhaps matters were not helped by the fact that they lived with Oskar's drunken father and invalid mother.[20] There were no children; however, she was extremely supportive to Schindler in his work to help Jews, even though he was not particularly loyal to her:

I saw these unfortunate Jewish people reduced to slavery, treated like animals deprived of everything – including the use of underwear, regardless of the season, under their uniforms. Seeing them that way, with all their possessions and even their families taken away from them, and without the right to a dignified death, I could not but feel sorrow for their terrible fate.[21]

The incident of the Golleschau/Goleszów Jews demonstrates not only the barbarity of the Nazis but also Emilie and Oskar's courage and humanity in dealing with such a horror.

Emilie wrote her memoir to counteract the way her husband 'was bathed in all the light that history accorded him and I feel that is not entirely fair. I am doing this not for him but for the sake of truth.'[22] She gives an insight into their motivation:

> Steven Spielberg's film, Thomas Keneally's book and all the rivers of ink spilled fifty years after the facts depict my husband as a hero for this century. This is not true. He was not a hero, and neither was I. We only did what we had to. In times of war our souls wander aimlessly adrift. I was one of those fleeting shadows affected by atrocity, by all its misery and vehemence, suspicion and contradiction, which have left an indelible mark in my memory.[23]

Her book concluded with a simple statement:

> The moral of my story is simple: a fellow human being always has the right to life. Like so many others during the war, I think I have experienced in my own flesh that 'Love one another' is not an empty phrase but a maxim worth living by, even in the worst of circumstances. The descendants of those on Schindler's list have shown this to be true; they are living, having children, remembering.[24]

In 2001 Emilie undertook a lawsuit to obtain the original copy of Schindler's list.[25] She died that same year.

Steinhouse's article rested in a trunk for forty years, because in the immediate post-war period no one wanted to publish it. When *Schindler's List* was released in December 1993, he dug it out and it was snapped up. He brought it up to date with Schindler's departure for Argentina in the summer of 1949 funded by an American Jewish charity (JDC). Schindler was treated generously, with enough money (around $15,000) to start a fur business, but it failed and then he tried being a farmer but that was unsuccessful too. 'He was optimistic and hopeful – as he always was.' According to his wife, 'in Argentina he was just lying in bed', though he got up in the afternoons to see his girlfriend. He owed 500,000 pesos when he left Emilie in Argentina in 1958 and returned to Germany. She paid the debt off herself and was left with nothing.[26] In Germany, too, he failed and again lost his benefactors' money – this time in a cement factory. His wife said he was 'a salesman, a dreamer and a very bad honest businessman':

> He knew how to play the black market and he had known how to become a millionaire. Under wartime conditions of bribery and gifts he made money. But as a straightforward entrepreneur he apparently made a mess of things, in Argentina and back in Germany.[27]

His story was told briefly on German television in the early 1960s. He was living in Frankfurt and someone recognised him in the street and spat into his face calling him a 'Jew kisser'. Although Konrad Adenauer, West Germany's first Chancellor, gave him a medal and a small pension he was miserable. He lived in one room near the station in Frankfurt and was still living on handouts from the *Schindlerjuden* (Schindler's Jews). Although he was recognised by Yad Vashem and feted by Jews in Israel when he visited each year, he was drinking too much. He died in 1974, aged only 66, of 'poverty and alcoholism' according to Steinhouse. Unfortunately for him, this was six years before Thomas Keneally entered Poldek Pfefferberg's luggage shop in Beverly Hills in 1980 and heard the story of a lifetime.

Trude Simonsohn had known Schindler when he moved to Frankfurt in 1958. She was active in the Frankfurt Friends of the Hebrew University of Jerusalem. Aged 73 she told a Reuters' journalist: 'He was a burned-out soul. It was as if all the energy which he had in his life was exhausted in this rescue action … You could sense this from him. A person who had so much strength in those terrible times couldn't find his feet again.'[28]

Yitzhak Stern, who worked with Schindler all through his rescue, gave testimony in May 1962 at a meeting of survivors with Schindler. He said:

> I met Schindler on 18 November 1939 … when he extended his hand to me, I said, 'I'm a Jew' because a Jew had to announce he was a Jew when talking to a German. Schindler dismissed this and said 'nonsense. Why do you remind me that I'm a German. Don't I already know it?'

On 4 December 1939 Oskar rushed in and told them about the creation of the Ghetto and the rounding-up of Jews, but no one listened to him. Later they remembered: 'Schindler had told us about the plans, and we, stupid people, didn't pay attention.' Stern's testimony even covered Schindler's respect for Jewish traditions: he created a special Jewish cemetery when a Mrs Hofstater died and she was buried with all appropriate ritual. As Stern said: 'It was the only establishment of a Jewish cemetery in occupied Europe …'

After describing the horrors of the Goleszów train rescue, Stern concluded: 'In the Hebrew language there are three terms, three grades: person, man, human being. I believe there is a fourth one – Schindler.'[29]

The final word on Schindler should be given to someone who knew him well over a long period: Dr Moshe Bejski, who described him with a Yiddish word, *mensch*. This is usually translated as 'a decent fellow' or 'a good person'.[30] He said Schindler had been brought up as a *bon vivant* and liked the good life. Born in 1912, he was only in his early thirties when he came to Poland to make money, but when he saw the way the Jews were suffering, he felt he should do something:

> He was a true human being and very sensitive to human suffering. At the Brinlitz factory there was an infirmary in the camp. There was a young Jewish girl aged 22/23 who was terminally ill with TB. Schindler went to see her and asked if she wanted anything. She said she would like an apple. This was the winter of 1944/45 but he went to Zwittau and came back with a bag of apples for her.[31]

Dr Bejski said this was an example of his great kindness, but he admitted that he treated his wife badly. 'He was very cruel to her.' Bejski told me he was the only German he did not fear. Bejski worked doing technical drawings in the office: 'When Schindler visited he would sometimes light a cigarette and then leave the rest of the packet on my desk. They were extremely valuable. Two cigarettes could buy half a loaf of bread in the camp.'

Schindler was a man of complex motivations like many of the rescuers. He found his niche during the war but his life after it was a disaster, and in fact he was bailed out by the Jews he had rescued for the rest of his life. Nevertheless, at the crucial moment in his life he was a benevolent and true rescuer to his 1,100 Jews.

RESCUERS INVOLVED IN THE RESISTANCE

Henk Huffener (1923–2006). Henk's family were all involved in the Resistance. His father, Hendrik, who was an active anti-fascist from 1935, began holding Resistance meetings at their home in 1941. 'My father was an incredibly kind, brave person. He never showed any anxiety at all.'[32] The family consisted of Hendrik, his nine children and their stepmother. Their own mother, Wilhelmina Huffener-Merks, had died in 1932. The family were Catholics, which Henk said has no significance for him.[33] They lived in a remote area in Bilthoven on the edge of a very large estate because his father became site manager for a hospital and sanatorium for TB patients. Its isolation was invaluable for the Resistance work.[34]

Henk's family was musical and at weekends they gave chamber concerts with friends who joined their Resistance group. However, their first exploit in 1941 was disastrous, when a Dr Browser, who had established radio contact with the Dutch government in exile in London, asked Henk and his younger brother Joep to report on German military establishments and troop movements. Henk admitted:

I was 18 but I looked 14 and I'd chat to the soldiers. I'd be cheerful and gormless and say 'gosh, are you really going in that direction?' The

Germans eventually detected the doctor's aerial and stormed his house. They caught him red-handed; he was taken away and shot.[35]

Henk, who was born in Utrecht on 24 February 1923, says he was a precocious youth and by the age of 15 already had a mix of friends which included Jews, atheists, Quakers and Protestants.[36] His formal education ended when he was 17, when the Germans occupied the Netherlands. He was very close to his older sister Ann and brother Joep who were the most involved in the Resistance.

Henk has also written of the great influence on him of Betty Cadbury, a Quaker from Birmingham who married Kees Boeke, who ran the Werkpaats School – 'an eccentric, progressive boarding school'. Betty introduced him to several interesting people – Victor Gollancz, the publisher; Fenner Brockway MP; and Corder Catchpole, another Quaker who was actively involved in alleviating distress caused by the Nazis and who was very clear about the fate of the Jews. He, like the Boekes, had been interned during the First World War for pacifist activities. However, in Europe in the 1930s, 'Quakers decided to avoid the word "pacifist" and described themselves as "Friends of Peace", because the Nazis assumed that pacifism demonstrated a political involvement with the Communists, who were regarded as traitors'.[37]

Henk wrote: 'Because of her [Betty] I became an ardent pacifist and saw little point in armed resistance. Armed resistance was mainly counter-productive and at the time cost countless lives.'[38] The Boekes had employed two German Jewish teachers in their school in 1940, but at the end of 1941 it became forbidden to employ Jews. Betty, as an English woman, had already attracted the Nazis' interest and as she had considerable incriminating material at the school, such as the addresses of German Jews and books written by them, Henk offered to move the stuff to a safe hiding place, in case the Nazis came searching. He wrote: 'I filled up a handcart with boxes not knowing what was in them.'[39] But not all their work involved helping Jews: his sister Ann, with her husband Jeff Le Jeune and brother Joep, ran a 'Swiss road' escape route which:

was primarily intended with getting former Dutch parliamentarian figures back to London via Geneva and Dr V. Hooft, Head of the

International Council of Churches, smuggled micro-photographs of material – mainly secret documents – military installations went the same way. The official London agreed organization involving over 50 couriers working in relays began in Holland where Ann managed a safe house, where a lot of material was gathered and packed in safety razors, fountain pens and hair brushes etc. Finally I know that about 50 baled out aircrew were sent to route 2 to Spain and Portugal. In 1942 I persuaded her and her Swiss route courier husband to help Jews get at least to Belgium. Jews were the exception not the rule.[40]

In 1942 the group had their first major challenge when they were asked to evacuate a kibbutz of German Zionists, known as the Hachshara home, in Loosdrecht:

The resistance group received a tip-off that the Germans would raid the Kibbutz and send its occupants to concentration camps. The group dispersed the Kibbutz in just a few weeks. They were spirited out in small groups, some dressed as hikers and cyclists. Mr Huffener and his sister moved all the Jews to secure permanent accommodation. Mr Huffener even managed to place a Down's Syndrome girl in a home for mentally handicapped children. He took her to the home by train and bicycle.[41]

It was of course very dangerous and on one occasion, when Henk was escorting a very Jewish-looking girl who spoke no Dutch, he was stopped by some German soldiers. 'He kissed her, explained to the Germans that they must be off or they would be in trouble with their parents and got away with it.' However, it was that girl's father who subsequently showed Henk his First World War medal sitting on a black velvet cushion, with the words: 'That is an Iron Cross First Class. I am exempted from deportation.' Henk pleaded with him not to believe that, but unfortunately the advice went unheeded.[42]

The question of Jews and the Iron Cross was of great significance, particularly amongst assimilated Jews. Jews who saw themselves as quite assimilated felt safe in many countries. At the start of the First World War, the main Jewish organisations encouraged Jews to sign up to the armed forces to show their commitment to their homeland.

One hundred thousand Jews fought for Germany in the First World War, including Anne Frank's father Otto and Wilfrid Israel's uncle Richard and his cousin Ernst. They represented one-fifth of the Jewish population and, whilst 12,000 fell in battle, 30,000 were decorated and 2,000 became officers.[43] The graves of those who fell can still be seen in the Weissensee cemetery in Berlin – the largest Jewish graveyard in Europe. 'An entire section honours the fallen of 1914–18 with rows of little white headstones lined up with military precision.' They were erected in 1927 when 'it is still possible to honour German Jews for having died as patriots for the Fatherland'.[44]

Those surviving soldiers, particularly those who had been decorated, felt very secure. But German Jews who regarded themselves as 'Germans of the Mosaic Persuasion', who had joined wholeheartedly in Prussian jingoism in 1914, were eventually to be disappointed.[45] They had believed they were an integral part of German culture:

> After 1933, they were stunned to realize that they were targets of the Nazi racial laws – that Hitler's diatribes were directed at them. Convinced that there had been some mistake, World War I veterans pinned on their medals and visited local Nazi officials to emphasize their patriotism. In March 1933, the Jewish congregation of Berlin sent a statement to Hitler affirming 'the pledge that we belong to the German people; it is our sacred duty, our right and our deepest wish that we take an active part in its renewal and rise'. As late as 1936, the 'Reich Association of Jewish Front Soldiers' commemorated their fallen comrades from World War I with a ceremony in Berlin that stressed their loyalty to the Fatherland.[46]

Else Pintus described an incident in Danzig in the summer of 1941. Mr David, who owned a furniture store, was queuing for food when a woman told him it was just for Germans. He replied, 'I'm just as German as you. I served four years on the German front.' Someone must have reported this to the Gestapo, and although he was ill in bed, they dragged him off and eight days later he was dead.[47]

Dr Arthur Arndt, who was hidden in Berlin with six other Jews throughout the war, had been awarded the Iron Cross for his services as an army doctor in the First World War. On 16 August 1935, one month before the Nuremberg Laws were passed, he was awarded a Cross of Honour certificate, again for his work during the First World War. In July 1938 he was told that Jewish doctors were being taken off the Medical Register and could no longer call themselves physicians or treat Aryan patients. The Jewish doctors were to be known as *Krankenbehandler* (healers for the Jewish infirm).[48] Finally, in Hungary, all exemptions for Jews, even war heroes, were revoked on 15 October 1944 when the Szálasi government came to power.

These proud soldiers would have done better to remember the events of 1 November 1916 when, as the war began to go against the Germans, the High Command – in the person of the Prussian War Minister, Adolf Wild von Hohenborn – thought the Jews would make a good scapegoat for the Germans' lack of success. It was decided that a census of Jews would show that they were shirking their military duty for the Fatherland. However, because of the Jews' earnest patriotism, the *Judenzahlung* (Jew Count or Jewish Census) demonstrated that not only were the Jews serving enthusiastically, but they were volunteering disproportionately for front-line duty. The results of the survey were never published because they did not serve the purpose for which the exercise had been intended.[49]

Henk found hiding places for many Jews, including the Da Costa family and Bep and Mani Aalsvel, who were temporarily sheltered in the family home:

> When a Jewish boy of Austrian origin, whose alias was Jan Boon, needed an operation, Henk rented a cart and took him to the city of Utrecht, where he was treated by, of all people, a surgeon with German sympathies. The enterprise was very dangerous since Jan spoke very little Dutch.[50]

Henk and Joep needed money and ration cards to look after their charges. Joep raided distribution offices and:

> Henk made welfare collection rounds, calling on wealthy Jews in hiding such as Kurt Leipziger, who owned a cinema in Berlin, Eddy Salm, a former publisher from Amsterdam and the philosopher Wolfgang

Frommel. To Henk these eminent Jews represented not only a source of money but also a wonderful underground university.

Henk was arrested in Arnhem in March 1943 while visiting some of his kibbutzniks in hiding there. He was only arrested for minor offences and eventually found himself as a slave labourer in Germany. He got out in a poor condition. He was anxious to return to his underground activities and some friends gave him the key to their empty apartment in Amsterdam. It appeared that a young Jewish violinist and his wife had taken refuge there. They had no food and no ration cards, so could not buy anything. They were so desperate that they said they wanted to kill themselves. Henk promised to help them, but when he woke up the next day, he found he was too late. He was inconsolable and this led to a nervous breakdown. He was prescribed pills and told to rest but, as the Germans were after him again, he had to go into hiding.[51]

Henk is among those whose desire to help minorities in trouble continued after the war. He was upset at the racism he came across in London when he first arrived there in 1950, when he was helping a colleague sell African art. Later, in 1972, he helped Chilean refugees, and he also helped West Indians living in Notting Hill through the 1970s who were suffering from the 'Sus' laws. He set up a Legal Defense Association (LDA) 'whereby families would contribute 50p per week to be guaranteed access to a solicitor in case of arrest and charge'.[52] However, Henk himself saw at first hand the racism and prejudice in post-war England; as a result of being seen attending the meeting to create the LDA, at 'a friend's posh Kensington house with West Indians and Africans', within minutes of leaving he was stopped in Kensington High Street by an unmarked police car. He was accused of stealing from cars and his was searched. 'In the boot of my car they found a piece of worm drift-wood which was called an offensive weapon and so was my umbrella.'

He later set up an arts centre called Atlantis in a disused church in Bruton, Somerset, for people of all races – including West Indians, Africans, Jews and a variety of continentals – which he ran for about ten years. He wrote: 'They all contributed to the culture of this nation.'[53] He added:

> [It was] intended as a meeting place for Guildford staff who had not
> been reinstated, studio spaces for postgraduate art students and musi-
> cians to further their careers, also as a social centre for local pensioners.
> Socials, concert (classical, chamber, orchestral) and theatre. 36 Students
> spent time working there. The facilities were free.[54]

He encouraged the late Maria Sax Ledger in her painting.[55] A group
called Treatment recorded in his studios there from 1981–85. They
thanked him on the sleeve of their record *Cipher Caput* in 1993,
with the words: 'Back Cover Montage: Henk Huffener – Who also
deserves our eternal thanks for the energy and magic we found lying
long ago in Atlantis, Bruton – Thanks to his accommodation then.'[56]
Philip Hardaker, the sculptor, had a studio there during 1980–85 and
told me he remembered Treatment, who had played at Glastonbury.
He said there was a rather primitive recording studio in the basement of Atlantis which different groups used, and when Glastonbury
first started lots of them stayed at the centre which was quite nearby.
Tenants only had to pay for the utilities, but some people abused
Henk's generosity. There were lots of different people there including
weavers, a guitar and mandolin maker and photographers:

> As he was a painter and a creative practitioner he was also a great sup-
> porter of young artists. I will always remember him as being one of the
> most generous and supportive patrons and one of the funniest men I
> have ever met. He had a great spirit and a passion for life that was infec-
> tious to all around him.[57]

Henk had told Philip about his work in the Resistance but obviously found it painful to discuss. He told him about when he
was arrested and worked in a U2 factory, where he sabotaged the
parts he was making. Henk told him he came to England after the
war because in Holland many of the people who had collaborated
with the Nazis were still holding high office. He and his wife Margaret
had three children – Guy born 1952, Clare born 1955 and Josephine
born 1961. Unfortunately, Guy and his wife Gabriele died in September
2001, having contracted cerebral malaria in Malawi, and both died on

their return to Germany. Philip concluded by saying how much he missed Henk.[58]

After the war, Henk received the Resistance Commemorative Cross. Henricus (Henk) Huffener was recognised by Yad Vashem as a Righteous Among the Nations on 23 July 1998 and was honoured in London on 3 February 1999. In his speech on that occasion, the Israeli Ambassador unusually commented on Henk's post-war work:

> After the war, Mr Huffener wanted to help the victims of the Nazis and went to great lengths to find useful work in this area. He eventually worked as a psychologist with UNESCO in Paris until 1950. After coming to England and marrying his wife Margaret, he owned and ran a Cultural centre in Somerset helping young people with their careers.[59]

Henk was modest about his achievements. When asked why he risked death to save strangers when so many others did not, he said: 'I had Jewish friends. It's difficult to say. I'm a bit odd in that I love cultural diversity.'[60] Sadly, Henk died in 2006, but the words of HE Dror Zeigerman at the Israeli Embassy will last for eternity: 'You are a shining light amidst the darkness of the Holocaust, your stunning bravery is a testament to all humanity.'

Claire Keen-Thiryn (1924–) was a young girl living in Brussels when she became involved in her parents' Resistance work. She said: 'Like so many resistance workers, we became involved with the Jews, unwittingly as it were, but so many of us did.'[61]

Claire regarded her family as very 'establishment' as her father, Eleuthere Thiryn, was a professional soldier, an officer in the Belgian army. He had served throughout the First World War without being wounded and afterwards he became a lecturer at the Military College. Her mother went to England as a refugee during the war and stayed for four years in Bexhill. Claire's brother Louis was born there in 1918. The experience made her parents liberal anglophiles. Claire recalled that she and her brother begged her mother to vote for the Nazis in 1936, when women first got the vote. They felt it was the beginning of a new period, with the right-wing government of Belgium sweeping with a new broom.[62]

Claire thought Jews were well integrated in Belgium, as in France, because of the influence of the French Revolution which gave Jews equality of citizenship. She spoke of her mother 'visiting the only Belgian Kosher restaurant with her Jewish best friend and commenting that she had eaten Kosher food as though it was exotic. Claire herself knew there were Jews at her grammar school but she did not know who they were until they and a teacher disappeared after the invasion on 10 May 1940.'[63]

Claire's father was put in charge of the Ministry of Food, which rationed food for everyone in the area around Brussels known as Brabant. He was in constant contact with the Nazis and had to feed their troops. It was in June/July 1940 that the family joined the Resistance and almost immediately a Jewish couple in their fifties or sixties came to live with them. The man had been in the army with her father during the First World War, so this may have been a matter of loyalty. They stayed only six months and Claire believes they had an escape route out of Belgium. She knew the couple did not eat with the family – perhaps they ate only kosher food, as the man often went out.

In November 1940 Claire's family suffered a catastrophe when their wealthy grandmother, who had been a great hoarder, was forced to hand over to the Nazis her collection of gold and antique coins. She died of shock shortly afterwards and at that point the family became determined to act as intelligent resisters. Claire's brother Louis became actively involved in the Resistance with a woman they knew as Madame Hardy. She was a British woman working with MI5 or MI6. Louis worked with Madame Hardy to prepare for Allied landings:

> Claire said she did not know anyone who worked in the Resistance who was not helping the Jews as well. They were pro-Jewish. Her family resisted because of her father's fight in WWI and he saw this as a continuation of the war. Her mother saw it as anti-German rather than anti-Nazi. They hid British airmen and someone who had shot a soldier and had been condemned to death. They were already living on the fringes of illegal activities and hiding the Jews was part of the anti-Nazi activity.[64]

In 1943 Madame Hardy asked the family to look after two young Jewish girls from Antwerp, whose father was a diamond cutter. Their older sisters had been taken by the Nazis to work in a brothel in a concentration camp. Claire said that all the concentration camps had brothels, as the Germans believed that men worked better if they had sexual satisfaction. The two girls were known as Fadette, who was 13 or 14, and Yvette, who was 17 or 18. Only Fadette lived with them; Yvette was based somewhere else but was in and out visiting her sister. They could not have them both because there were lots of airmen in the house as well. All their friends had Jewish visitors who were moved around in case the Gestapo called.

Fadette was a very quiet girl. She ate with the family but hardly spoke and spent most of her time in her room. She was obviously very frightened. Claire thinks her mother was in another house somewhere. Claire's father knew the girls' real names and that after the war they went to Tel Aviv. They were the only members of their family to survive.

Both Louis and Madame Hardy were eventually betrayed by a man thought to be a friend – Prosper De Zitter. He was born in Flanders and had been a soldier in Canada. It appears he offered his services to the German Embassy even before the occupation. It has been calculated that he was responsible for the betrayal of several hundreds of members of the Resistance, Allied airmen and escaped POWs by leading them to safe houses in Belgium and France and then sending them to Paris by train, where they were picked up as soon as they left the station. Both he and his accomplice, Flore Dings, were sentenced and shot on the same day, 17 September 1948.[65]

When Claire first told me about her brother she said that the mysterious Madame Hardy was arrested in January 1944, was sent to Mauthausen to be gassed at once and was listed as a Belgian hero. The wonders of the internet have now enabled me to find out that Madame Hardy was very influential in organising escape lines, Resistance work and hiding evaders. Although she was known as Edith Hardy in the Resistance, she was born Edith May Bagshaw in 1899 in Aston, Birmingham. Her father was a grocer and she was the fourth of five children – all the rest were boys. She served in the First World War as a member of the Women's Army Auxiliary Corps in January 1918 and then in the Women's Royal Air Force. On 11 December 1919 she married a Belgian gentleman by the name of Van-den-Hove in Birmingham Cathedral. He was 29 and she was 20.

The next that is known of Madame Hardy is following the invasion, when she was married to another Belgian, Felix Hardy. Whatever her activities, she was arrested at home on 26 January 1944 for assisting the enemy – she was a member of the *Service de Renseignements d'Action* (SRA), the general name for intelligence services. She was sent to Saint-Gilles prison in Brussels, which was the normal destination for members of the Resistance, and stayed there until 21 July 1944 when she was sent to Germany. Apparently she arrived at Ravensbrück camp, which was mainly for women, on 30 December 1944 and then on 7 March 1945 she was sent to Mauthausen camp, where she was gassed on 15 March 1945.[66] Claire told me that after the war her Belgian husband came to see them and told them Edith had been Jewish. This seems unlikely given that her first marriage was in Birmingham Cathedral, but she may have converted at some point.

Louis was sent to the Dora-Mittelbau camp in the Harz mountains, which was established in 1943 as a sub-camp to Buchenwald. Sixty thousand people were sent there, of whom 20,000 perished. The labour camp Dora is not as well known as many of the other Nazi camps. Its horrors were described by one of its inmates, Guido Zembsch-Schreve, a member of the Special Operations Executive (SOE). He arrived in late 1944 and described the fear he and his chums felt when they discovered where they were: 'a labour camp so secret that it rated a "Nacht and Nebel" ("night and fog", or top secret) classification, meaning that the only way an inmate could be permitted to leave there was by way of the crematorium chimney'.[67] The inmates were forced to produce V2 missiles for the Germans:[68]

Though every slave labourer had a German soldier at his elbow, more than half the V2s made in Dora misfired; so badly had they been built. Zembsch-Schreve's own team was once visited by Wernher von Braun, who spotted at once that they were saboteurs; they were all instantly shot by von Braun's Gestapo companions, except for Zembsch-Schreve, who had taken the precaution of standing back against the wall behind the gunmen, where he was overlooked.[69]

Claire's brother died on a train in 1944 aged 27, whilst being evacuated from camp Ellrich which was near Dora. There the prisoners performed the:

> same work but ... things were much tougher. He [Louis] survived illness thanks to his friends, but weighed only 48 kilos in the end. Ellrich was evacuated, some by foot and almost all died and by train. Loulou [Louis] was in the train and that transport was also lethal: those who survived the lack of food and drinks were eventually machine-gunned by the RAF and that is how Loulou died. All 186 who died with him are in an unmarked grave in Dreetz on the railway line between Hamburg and Berlin.[70]

Dora camp is not very well known and a former inmate, Freddie Knoller, has suggested that this is because Wernher von Braun was in charge of the scientific work being done there. After the war, both America and Russia were fighting for supremacy in missile technology and when von Braun became an American hero, it was inconvenient to remember his work in Dora and all its associated horrors.[71]

Claire has said that the family heard of Louis' death in July 1945 and that her mother died of a broken heart in 1950. I found Louis Thiryn listed with thousands of other Belgian political prisoners as No 60511, and listed as a 'maler' which translates as a painter on a prisoners' website.[72]

Claire's family, like so many others, paid heavily for their involvement in the Resistance, with the death of her grandmother, the premature death of her mother and the murder of her brother. However, it is impossible to know how many people were saved by their Resistance work. Claire and I appeared on BBC Radio 4's *Woman's Hour* to talk about her story and other Holocaust rescuers on 6 January 2005, and she participated in the national Holocaust Memorial Day event in Cardiff in 2006 and was introduced to Tony and Cherie Blair.

Jacob (1881–1953) and Hendrika (1889–1971) Klerk. Henri
Obstfeld, who now lives in London, was left with a couple called the
Klerks in Arnhem in 1942 when he was 2½ years old. He stayed with
them until he was 5. He does not know how contact was established
with the Klerks and neither did their adopted daughter Els Willemsen,
with whom he was in regular contact until she died in January 2003
aged 87. She was married in 1942 and the Klerks, who were then in
their fifties, were left with a large house. Jacob Klerk was an estate
agent and insurance broker, with an office at home. He was a dedicated
Freemason, having been initiated in 1909, and he became a Master
Mason in 1920. In 1932 he joined a new Lodge in Arnhem and was its
secretary for many years.[73] He was also an elder of the Baptist church.
His wife was called Hendrika. Henri has assumed that his parents made
contact with them through the Freemasons, although his own father
was not a member.[74]

Henri's father originally came from Krakow, now in Poland, but
lived in Vienna from 1910 to 1925. He moved to Amsterdam in 1925
where he joined other members of the family who had arrived earlier.
He became a shoe designer and eventually took over the family slipper
business with his brother Simon. He married Henri's mother in 1933.
Her family had lived in Holland since before 1800. Henri was born
in April 1940 and a month later the Germans invaded. Gradually, life
became more difficult for Jews as restrictions on their activities were
increased. In 1942 the Jewish Council was ordered to arrange for Jews
to be chosen for work in the East, and the Obstfelds received call-up
papers for Henri. Not surprisingly, his parents were alarmed when they
realised that their 2-year-old son had to present himself with a ruck-
sack, clothing and food for a few days, in order to be sent off to work
in the East. They immediately took him to his Uncle Dolek's whilst
looking for somewhere permanent to leave him.[75]

Henri has described how initially he was taken by train to Arnhem
to meet the Klerks:

Apparently, I was most taken with the pictures on the Delft blue tiles
which decorated their toilet. Having returned to Amsterdam, my mother
started to tell me frequently that they would have to give me away for a

while, but they would come back for me later. Some time later, we went to Arnhem again, to visit the Klerk family. While I was kept busy with the picture-tiles in the toilet, my parents left quietly.[76]

He concedes his life was pleasant enough as he was not aware of shortages, but he had no knowledge of how the Klerks managed these matters when everyone had ration books. He only played with Emmy Willemsen, the Klerks' granddaughter, who was three years younger than him and with whom he stayed in touch.[77] Sadly, she died in January 2006.[78] Apparently Henri was passed off as a nephew whose parents had been killed in the German bombardment of the city of Rotterdam in the early days of the German invasion. Many people died at that time and many 'hidden' children were explained away in this way. Only in 2001, Els told him that when she had taken him for a walk one day with Emmy in her pram, someone had asked her whether he was, by any chance, a Jewish child. She had replied: 'Oh no, he is a nephew.'

Even after Henri had been returned to his parents, at least one shopkeeper had enquired whether that little boy had been a Jewish child.[79] This curiosity about his presence must have created anxiety as the Klerks could have been betrayed by nosy neighbours at any time. However, he was not physically hidden and recalls playing in the back garden from where he watched the trams go by. He also went out shopping with his 'aunt'. He remembers playing in the part of the house used as an office and so the staff and the visitors would have seen and been aware of him.[80] He remembers visiting one of Klerk's employees with his 'aunt' on one occasion. It was only just round the corner and the house overlooked the sidings of Arnhem railway station and he enjoyed watching the trains. Although nothing unusual happened, he remembers the Klerks talking about it and deciding not to do it again.

When I asked him about how risky this must have been, he said anyone could have gone to the Nazis; in fact, many did and just supplied an address. A Jewish life was worth 7.00 guilders which is what was paid to the informer. Henri was not sure what this was worth at the time but in 1961 £1 equalled 10 guilders.[81]

In September 1944 they were evacuated, prior to the battle of Arnhem featured in the film *A Bridge Too Far*, to Harskamp, a hamlet 20km away, and were liberated by the Canadians on 17 April 1945. As the war was over, the Klerks sent a postcard with their new address from Harskamp to the last known address where his parents had hidden. Fortunately, they too survived to claim their 'baby' – now 5 years old.[82] Apparently, when Henri saw his mother again, he recognised her and said: 'You stayed away a very long time.'[83]

Henri's conclusions on the Klerks' motivation, following discussion with their daughter, are these:[84]

Firstly, they were religious people who were prepared to look after me for humanitarian reasons. Secondly, the Nazis had forbidden Freemasons to be active. That in itself would have been a good enough reason for my foster father, a dedicated Freemason, to act contrary to their dictats.[85]

Henri proposed the Klerks and their daughter and son-in-law to Yad Vashem, for recognition as Righteous Among the Nations, which was awarded on 10 April 2000 in the synagogue in Arnhem.

I was quite unaware of the Nazis' obsession with Freemasons until I looked into Henri's story. The Nazis regarded all Freemasons as allies of the Jews, and both were regarded with suspicion by right-wing bodies in Germany and France from the 1840s. The infamous publication *The Protocols of Zion* linked Jewish and Masonic conspiracies arguing that Freemasons were in league with the 'Elders of Zion'. In Sweden the notorious anti-Semite Elof Eriksson from 1932 focused on the Freemasons 'as the Jews' main associates and vehicles of propaganda in their quest for world dominance'.[86] When the Nazis came to power they created an anti-Masonic museum. Members were ordered to leave their Lodges, and those who had not done so prior to the Nazis' rise to power on 30 January 1933 were not accepted into the Nazi Party, and some were sent to concentration camps. In September 1935 all Lodges were forced to dissolve themselves and property was confiscated.[87]

The fall of France in June 1940 led the German Foreign Minister, Alfred Rosenberg, to raid Masonic premises; documents were seized and Lodges were looted. On 1 May 1942 Hermann Göring, the most powerful Nazi after Hitler, said:

> The struggle against the Jews, the Freemasons and other ideological forces opposing us is an urgent task for National Socialism. It is for this reason that I welcome the decision of Reichleiter Rosenberg to establish special task forces whose job it will be the safe keeping of all the documentary material and the cultural assets from the above mentioned sites. [88]

This loot was confiscated by the Soviet forces in 1945 and only returned to France after the collapse of communism in 1990, following their discovery by an American researcher, Kennedy Grimstead. In total, 750 boxes of material were sent from Moscow to Paris by lorry in December 2000.

Evert Kwaadgras provided me with a great deal of information on Jacob Klerk's early life. He was born on 19 April 1881 in Warder, a village in the Dutch province of Noord-Holland. He appears to have first applied to be a Mason in 1909 in Hoorn, close to Warder. He was accepted and initiated on 26 October, but at the time was living temporarily in Germany, in Essen on the Ruhr. His job was as a 'representative of a Dutch vegetable transport company'. Evert stressed to me that Holland has always been a great exporter of vegetables, especially to Germany. Some time before 1915 he moved to Breda, and then in 1916 he moved to Arnhem. He joined the local Lodge and became a Master Mason. In 1923 he joined a new Lodge called '*De Oude Landmerken*' and he was the secretary for many years. [89] The Masons have no record of his looking after Henri:

> But that would not be the kind of thing about which to spread the word during the war or to boast of unduly after. We know that he had a sharp sense of justice. When after the war some lodge members were expelled on account of pro-German attitudes or activities during the occupation years, he took up the defence of two of them, claiming that they were being falsely accused … this would characterize him as a man who liked to be fair and square in his opinions and actions. [90]

The Dutch Freemasons have no records from the war years: 'The Nazis banned and suppressed all Masonic organisations, including ours, so in the years 1940–1945 there were no regular Masonic activities such as Lodge meetings, and, accordingly, there are no normal records available.'[91]

Kwaadgras concluded:

Anyhow, by the time the shoa(h) got under way, the Freemasons were already a thing of the past in the eyes of the Nazis. They had already been suppressed and their possessions looted or destroyed in Germany and all German-occupied or dominated countries.[92]

Henri remained as an only child, growing up with an extended family of cousins, aunts and uncles, most of whom had also survived by hiding. As a young teenager Henri joined Jewish youth groups and became involved in camps and Hebrew educational seminars. When he was 16 he started the Dutch opticians' course in Rotterdam, after which he started working in a few practices. One of his bosses did some lecturing on a part-time basis and sent Henri to do so in his place. He realised he needed to broaden his optometry skills and applied to study in London in 1961. He stayed in London doing research and developing his skills until he became Senior Lecturer at City University. He has been involved in developing optometry courses in his native Holland and also lecturing abroad.

In 1972 he married Dorothy who was born in Cape Town. They have two sons and two grandchildren. In the 1990s he met an old acquaintance from Amsterdam, also living in London, who introduced him to a group of Jewish child survivors. He and Dorothy are now active in the World Federation of Jewish Child Survivors of the Holocaust (WFJCSH) where Henri holds the office of vice-president. He is also involved in the European Association of Survivors.[93]

Jacob Klerk died on 2 February 1953, a fortnight before Henri's Barmitzvah.[94] His wife Hendrika died on 18 July 1971. Their grandchild, Henri's foster sister Emmy, died on 28 January 2006.[95]

Robert Maistriau (1921–2008) was only 22 when, on 19 April 1943, he led a daring raid on a train carrying 1,600 Jews from Belgium to

Auschwitz. His two colleagues, Youra Livchitz and Jean Franklemon, were both 25 when they set off on their bicycles with their equipment – a pistol, three pairs of wire cutters, a lantern and red paper. This was also the day the Warsaw Ghetto Uprising started.

The three had cycled the 40km from Brussels to Boortmeerbeek in Flanders and used the red paper to turn the lantern into a temporary red signal to stop the train on its way east. The train was taking 1,631 Jews from Mechelen (Malines) transit camp to Auschwitz – a full list compiled by Nazi officials at Mechelen gives names, dates of birth, places of birth and occupation. It shows a great many schoolchildren were on the train.[96] As soon as the train stopped they used the wire cutters to cut the doors open and encouraged people to jump out, and seventeen people did. As the guards opened fire, Livchitz fired their pistol while the other two opened another carriage and again urged people to jump. Some people on the train had been warned of the rescue and managed to cut open a third carriage and escape. A total of 231 Jews escaped, and although twenty-three died, most got away and were helped in some way by Belgians. Some, like Simon Gronowski, an 11-year-old boy, jumped once the train started moving. He walked all night and eventually approached a house with a tale of having got lost from his playmates. He was taken to the local policeman and was terrified of being handed back to the Germans. The policeman said to Simon: 'I know everything. You were in the Jewish train and you escaped. You don't need to worry. We are good Belgians, we won't betray you.'

Maistriau told of one woman who asked him what she should do as she looked around in the dark. He said to her: 'Madame, Brussels is that way, Louvain is that way. Sort it out for yourselves. I've done all I can.'[97] Jacques Grauwels and his friend had jumped from the train and, whilst waiting for a tram, worried that their filthy appearance would draw attention to them. They chose to wait on the stairs to escape quickly if necessary:

And then something happened that Jacques Grauwels would never forget as long as he lived: 'The workers had probably noticed that there was something up with us both, that we had some sort of problems. As

though in response to a silent order, they circled us both on the platform
so that we were protected against prying eyes.'

Another couple limped into a church and told the astonished priest
that they were Jews who had escaped from the train to Auschwitz and
they had no money. He gave them a 50-franc note, said 'God bless
you', and told them how to get to Liège, where they had a relative to
help them.

None of the escapees were betrayed by a Belgian – *L'honneur des
Belges*.[98] Marion Schreiber attributes 'national modesty' as the reason
no one knows how much the Belgians helped their Jewish neighbours.
Additionally, she comments that her book has had little media attention in France and the Netherlands, 'countries which have trumpeted
their resistance past while being rather less open about their collaborators'. She puts it down to jealousy.[99]

Maistriau did not speak English and I asked a bilingual secretary to
visit him on my behalf, which she did on 2 August 2004. He told her
that although he claimed in the book that he was bored with his job, he
had actually been 'drilled' against the Germans since he was 5 years old.
His mother's first husband had been a Jew and was in the French army.
After he died in the First World War, she married a Belgian who was a
doctor in the Belgian army.[100]

There is a tendency in the UK to look at the Low Countries as one
homogeneous area. This is particularly incorrect when it comes to
Jewish rescue in the Holocaust:

> Four thousand children like myself survived the Holocaust living under
> false identities with families, in boarding schools, monasteries and chil-
> dren's homes. Sixty per cent of the sixty thousand Jews living in Belgium
> at the time were not deported because they were able to escape the
> clutches of the German racial fanatics with the help of neighbours,
> friends and strangers.[101]

In fact, more Jewish children were saved in Belgium than any other
occupied country. Why? One answer is given by Steve Jelbert. He
suggests that Belgians, unlike the Dutch, were bitterly anti-German

having experienced 'brutal German occupation in World War I'.[102] He also suggests that Belgians have a strong individualistic streak: 'Given to unforced bourgeois individuality (it was, after all, the home of Surrealists such as Delvaux and Magritte), the strength of its civic society hampered the Nazis' attempts to carry out their murderous policies.'[103] He concludes that 'the Belgian bourgeoisie of the era apparently recognised themselves by lifestyle and culture, the idea of discrimination against minorities who clearly share the same values clearly contradicts the core beliefs of their civic society'.[104]

When deportations first began in 1942, the patriotic underground newspaper *La Libre Belgique* urged its readers to show Jews support: 'Greet them in passing! Offer them your seat on the tram! Protest against the barbaric measures that are being applied to them. That'll make the "Boches" furious!'[105] The bureaucrats played their part too, in spite of the posters warning against helping the Jews, and some were discovered and punished:

> In all the city halls and council houses there were officials who quietly issued additional food cards for people's relatives who had supposedly been bombed out, or whose nieces had suddenly turned up out of the blue. There were city officials who gave the Resistance blank forms to which only the false name had to be added and the right passport photograph glued. And then there were postmen who intercepted letters addressed to the Gestapo and the war commands if they suspected they might contain denunciations. They opened the envelopes, warned the people denounced in them and delivered the letters two days late, to give them time to go into hiding. 'Service D' – against defeatism and denunciation – was the name that the members of this group gave themselves. They probably saved 5,000 people from being handed over to the occupying police.[106]

It has been estimated that about 200,000 Belgians were in the Resistance, many motivated by strong anti-German feelings resulting from the First World War. Robert Maistriau was perfect Resistance material.[107] He was desperate to help damage the Germans because of their 1914 atrocities:

It wasn't just that everything the Belgians had saved by careful husbandry – food, fabrics or coal – was going to Germany. Now young people were going to be forced to work in German factories to keep the wheels of Hitler's arms industry in motion. Around this time, Robert found himself thinking about his father. A military doctor, and originally an ardent admirer of German culture, with its poets, musicians and philosophers, he had lost all his respect for the German nation in the First World War, at the Front at Yser. He considered it particularly barbaric that during their invasion in 1914 the Germans had set fire to the precious library in Leuven with all its irreplaceable books and manuscripts. 'In one way and another,' Maistriau recalls, 'we young people were opposed to the Germans even before the second World War.'[108]

The hatred felt for Germans in Belgium was confirmed by Bob Whitby, the son of an English major and Belgian mother, who, aged 19, was interned in Belgium in 1940. He said: 'We were very frightened because my mother had told us about the First World War, the cruelties and so on'.[109]

Paul Spiegel wrote:

Belgium is Germany's unknown neighbour. And that is particularly true as regards the chapter of resistance and civil disobedience against the Nazi regime in Belgium … These Belgians risked imprisonment or even transportation to a concentration camp because they were infringing the laws passed by the German military administration, according to which any help for the persecuted Jews was to be considered a serious crime.[110]

Another explanation of Belgium's success is based on their willingness to disobey. 'The Belgian police dragged their feet, railway workers left doors of the deportation trains open or arranged ambushes, and many Jews found hiding places.'[111] Whereas in Holland, where 20–25,000 Jews went into hiding, half of them were discovered 'no doubt through the efforts of professional and occasional informers', it is significant that 'of the ten thousand Jews who survived in hiding, about seventy-five per cent were foreigners – a percentage that testifies to the unwillingness of Dutch Jews to face reality'.[112]

In 1939 the population of Belgium was 8,386,600 and 1,537 have been recognised as Righteous Among the Nations (see Table 2 in Appendices). Perhaps the most remarkable rescue case I came across was of Gisele Reich, who in 1941 was at Malines awaiting deportation to Auschwitz with her parents. Her father was deported first and Gisele, aged 5, who suffered from a lung complaint, was waiting with her mother. A German officer took pity on Gisele and asked her mother if anyone would look after her. She must have mentioned their neighbours, the Van de Velde family, who were a devout Christian family. The Nazi telephoned them and they immediately agreed and came at once to collect her by car; they took her into their family even though their eighth child was imminent. The father was a chef in a hospital kitchen. Gisele lived with them until she was married. She had children and grandchildren of her own, but unfortunately had been severely traumatised by her experiences. Her son, Willi Buntinx, put the Van de Velde family's actions down to genuine neighbourliness, and had never told anyone about the story until Rose Marie Guilfoyle told him I had asked her to see Robert Maistriau.[113]

Maistriau was then very frail, with poor sight and mobility. He told Rose Marie about his childhood and his family's anti-German attitudes. He also revealed that he now felt he has been given less credit than was his due as it was he alone who actually opened the doors to the train on 19 April 1943. He claims Youra Livchitz was frightened when he saw a German officer close to the train who might have recognised him and disappeared. Robert was also upset that Youra seemed to have been given the credit for leading the event – especially in the Washington Holocaust Museum.[114]

Of the three, all were subsequently arrested for other matters. Livchitz was caught months later and was shot as a 'communist' in 1943. Maistriau was arrested in March 1944 and sent to Buchenwald but ended up in Bergen-Belsen where he was liberated in April 1945. Franklemon died in 1977. Maistriau was recognised as a Righteous Among the Nations in 1994 and died on 26 September 2008 aged 87. The attack on the twentieth convoy was historic – it was the only time in occupied Europe that Resistance fighters liberated a deportation train.[115]

RESCUES MOTIVATED BY LOYALTY

Maria (Mitzi – *née* Müller) Saidler (1900–94) was a Roman Catholic woman born in rural Austria. She had acted as a live-in cook to Hermann and Camilla Fleischner for fifteen years when, due to a Nazi decree, she had to move out. It was no longer permitted for an Aryan woman under 50 years of age to live under the same roof as a Jewish man. In any event, since Hermann could no longer earn his livelihood because his wholesale button business had been 'aryanised',[116] they could not afford to keep her. Nevertheless, Mitzi continued to come to their flat to help Mrs Fleischner who had been an invalid since the early 1930s.

When they had to leave their home, 'because a Nazi "required" it', and had to move elsewhere where they shared a flat with several families, Mitzi continued to visit them and even brought them food. When they were ordered to be resettled at Theresienstadt, Mitzi advised them not to comply and offered to hide them in her own little flat. Because Camilla suffered from poor health, the offer was felt to be impracticable and was declined. Mitzi promptly approached a friend of the Fleischners, a Mrs Sommer, who accepted the offer and stayed with Mitzi from 1942 until the end of the war. Mitzi fed her by sharing her ration card with her. Hiding Jews could incur the death penalty, or at least deportation to a concentration camp, and Mitzi risked that willingly.[117]

Otto Fleming, the Fleischners' son, told me that even after his parents had been sent to Theresienstadt, Mitzi continued to send them food and also co-operated with the Chief Rabbi of Vienna and his wife in sending food parcels to others in Auschwitz. Chief Rabbi Öhler himself was living in the same flat as Otto's parents, but was protected by a senior Nazi who found him work with the Jewish Archives.[118] It appears that the Fleischners were sent to the Chief Rabbi's own flat along with four other families, so each one occupied a room in the six-bedroomed flat. As a result of the many visits she made, Mitzi and Mrs Öhler became good friends. When Otto and his wife Dorothy went back to visit Mitzi in May 1982, and to collect some valuables that the Fleischners had entrusted to Mitzi, she took them to meet Mrs Öhler, and they saw the room where they had lived.[119]

Otto brought Mitzi's actions to the attention of Yad Vashem, as did Mrs Sommer's daughter Resi, who had worked as an interpreter in the British Embassy in Tehran during the war. She was honoured by attending with her daughter, planting a tree in the Grove of the Righteous Gentiles at Yad Vashem in March 1981; subsequently Mitzi was honoured by the Israeli Embassy in Vienna.

My informant, the Fleischners' son, Otto Fleming, died in 2007. He had written about his family and their life in Vienna. He explained that he only experienced anti-Semitism at the end of his time at the *gymnasium*, which must have been around 1932 as he was born in 1914. Apparently the head boy took him on one side:

> He said that we had always got along well but he had now joined the National Socialist Party (the Nazis). He had nothing against me person-ally but I should understand that, from now on, he would no longer be able to speak to me. I think that was very decent and when I saw him again in 1980 and he was suffering from Parkinson's disease, I felt very sorry for him.[120]

After he had matriculated, he decided to study medicine, even though life was becoming difficult for Jewish students, who were being attacked and beaten up even on university premises. He started in 1933 and suffered considerable prejudice from all sides, but one of the most memorable occasions was when a lone woman harangued him and a friend in the street. In March 1938 he was about to take his final medical examinations when the Anschluss prevented Jews from taking finals. Jews began to be attacked in the street or dragged off to camps. He rarely left his home and eventually decided to leave Austria. However, it was not easy to find a country willing to take desperate Jews, who could be dragged off as they waited in long queues outside various embassies. Otto managed to get a ticket to Shanghai but, as he also acquired a visitor's visa to Palestine, he left Austria in July 1938 and spent some years there. In 1942 he joined the British army, and after the war completed his medical qualifications, eventually becoming a GP in South Yorkshire. In 1999 he was invited back to Vienna to receive an honorary doctorate from the university, sixty-one years late.[121]

Otto wrote of returning to Vienna with apprehension:

> All the time we were in Vienna I felt uneasy every time I met a man
> in my age group. I always had to think, 'Is this the man who killed my
> parents?' But I was also reunited with some old schoolfriends who
> greeted me very warmly.
>
> In the '80s my wife and I were holidaying in Seefeld. As we walked
> past an elderly man, we heard him murmuring, 'There's too many for-
> eigners here again, we should do some gassing and injecting'. It was after
> that that we decided not to take holidays in Austria again. [122]

Otto's wife Dorothy, who came from Vienna on the Kindertransport,
told me the first time she met Mitzi was in August 1958 when they were
staying with a family friend of Otto's near Saltsburg. Otto became ill
and Mitzi brought him traditional chicken soup and *Knaidlach* (matzo
dumplings) which his mother had taught her to make. She gave them
some family possessions she had been guarding since the war. After
that visit, Mitzi married a railway worker by the name of Saidler and
had a daughter but was later widowed. The next time they saw her was
at Yad Vashem when she was honoured as Maria Saidler on 29 March
1981. The third time they saw her was in May 1982, when the Flemings
took their three children to Vienna and Prague to show them their
'roots'. They saw Mitzi in her flat and met her daughter. Mitzi took
them to see the Öhler flat where Otto's parents had lived until their
transportation to Theresienstadt in 1942; they had subsequently been
murdered in Auschwitz in October 1944. [123] Hermann was 63 and
Camilla 62.

During this 1993 trip they also visited the Fleischners' former home
where they were welcomed by Resi Sommer – the daughter of Mrs
Sommer whom Mitzi had hidden in her tiny flat. As the Russians
attacked at the end of the war, Mrs Sommer had rushed back to the
Fleischners' flat and claimed it back from the Nazis living there, in case
the family returned. Apparently, not long after this 1993 visit, Mitzi
moved into a retirement home run by the railways, as she was becoming forgetful and was not deemed safe on her own. She died in 1994
aged 94. [124]

It appears that Mitzi's motivation was loyalty to the Fleischners and a desire to help people for whom she had worked for many years and with whom she had a good relationship. This loyalty was extended to their friend Mrs Sommer. Otto has said of her: 'She was a simple woman who knew what was right and wrong.'[125]

Mr & Mrs Stenzel. Else Pintus (1893–1975) was hidden for two and half years by a family called Stenzel in Danzig.[126] Else was born in Chmielno, the youngest of eight children. She never married and kept house for her brother Heinz, a watchmaker in Kartuzy (formerly Karthaus). In 1947 she wrote a war memoir in the format of a letter to her brothers Gustav and Paul, who with Else were the only three to survive the Holocaust. Gustav was hidden in Germany and Paul lived in Shanghai with his wife and child during the war.

Else claimed the Stenzels hid her because they had a good relationship with her parents. When the Stenzels' last cow died, they were in desperate financial straits, and Else and her brother Heinz were the only ones prepared to lend them money. The Stenzels therefore hid her out of loyalty. Doris Stiefel (*née* Pintus) translated Else's diary from the original German in 1998. Doris' father Richard Pintus was one of Else's first cousins and they corresponded regularly after the war. Doris, who now lives in Seattle, thinks the reason they helped her was as follows:

> It seems that in the case of the Stenzels, as in others, humanitarian motivation, depending on how that is defined, was based on a warm, personal and long-lasting relationship that existed between those doing the saving and the individual saved. [The] Stenzels willingly risked their own lives for Else Pintus but it is hard to imagine that they would have done it for any Jew who happened along. Else repeatedly remarks on their kindness to her. To my thinking, [the] Stenzels were very decent simple country folk, who obviously were not of Nazi ideology.[127]

Else described in her diary how they took her in on 14 December 1942:

Mrs Stenzel immediately recounted the time when things had gone badly for them and the sheriff was after them, when even the last of their cows succumbed, and then Heinz, without being asked, had loaned them money. She had come at that time and talked about all their bad luck. She had not asked for anything, just mentioned that neither family nor friends were willing to help. We had just received the rent for the lake. I happened to be busy in the kitchen at the time and Heinz came to me and asked if we shouldn't give them the rent money, things were going so badly for them. I immediately agreed, and so she took the rent – speechless, because she had neither asked for nor expected to receive any help. With our money then they pulled themselves up again. First they got the sheriff off their back, bought another cow, and then started taking in summer guests.[128]

Else continually stressed the Stenzels' goodness in spite of the great personal risks they were running. However, she had a very difficult time at the hands of Regina, the elder daughter of the family, who treated her like a slave and severely exploited the situation. Else had arrived at the Stenzels in December 1942, initially to stay only until the following summer, but in fact she remained hidden until 25 March 1945 and did not experience any fresh air in all that time. Her room was an attic room under a 'low cardboard-thin roof, the place approximately 3 meters long, 2 meters wide – where they stored junk. In the summer it was hot like an oven, in the winter icy cold. In the winter my breath froze the bed to my nose.'[129] She describes how difficult it was to be incarcerated:

On the street I could see and hear acquaintances. The window I dared open only a tiny crack. I was afraid that I would be seen from the street and recognized. Would I ever walk that street again, as a free person? Often I despaired of it. How often I was reminded of the song, 'Freedom, it is mine.' One had sung it at school without understanding its meaning. Now I knew what it meant to be free. [The] Stenzels brought the food up to me; but had to make sure that neither the maid nor the children noticed it. For me, the worst and most embarrassing was the toilet arrangement. A bucket for the night was placed in the hallway at the window next to my door, ostensibly for Regina, who also lived upstairs. In the morning the children had to bring it down. [130]

The ordeal of being confined but yet hearing ordinary lives going on is a common theme in the memoirs of persecuted Jews from the Holocaust. One experience that has always stayed in my mind since I first read it in 1995, is that of Eva Heyman who could be described as a Hungarian Anne Frank – she even addresses her diary as a person like Anne did.

Eva was a 13-year-old girl in the Ghetto in Nagyvárad, where my father was born. She kept a diary for a few months in 1944 before she was deported to Auschwitz, where the notorious Mengele selected her and himself pushed her onto a truck to be killed on 17 October 1944. [131] Eva chronicled her time in the Ghetto and on 14 May 1944 describes hearing the ice-cream seller's bell ringing outside. She comments that looking out of the window was punishable by death, so she could not see him, but she and her cousin Marica heard him:

This afternoon I and Marica heard the icecream vendor ringing. As you know, we can't look out through the window, because even for that we can be killed. But we're still allowed to hear, and so I and Marica heard the icecream vendor ringing his bell on the other side of the fence. I like icecream, and I must say that I like the icecream they sell in cones on the street much more than the icecream they sell in confectionery shops, even though in the confectionery shops it's much more expensive! Formerly, whenever I used to hear the icecream vendor's bell, I would dash to the gate. Mostly I would ask for a lemon cone. But if I didn't hear the bell, Ági [Eva's mother] and Grandma or Juszti or Mariska would rush outside and bring the lemon cone. Ági liked to say that in front of our house, the icecream vendor 'is sure to earn something' – that is, he was certain to sell at least one cone.

Once that poor icecream pedlar was very sad, because one of his children was sick. I went with him to grandpa's pharmacy and he gave him medicine free of charge. I remember that for a long time he didn't come, but then he brought a huge lemon cone and wouldn't take any money for it. Of course, I don't know, because I can't see, if the one ringing on the other side of the fence is the same icecream man who used to come to us, but in all of Várad there were just two icecream pedlars. Maybe it really was him, and now he is sad because his customers are locked up behind the fence. I think he must remember me, because I went with him to Grandpa that time for the medicine for his boy. Marica and I even told each other how well off the icecream man's boy is now, better off than we are; anybody in the world is better off than us, because they all can do whatever they want and go wherever they want, and only we are in the Ghetto.[132]

Adina Szwajger, who was a 22-year-old medical student working in the Ghetto hospital, recalled the defeat of the Warsaw Ghetto revolt on 19 April 1943, when the Luftwaffe dropped incendiary bombs until the place was engulfed in flames. There was shooting and Jews leapt from burning buildings, but meanwhile, literally a few feet away outside the Ghetto, 'the merry-go-round went round and jolly music played. And people enjoyed themselves.' Polish families had come from Easter services in nearby churches to spend time in Krasinski Park just outside the Ghetto wall. She later returns to the same theme: 'But I remember the laughter of the children. Because they were playing, and going round on the merry-go-round. And the music was playing.'[133]

To return to Else's story, she wrote that the Stenzels' house was geared up to having guests in the summer – presumably paying guests, because she describes a variety of different people who stayed in the house whilst she was incarcerated. She records at various times police boarding at the house, and fanatical Nazis who were relatives from Berlin with two children aged 3 and 6. She describes her difficulties with these curious children around:

Often they try the doorknob, rattle the door, spy through the keyhole and cuss at Regina – I had to cover the keyhole and all cracks. [The] Stenzels warned me whatever I did, not to reveal myself. The Berlin children were all over the place. To bring food up to me was very difficult. Even worse was the toilet business. In the oppressive heat, under the cardboard-thin roof, I didn't take a drop of liquid, suppressed my thirst, just to dry up my bladder. I couldn't fall asleep at night for fear that I might give myself away whilst I slept; I was afraid I might sigh.[134]

1. Bertha Bracey with her great-niece Pat Webb around 1938. *Pat Webb*

2. Charles Fawcett and the author in London, 1998. *Author's Collection*

3. Charles and April Fawcett with Tony and Cherie Blair at the national Holocaust Memorial Day Event in Cardiff, 2006. *HMDT*

4. Left to right: Miriam Ebel-Davenport, Charles Fawcett and unknown man, 1999, *Author's Collection*

5. Annette Fry (Varian's widow) at the Varian Fry Colloque in Marseilles, 1999. *Author's Collection*

6. The Stenzels' house, where Else Pintus was hidden, 1980s. *Doris Stiefel*

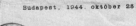

SVÁJCI KÖVETSÉG	SCHWEIZERISCHE GESANDTSCHAFT
IDEGEN ÉRDEKEK KÉPVISELETE	ABTEILUNG FÜR FREMDE INTERRESSEN
KIVÁNDORLÁSI OSZTÁLY	ABTEILUNG AUSWANDERUNG
V., VADÁSZ-UTCA 29.	V., VADÁSZ-UTCA 29.

4371/CW.

1944.

Die Schweizerische Gesandt-schaft, Abteilung fremde Inte-ressen, bescheinigt hiermit, dass	A Svájci Követség, Idegen Érdekek Képviselete, ezennel igazolja, hogy
KRAUSZ ISTVÁN & Frau geb. Rosenberger Rózsa	KRAUSZ ISTVÁN és neje sz. Rosenberger Rózsa
im schweizerischen Kollektiv-pass zur Auswanderung einge-tragen ist, daher ist der (die) Betreffende als Besitzer eines gültigen Reisepasses zu be-trachten.	a svájci csoportos (collectiv) utlevélben szerepel és ezért nevezett érvényes utlevél bir-tokában levő személynek tekin-tendő.

Budapest, 23. Oktober 1944.　　Budapest, 1944. október 23.

7. Jews queuing outside the Glass House, the Swiss Immigration Office, waiting for the issue of *Schutzpass* (Letter of Protection), 1944. *Agnes Hirschi*

8. *Schutzpass* issued to Istvan Krausz and his wife Rozsa, Tom Keve's parents, 23 October 1944. *Tom Keve*

Clockwise from above

9. Carl Lutz aged 55, 1950. *Agnes Hirschi*

10. Agnes Hirschi. *Agnes Hirschi*

11. Hermann Maas. *Paul Mower*

12. Vali Rácz at her home in Budapest during the war. Marietta Herzog hid behind the bookcase during a Gestapo search. *Monica Porter*

13. Vali Rácz. *Monica Porter*

14. Soeur St Cybard, aged 59. *Louis Lacalle*

15. Pupils at *École Saint-Gauthier* in Confolens, 1944/5. *Louis Lacalle*

16. Josie Martin Levy and the author, 2003. *Author's Collection*

17. Józef Barczynski
& his wife Anna,
1970s.

18. Anna Barczynska
with Józef's Yad
Vashem award, 1998.
Olympia

19. Guicherd family with Betty and Jacques, 1943. *Betty Eppel*

20. Betty Eppel and Victor Guicherd, 1983. *Betty Eppel*

21. Victor, Josephine and Betty, 1983. *Betty Eppel*

22. Betty in the kitchen with the bread and flour store in which she and her brother used to hide, 2009. *Betty Eppel*

March'81
Yad
V'shem,
Jerusalem

↑
Mitzi planting her tree,
a holly-oak

Mitzi's tree is planted and the identifying plaque says:
Maria Saidler
Austria

23. Mitzi Saidler at Yad Vashem, 1981.
Dorothy Fleming

24. Mitzi with Otto Fleming, 1993. *Dorothy Fleming*

25. Mitzi, 1988. *Dorothy Fleming*

Above left 26. Dr Ho, 1937. *Manli Ho*; *Above right* 27. Shanghai monument. The inscription on the monument reads: 'From 1937 to 1941, thousands of Jews came to Shanghai fleeing from Na persecution. Japanese occupation authorities regarded them as "stateless refugees" and set up thi designated area to restrict their residence and business.' *Author's Collection*

28. Vytautas Rinkevicius' family, 1950s. *Margarat Kagan*

29. Vytautas, 1970s.
Margarat Kagan

30. Margaret and Joseph
Kagan with Vitalija,
Vytautas' youngest
daughter, 1989.
Margarat Kagan

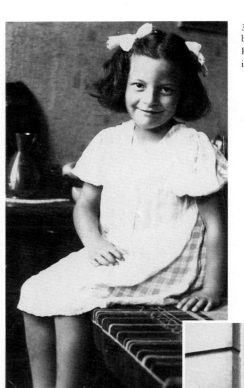

31. Suze van der Bijl, rescued by the Schoen family aged 4. Photograph taken by the Schoens in May or June 1945. *Peter Schoen*

32. Joost and Anna Schoen, 1945. *Peter Schoen*

33. The Klerks' visit to Heemstede with Henri Obstfeld, July 1946. *Henri Obstfeld*

34. The Klerks with the Obstfelds at Arnhem, April 1947. *From left to right:* Jan Willemsen, his wife Els (daughter of the Klerks), Henri Obstfeld (age 7), Emmy Willemsen (age about 5), Hendrika Klerk, Henri's mother and Jacob Klerk. *Henri Obstfeld*

Tanzkünstlerin Hilde Holger
Inhab. der Neuen Schule für Bewegungskunst
Wien, I., Singerstraße 16

35. Hilde Holger's dance school poster, 1930s. *Primavera Boman-Behram*

36. Henry Walton's father, Siegmund Weltlinger, with the Queen and Willy Brandt, 1965. *Henry Walton*

The continual fear of being betrayed tormented her and her rescuers. The Gestapo used to come at night and she always got dressed so that she could claim that she had just arrived. Towards the end of the war, in January 1945, Else writes of eighty SS men being quartered at the Stenzels'. They were searching for deserters and partisans. They were 18- to 20-year-old hooligans who terrified everyone because they had some dangerous Ukrainians with them. They ransacked houses, searching with dogs. She wrote:

> Now I thought my final hour had come, five minutes before the closing of the gates. Even [the] Stenzels, who had always appeared very calm or at least never showed me otherwise, now got very nervous. They wanted to entrust someone to get me some kind of papers but I was afraid again of bringing another person into the know. I didn't want to have the whole family Stenzel on my conscience and now had to prepare to end my life.[135]

Although Else had some poison, her courage failed her, so she was still alive when suddenly, after four weeks, the SS left. The Russians finally liberated the area on 10 March 1945; however they all hid in the cellar due to fear of the Russians' activities, and Else later found them to be anti-Semitic. She describes her emergence from hiding:

> That was the first time, from December 14, 1942 until March 25, 1945, that I got out into the fresh air. The last few days spent entirely in the cellar. I came outside and immediately became dizzy. And, to my dismay, I could hardly walk. Through my thin shoes the cobblestones dug into my feet like pins. The soles of my feet had become soft like an infant's. I had become so afraid of people that I didn't want to be seen by anyone. On top of which there was the fear that the Russians might yet be beaten back. On the move to the parsonage though, I was seen. It went like wildfire through the village. People I knew came to visit and to invite me. But I didn't want to go anywhere; it took a long time till I got used to the fresh air.[136]

Else survived the war thanks to the Stenzels. Ironically, after the war they had to prove that they had not been Nazi supporters and had been good to the Poles. The fact that they had protected Else was in their favour and she was the major witness for them. Else told her brothers that she was the only Jew to have survived in the Kartuzy region, and the only Jewish people in Danzig came from the East. 'Of the Jews we had once known, no one is left here.'[137]

In 1949 Else wrote of her life to Erich Pintus, an uncle of Doris Stiefel. She wrote very sadly:

> I'm alive, more or less healthy and you've got to be pleased with just that. Apart from that I vegetate here, lonely, deserted and forgotten by everybody, the only Jewess in the whole area of Karthaus, no relatives or acquaintances here – all either murdered or emigrated. I get by as a housemaid … What that means for me at 56 only you can tell. Lucky the people who were able to turn their backs on Europe in time.[138]

She moved to Berlin after the war and died in 1975 in the Jewish old-age home. She left all the family property in Chmielno to the Stenzels in gratitude for what they did for her. Doris Stiefel, whose father was one of Else's cousins, met the Stenzels' daughter, Dorota Prycskowska, in 1992 when she took the photographs. Dorota had been a young girl during the war and she still lived in the family home where Else was hidden, with some memory of those years. She died on 17 February 2006 aged 85.

János Tóth. Naomi Szinai (born 1924, *née* Mayer) grew up in Hajdudorog, Hungary, which was a village of 12,000 people with a few hundred Jews. Her father was one of five doctors in the village:

> He must have built up a busy practice fairly quickly which provided them with a reasonable, rather than big income as the largely peasant population could not afford to pay too much for their health care. Furthermore, Father treated lots of his patients who could not afford to pay free of charge or for a nominal fee.[139]

Naomi was the eldest of three children and had a happy childhood. Their father's surgery was in their home so the family were involved in opening the door to patients and answering the telephone. They also sometimes accompanied him on house calls when they could have private chats. In the winter they went on a toboggan in the snow which was great fun. They were educated up until the age of 14 in the town and lived in a Jewish circle. Many of this circle were murdered by the Nazis. Life was relatively primitive with limited running water in the houses and drinking water brought up from the well by the maids. They took holidays at a Jewish hotel in Ujhuta in the Bukk mountains: 'In the summer we used to go on holiday with Mother; Father would only come for a day or two as he wouldn't leave his patients for longer.'[140]

Anti-Semitism was a fact of life from an early age. The Hungarians broke windows in Jewish houses when drunk and shouted nasty things. In school there were many comments – some more unpleasant than others. Once the war started, although Hungary was not occupied by the Nazis until March 1944, Jewish men were called up for forced labour and Dr Mayer was often called for medical service. Her parents listened to Hungarian broadcasts from London to hear the real news rather than Hungarian propaganda, but because it was forbidden Naomi used to stand outside the house and run in to warn them if anyone approached.

Naomi had decided to flee her hometown even before the Jews were sent to the Ghetto. She decided to get work as a servant, but to do this she needed false papers. She wrote of her father's influence on her success:

My father was the local doctor. He had always looked after his patients devotedly and one, in our hour of need, was willing to repay my father's kindness, although this put his job, his liberty and even his life at risk. He was a clerk in the registrar's office and so was in a position to provide false documents for me, with which I could pass as an Aryan.[141]

Naomi recalls the clerk's name as János Tóth and told me her sister Elizabeth had written to commend him to Yad Vashem.[142] As a result of her false papers, she was able to obtain work as a servant in a nearby town. She presented herself at a hiring market where the servants waited for prospective employees, who inspected them and negotiated wages – similar to the traditional 'hiring fairs' in rural England. Naomi has described what happened there:

> A large heavily-scented woman stopped in front of me and asked for my service book, a document which every domestic servant had to have. 'What's your name, girl?' she asked. 'Maria Falus', I answered, controlling the tremor in my voice as I pronounced my new name for the first time. She looked at my service book. 'Why, you have not worked before and you are 18 now.' Most peasant girls went into service at 14. I had my answer ready. 'My mother was ill, I had to stay at home and help with the household and the younger children.' This satisfied her and she started to bargain about wages.[143]

Naomi was taken on because she was prepared to take low wages. She worked in the dingy commercial hotel owned by her mistress and husband and looked after their spoilt 6-year-old son. It was very hard work from early in the morning until 11 p.m. and she slept on a camp bed in the kitchen. She was terrified to hear one day that the Jews had been sent into a Ghetto and feared for her family. One day, she was taking the little boy for his afternoon walk when she came across a new fence 20ft high – the Ghetto was behind it. The boy threw some stones at the fence and she was just about to stop him when the guard came up and joked with the boy about the locked-up Jews.[144]

One afternoon, when she took him to the playground, the children lost interest in the sandpit and said: 'let's play Magyars and Jews'. She was made to play the Jew and the boys pointed their toy guns at her. She was gripped by terror and passed out. As she came round she heard people claiming she was a Jewess and others agreed. Whilst they were considering getting the police, an old lady asked her twice if she was 'expecting'. Naomi took a minute to understand and then admitted she was three months gone and began to cry.[145] The old lady saved her by her compassion and presence of mind.

Naomi was so troubled and looked so pale that the master was concerned that she was ill and his son might catch something. They therefore sent her to the clinic:

The waiting room was full and I was rigid with fear that someone would recognise the doctor's eldest daughter. I hid behind a newspaper. This brought its own terror, with the news of the hunt for Jews. It described the heavy penalties for people who hid Jews or tried to help them in any way. It had news of the capture and execution of fugitive Jews ...

Just then the surgery door opened and I was the next patient. I looked at the doctor and we recognised each other instantly. He was one of my father's colleagues. 'My name is Maria Falus', I said quickly.

He shut the door and both the nurse and he were silent. I knew what went through his mind. Could he risk not reporting me to the police? Would the nurse give him away, or blackmail him later? I saw them exchange a long glance, while I held my breath in terror.

Then a nod signalled agreement between them. My luck had held. They were not going to give me away. He took my hand ostensibly to feel my pulse, but I knew he wanted to reassure me and to wish me well. I relaxed and smiled gratefully as I took my prescription from him. He too was to give me strength in the dark days to come, when I recalled his kindness and courage. [146]

But Naomi became scared and abandoned her job to return home. Now Hungary was occupied life became difficult for all Jews. Her sister noted that she was the one who made the yellow stars all Jews were forced to wear and stitched them onto their clothes. 'It had to be a certain kind of yellow, described as canary yellow. Ex-school friends made remarks on the street on meeting us with our yellow star. Life was becoming more and more unpleasant.' [147]

Their father was taken away to provide medical service and the women were sent to the Ghetto in Hajdudorog. Their father and the only boy Imre ended up in Mauthausen camp, but, miraculously, the family of five all survived the Holocaust and in 1951 were all together again safely in Israel, although Naomi had married in 1948. She now lives in North London. None of this would have happened if the registrar's clerk, János Tóth, and the doctor had not protected Naomi in war-torn Hungary out of loyalty to her father. As Mr and Mrs Bela Grunfeld declared, János Tóth continued to be a true friend of the Jews:

We have known János Tóth since his youth; he was well known in our township for his liberal attitude. In the 1940s he was a civil servant working for the district council. During that time, which corresponded with the years of persecution of Jews, all his actions were directed at supporting and assisting the victims of fascism. During those difficult times, he was the only source of news for us, especially regarding political developments.[148]

He later proved to be a real hero by personally saving a Jew from being thrown off a train by a group of Hungarian soldiers:

In this regard we can attest to the following: On a particular day in the summer of 1944, my brother-in-law/brother Arnold Weinstock was returning by train from Debrecen to Hajdudorog. A number of soldiers in the carriage started screaming at him, 'Don't you know, you stinking Jew, that you are not allowed to travel', they then grabbed him and wanted to throw him off the speeding train. Mr Tóth, having witnessed these events, stood across the door and managed to calm the raving soldiers somewhat – it was due to his decisive intervention that my brother(-in-law) was not thrown from the train. This incident was related to us by my brother/brother-in-law. He subsequently perished in a concentration camp.[149]

János Tóth himself added to the tale by describing the situation after this confrontation and, incidentally, showing how spontaneous his actions had been:

Following the events described, a man, a civilian, screamed at me in outrage from the far corner of the carriage: 'Your Lordship will pay for this!' I recognised the man as György Molnár, innkeeper, and one of the leaders of the local Arrow Cross [Hungarian Nazi Party]. It was only then that I realised that my action was likely to have dangerous consequences.[150]

János Tóth managed to get protection by asking the local medical officer, Dr Imre Olah, who was responsible for the health control of local inns, to help:

When the innkeeper returned home, he found the doctor at his premises, for the purpose of an official health inspection. The doctor informed Molnár, that if he discussed the events on the train with anyone, or if any harm were to befall my person, the inn will be closed down on health grounds. I was very much afraid, that Molnár would talk of my act to the Nazis and soldiers who regularly drank at his inn, which would undoubtedly have resulted in me and my family being deported.[151]

Tóth was really frightened and he was right to be scared. He was attacked twice. Once, in late October 1944, when he was passing another inn owned by József Révész, someone shouted: 'There goes János Tóth, the hireling of the Jews!' and six Arrow Cross thugs, including Molnár, came out and chased him. He ran but fired four shots with his pistol and wounded Molnár, so he got away. After the war, the Arrow Cross members formed a number of right-wing political parties and infiltrated the Independent Smallholders Party. At 10 p.m. on 6 March 1946, eighteen months after the liberation of his hometown, 'a band of 20 members of the Youth Movement of the Independent Smallholders Party attacked me with clubs in the presence of my wife. With the last of my strength, collapsed on the floor, I was able to shoot off my last two bullets. The sound of the shots caused my attackers to flee.'[152]

At the end of his declaration, Tóth wrote: 'After liberation, in my function as district notary, I was able to help returning Jews to trace and restore their property.' He was recognised as a Righteous Among the Nations by Yad Vashem in 1999.[153]

Karl (Charles) Petras (1896–1952). I have included the rescue of Hilde Holger (1905–2001) here because it was very difficult to establish exactly what the motive was for her rescue. Loyalty and friendship seem the most plausible. She was a famous dancer who lived in Camden Town for many decades, still teaching pupils into her late nineties. She was one of the first people to contact me when I advertised in the *AJR* magazine for people to come forward with their stories. She wrote to me originally in August 2000, when she was 95, to tell me about Karl Petras, an Austrian journalist who saved her life by providing her with a visa for India in 1939. She wrote: 'Karl Petrascu sent me a visa from India to escape Hitler's Concentration Camps. He was a Journalist. Unfortunately my whole family was gassed – the war broke out, the frontiers were closed. I can't be enough grateful [for] what he did for me.'[154]

Unfortunately Hilde died before I could get to meet her in London. However, I have recently made contact with her daughter, who is wrestling with her mother's enormous archive in the house where Hilde lived and taught since the 1950s.

Hilde was born in 1905 as Hilde Sofer into an Austrian Jewish family in Vienna. Her great-grandparents had shared a house with Johann Strauss:

> Holger's youth coincided with a cultural flowering in the Austrian capital – the era of the composers Alban Berg and Arnold Schoenberg, the painters Oskar Kokoschka, Gustav Klimt and Egon Schiele, the writer Stephan Zweig and the poet Hugo von Hofmannsthal. In her work she was to pay tribute to the spirit of those times.[155]

She started to dance as a child of 6 and aged 14 she became a student of the influential and pioneering dance teacher and choreographer Gertrud Bodenwieser, with whose dance group she toured Europe in the 1920s. In 1926 she started her own group, the Hilde Holger Tanzgruppe (*see plate 35*). She also worked as a model for many photographers such as Martin Imboden and Anton Josef Trcka (known as Antios), the painters Felix Albrecht Harta and Benedikt F. Doblin, and was the model for Joseph Heu's famous 1926 sculpture.

The Nazis were schizophrenic about her type of expressionist free dancing which they appropriated for use in the 1936 Berlin Olympics whilst at the same time condemning it as 'degenerate'. She realised difficulties lay ahead when her school was closed by the Nazis, but she and her pupils were desperate to continue expressing themselves through dancing. She wrote how her great friend Felix Harta, who lived and worked in a large warehouse, allowed them to use his studio for dance classes and secret performances. This was a risk because the Gestapo were watching and they had to leave in very small groups to avoid arousing suspicion. 'These classes, in spite of the dreadful pressure and fears, were of great comfort to us all as we danced and freed ourselves for some hours, from all the horror inflicted on us.' She subsequently heard from some of these students who survived the Holocaust how important these lessons had been to them at that difficult time.[156]

Her memoir records her awareness that failure to acquire a visa for emigration would mean ending up in a concentration camp. She describes how, armed with this knowledge, she contacted all her friends abroad asking them to help her get an exit visa to show the Gestapo she was entitled to leave. She wrote:

> On account of my profession I was known to American friends and I also had a dear friend in India, a Viennese Journalist Charles Petrasch [Karl Petras], to whom I wrote *Save my life!* And thanks to his prompt action he got an entrance visa for me for India and also found someone to give the guarantee for me not to be a burden on the Indian government.[157]

She describes how she had long had an interest in India and its dancing, as well as having Indian friends in Vienna. She received her papers through Petras. She describes how the money given to her for the trip by her kind aunts was stolen by a Nazi who threatened to denounce her to the Gestapo if she did not pay up. His behaviour was illegal but in those times 'there was no law and no justice'.[158]

She left for India on 6 June 1939 and was very upset at saying goodbye to her mother and sister who came to the station to see her off – they knew they would not see each other again, and, in fact, fourteen members of Hilde's family were murdered at Auschwitz.[159] She travelled to Paris and from there by train to Marseilles where she got the P&O boat to India. She arrived in Bombay on 21 June 1939 and was met by Charles Petras and Dr Trivikram. She lived with the doctor and his young pregnant wife when she first arrived. He had his surgery at home and she is said to have slept on his consulting couch.

Initially, Hilde's rescuer was a mysterious man because of the limited information I received from her about him, and the little written in her memoir. This was not helped by the variation in the spelling of his name.

I believe he changed it from Karl Petras to Charles Petrarch to make it more English sounding in a country that was part of the British Empire. However, the spelling Petrasch is also found.

Dr Margit Franz of Graz University is researching *Exile to India during World War II* and has examined Hilde's archive. I am grateful to her for sharing what she has uncovered. She has written that Hans Glas, an architect and one-time lover of Hilde, emigrated to India in July 1938. He had a contract as an architect in Calcutta and tried to get Hilde to come to India. There are several letters in the archive from him and one, dated 16 October 1938, explains how he had been finding out in Calcutta about earning an income as a dancer. He said it was not a good prospect as dancing was associated with prostitution, and apologised profusely for not being able to be more helpful. Apparently, he was also trying to help his two brothers get to India as well. As a result of this information, Hilde undertook a course for *heilmassage* (medial massage) prior to her departure from Vienna, presumably to provide another source of income.

Karl Petras was already in Bombay when Glas arrived in India in 1938. Glas wrote to Hilde that he had been unable to meet Petras on his way to Calcutta but would write to him. So far, all that Dr Franz has discovered about Petras before he came to India is that he was a journalist and interviewed Gandhi in London on 29 October 1931.[160] He appears to have been a Renaissance man who was interned as an enemy alien by the British between 1939–45, and during this period he wrote poetry and painted watercolours. He was interned with 1,500 other German, Austrian and Italian enemy aliens in the central internment camp Dehra Dun in the Himalayan foothills near the Nepalese border.[161] Hilde tried very hard to get him released. There is a letter in the archive from the Archbishop of Bombay, dated 2 February 1940, apologising for the delay in meeting. On the envelope Hilde has written: 'Historical letter when I tried to get out from the Camp for aliens my "Arian" friend Carl Petras who was accused to be a Nazi which was not true as he saved my life being Jewish.'

Karl and Hilde remained close friends during all these years and after his release from the camp he became her manager. Dr Franz surmises this was probably to prove that he had an occupation, because this was one condition for being allowed to stay on in India. He stayed in India for the rest of his life and, having been sympathetic to the Indian liberation struggle for some time, he set up an Institute of Foreign Languages in Bombay as a meeting and mediation place between India and the West. He was the director of what became a successful international centre and in 1950 it expanded to New Delhi as well. He arranged exhibitions, performances, cultural radio programmes, as well as the language courses. He helped young artists in Bombay by showcasing their experimental works in his centre – such as Sayed Haider Raza's 1950 show. Raza, who was born in 1922, has become one of the most distinguished international Indian artists and he still exhibits around the world. In December 2009 I tracked him down in Paris. Both Primavera and I spoke to him on the telephone but unfortunately, although he remembers that Petras organised the exhibition for him and ran his language centre, he was unable to tell us anything about Karl and what sort of a person he was.

In the Holger archive there is a press cutting on faded *Financial Times* pink paper, dated 13 February 1951, describing the cultural activities at the centre in New Delhi. It refers to language classes in Chinese, English, French, German, Hindi, Russian and Spanish. In January 1951 the Swiss inister in New Delhi opened a posthumous art exhibition by the Swiss artist Molly Ruetschi. A play by Shaw was presented and a recital by 'the British songstress Miss Victoria Kingsley'. Future plans were for an 'Indian Week' with dance and music events, and distinguished Indian guests were going to lecture on aspects of Indian cultural life.[162]

When I visited Hilde's daughter she showed me an invitation for Hilde Holger and Karl Petras to attend an Art Preview on 3 January 1949 in Bombay, and on 15 February 1951 Karl wrote to Hilde from New Delhi on rather 'art deco' notepaper for his Institute of Foreign Languages, where again he was described as Charles Petras, Director. I also saw wonderful photographs of Hilde dancing.

Hilde had a difficult life and her daughter Primavera enumerated her problems for me. She had become a dancer and then taught dancing to earn a living; she fled Hitler and lost many members of her family in Auschwitz and came with no money to an exotic country.

Having married a Parsee doctor and homeopath, Dr Ardeshire Kavasji Boman-Behram, her first child was stillborn. Then she had her daughter Primavera and a son Darius, who had Down's syndrome and holes in the heart. After the murder of Gandhi, whom she had met, she came to England in 1948, but around 1962 her husband left her for someone else. Her daughter eventually brought them together again many years later and they remarried. Subsequently, her husband said that although she was very difficult to live with, he had enormous respect for her.

Like many survivors, she suffered from guilt that she had escaped when relatives had not. She seems to have had the gift of friendship, supporting others and teaching young people right until the end. She kept up to date by reading the newspapers every day and the house was always full of people who she helped and who helped her. It is extraordinary to consider that but for Karl Petras, her eighty-year career as a dancer might have been tragically terminated with the rest of her family in the Holocaust.

Karl Petras, however, over-worked, and after suffering a heat-stroke, died in Delhi on 1 July 1952.[163] But the mysterious Karl/Charles had saved a most remarkable woman. As Julia Pascal wrote:

> Her achievements in Britain were more those of an educator than as a dancer, and her fame here never reached the peak it enjoyed in pre-Nazi Vienna. None the less, she gave to future generations a link to a rich cultural heritage that Hitler failed to efface.[164]

Dr Franz has explained the visa/affidavit situation for refugees from Europe:

Apparently, as a result of the number of refugees seeking entry to India, the British had annulled the visa-abolition agreement with Germany and Austria following the Anschluss in March 1938. The refugees had to reassure two authorities and administration units, the British in London and the British Indian government in New Delhi, of two essentials regarding their stay in British India:

1. not to be of any security risk
2. not to be a financial burden

The new rules for visas indicated that the applicant had to be in possession of a valid national passport bearing a visa for India given by a British passport or consular authority, a return-ticket — even if the possibility of return was restricted by Germany — and two affidavits signed and verified by British Indian or British citizens guaranteeing the refugee's maintenance in India or a possible re-patrification. Additionally, a guarantee of employment was very helpful, and in some cases essential, as the number of sponsorships British or British-Indian persons could offer to refugees were limited. After intense negotiations, the Jewish Relief Association was able to sign for refugees' maintenance and overtake these sponsorships with the beginning of the year 1939. Jewish families like the Ezras in Calcutta or the Sasoons in Bombay were able to offer financial guarantees that also contributed massively to the work of the Relief Association.

I note from my own parents' Austrian passports that we too had similar conditions imposed on our entry into England on 24 May 1947. We were initially only allowed in for two months and forbidden from undertaking employment, paid or unpaid.

PAID RESCUERS

Before we leave the subject of rescuers, we should note that not all rescuers were altruistic. Some did it purely for money without showing any concern about their charge other than to keep them safe to ensure maximum payment. One Polish woman, who may well not have been alone, was paid both by Jewish and Polish Resistance groups for one child. Pani Borciñska took a young Jewish girl, Margarita Turkov, into her apartment in Warsaw on 18 August 1942 when she was 8½ years old. Margarita was to be known as Maria Konrad, nickname Marysia. Margarita was fortunate that her looks were not typically Jewish. With light brown hair and hazel eyes, she could pass as a normal Polish child. Months later she noted: 'I was considered lucky to be able to go about freely, nothing about me to suggest I might be Jewish.'[165]

On her first night with this strange woman, an air raid forced them into the cellars. In a pause between blasts, someone commented, 'Nothing to worry, they just want to drop a few on the Ghetto – finish off the kikes' and giggled. This made her cry and say she wanted to go back to her mummy. To cover up, Pani Borcińska told everyone in general: 'this relative of hers had just arrived from the country because her parents had been sent for labor in Germany and the child was still confused'.[166]

Her recent traumatic experiences left her fearful, compounded now by the harsh treatment she was receiving, and she began to wet the bed. This caused her endless unpleasantness with her guardian who was not a kindly soul and beat her incessantly.[167] But Margarita writes that she was not really cruel just bad tempered:

> Pani Borcińska did not want me to stay in order to have a victim to torture. She originally agreed to temporarily take in a Jewish child for the money she would get for it, and she ended up getting paid from two sources, the Jewish and the Polish underground resistance organizations, one not knowing the other was paying. She did not intend to be unkind but could not help it that I provoked her so.
>
> Pan Borciński, her husband, was a blond, blue eyed, squat man with a gentle mien. He never wanted to take in a Jewish child because he did not want to endanger the family, especially his beloved Bozenka [their daughter two years older than Margarita]. But his wife prevailed and he agreed to the temporary arrangement. Then, when the money began to make a difference in their lives, she convinced him they might as well continue, their lives being in danger anyway since he belonged to the Resistance in which also Danusia [the eldest daughter aged 20+] and Bogdan [son aged 15] began to play increasingly active roles. And so he agreed to that as well.[168]

She contrasts his kindness to her with his wife's behaviour, and notes how difficult she found it:

The constant terror in which I lived made it impossible for me to respond affectionately and I just wished he would stop being kind. I learned how to brace myself to bear cruelty – the feeling of gratitude for all his small gestures of kindness and sympathy was too much of a burden. What I found especially hard to bear were the nights he would come home drunk and berate his wife for treating me the way she did. They would start fighting and it invariably ended up with her beating him up. I would rather take the blows myself than have that sweet, gentle man suffer them for trying against the odds to protect me.[169]

Perhaps the greatest shock Margarita received, not long after her arrival, was when she was told to call her hosts uncle and auntie. On that particular evening she was washing her feet before going to bed when the son, Bogdan:

A lanky, blond boy with gray-green eyes and a streetwise air kept watching me and asked with a smirk, 'How does it feel to wash yourself with a soap made out of your brothers and sisters?' I looked up uncomprehending while Auntie hissed at me to be careful lest I leave some spots, at the same time telling Bogdan to shut up. I was looking now at Uncle who was seated at the kitchen table and had put down the newspaper he had been reading. There was pain on his face as he gently answered my look, 'Yes, it's true, I am afraid. The soap we get is made in the camps of Jewish fat.' I stared at him while this information was sinking in. I still did not know about the camps. Bogdan could not stop himself from adding, 'And new lamp shades from their skin.' At this point he received a blow from Auntie who advised him to keep his trap shut or he would really get it from her, while he protested that I might as well know what was what.[170]

Margarita's memoir is quite terrible to read as it narrates the way she hardened herself to the treatment which was so alien to her previous experience. She writes of auntie's nastiness to her own children which alternated with demonstrations of affection, particularly to Bozenka, who was obviously her favourite. Both in the memoir and in subsequent correspondence she stresses her shock:

When she got into one of her fits, she was liable to hand it out to them as well, but they were used to her and had learned how to protect themselves. I had never before experienced anybody talking or behaving in such a manner and my constant state of shock was only slowly turning into numbness, my being encased in a hard shell.[171]

Although Pani Borcińska treated her with utter contempt, she never accused her of stealing, and when her little hoard of money disappeared she asked Margarita who had taken it. She knew it was Bogdan, but before she could respond Pani had confronted him:

he wanted to know why she should suspect him and not the Jewish bitch. She began to beat him but he managed to escape and run out into the landing. Convinced that I had told on him, he screamed at the top of his voice, as he started running down the stairs, 'Yes, believe a slandering Yid! The f***ing good for nothing kike is now more valuable to you than your own flesh and blood!!' Fortunately nobody was around to hear this and Auntie managed to run after him and drag him back into the apartment. This time he really got it from her.[172]

Actually, auntie kept her until Russia liberated Poland and her father came for her:

She had been keeping me now for a long time without any money for me coming in and she was willing to continue keeping me on the chance that my parents or some other relatives had survived and would handsomely remunerate her for all the trouble and expense I caused her. Otherwise, she had a plan to sell me to some peasants.[173]

Pani was lucky and so was Margarita, who was planning how to escape if she was sold. When Margarita's father turned up to collect her in the spring of 1945 he settled the debt. Margarita recalls that he went back to his office and borrowed from whoever he could, and then returned a few hours later 'with the cash and I left with him'.[174]

Margarita was thoroughly traumatised by her whole experience, and even though her parents survived to take her to America in December 1947, her life has been scarred by these events:

> Counselling was not known in those days. My parents thought it was enough to have me back with them and while they were aware (at least to some extent) of what I went through during the time with Mrs Borcińska they had no clue to what extent I was damaged. Years of therapy after I grew up did not touch upon that experience and only recently, a new therapeutic approach helped me relive and accept those emotions which were buried and denied all the years and which, among other causes, prevented me from having any fulfilment in life – till now; and this therapy was what enabled me to write about those times.[175]

A final case of someone who paid for safety was Lea Goodman's parents, who voluntarily entered the Kostrze camp near Krakow in September 1942. Lea had been born in 1935 in Krakow and was an only child. In 1941 the family of three moved to Dzialoszyce, her mother's hometown. However, on the eve of the mass deportation of Jews they travelled to Kostrze. Lea was 7 at this time.

The camp's commandant was a German engineer called Richard Strauch whom Lea described as an opportunist like Schindler. She believes her parents may have paid to stay. The camp had Jewish guards and there were Jewish secretaries in his office in the town. Lea remembers visiting the office. After they had been there a short time, Richard Strauch told Lea's parents that the authorities had learned there were children in the camp and he could not keep them anymore. He found places for them all in an orphanage in the Ghetto:

> We were about twenty children in a horse-drawn cart. We were all quite happy; it seemed as we were going on an excursion. My father followed the cart and after some kilometres, in a suburb of Krakow, my father took me off and said I was going to say goodbye to friends, and rejoin the children in the Ghetto, which of course I did not. If I had I would probably not be alive.[176]

Lea was placed with a Christian family, Mr and Mrs Soltisova, who were business friends of her father, and she believes her survival was due to being with them. Lea's father was arrested by the Nazis at the end of 1942 when he left his work party to go into a shop which was forbidden to Jews. He did not survive the war.

Her mother then joined Lea and they moved from place to place. Eventually they heard that travel to Hungary from Poland through Slovakia was possible with the help of the Underground. Lea's memories of their journey from Krakow are clear; as there was snow on the ground she thought it was February or March. In the small group of six or eight was a girl strapped to a relative who carried her – she had lost the use of her legs from being hidden in a confined space. The guide disappeared and they eventually found their way back to Krakow.[177]

Left with nowhere to go, they turned up at her mother's old dressmaker who took them in. She kept them for free – perhaps out of loyalty. There was also a Christian teacher who her mother used to meet in the street, who she believes gave her money and addresses of places to stay. They stayed in three different places and had to pay 'danger money' to be lodged. However, Lea and her mother made another attempt to reach Slovakia – and survived – and she remembers the drama of crossing the border at night. She commented: 'The Slovaks, who at that time were still an axis power of the Germans, behaved with humanity towards illegal refugees and that could not be said most of the time of the neutral Swiss, who in similar situations like ours sent people back to occupied France.'[178]

Their real good fortune was that they started their journey late in the war, March 1944, and never reached Hungary where they might have joined the thousands sent to their deaths in Auschwitz. As Lea has written: 'We stayed in Slovakia, where we were liberated by the glorious Russian army.'[179]

Lea always wondered how the guides and the forays across the borders were organised. She eventually read Robert Rozett's article which told her:

From February 1943 until March 1944 an extraordinary and, in many ways, unique rescue operation took place. Zionist youth-movement

members, veteran Zionist and Orthodox anti-Zionists in Slovakia and
Hungary, backed by representatives of the Jewish Agency from Palestine
in Turkey and aided by gentile couriers (guides), strove in loose federation to extricate Jews from Nazi-occupied Poland. Those who were
smuggled out of Poland were brought to Hungary, generally by way of
Slovakia, with the hope of eventually bringing them to Palestine.[180]

They arrived in the town of Kezmarok, where they stayed until the
end of the war. Her mother found work as a mother's help, passing as a
Polish Christian. After the liberation they went to Prague and at Easter
1946 they went to France. Her mother remarried and had another
daughter in 1948. Lea married Dennis Goodman in 1954. He had been
sent to school in England in 1936 from Germany aged 13. His parents
had moved to Holland and did not survive. Lea has lived in London
since the age of 18 and is a sculptor. Dennis died in 2007 aged 84.

Lea concluded that the fact she and her mother survived in Krakow,
on the Aryan side, was very unusual. Very few Jews managed to do so in
a town which was the headquarters of the Germans in Poland.[181]

CONCLUSIONS

Now that we have read the narratives about the rescuers and the people they saved, in this section I would like to compare the rescuers, the wider issues of rescue and also show the relevance of their courage to the world in which we live today.

COMPARING THE RESCUERS

We have seen that the rescuers came from varied backgrounds. We find that some rescuers, such as Józef Barczynski and Dr Ho, had experienced hardship in their youth. Barczynski's family had been displaced and he therefore identified with the Jews. Dr Ho had grown up at a time when the Chinese were badly treated, so he too could empathise with persecuted Jews.

The Italian Costagutis, Mitzi and the Stenzels all helped people they knew and felt a loyalty towards, either because of previous relationships or living in close proximity. This can also apply to János Tóth who certainly was consistently good to Jews without even considering his own position. The Costagutis knew the people they helped because they were neighbours in Rome. They were not particularly pro-Jewish and some of those they assisted were early members of the Fascist party, so the rescue was really based on their neighbourly relationship and humanitarianism.

Vali Rácz also had mixed motives: loyalty to Jews because she had worked amongst them for years, but also great compassion for those who needed help. Her daughter described her as brave, humane, generous to a fault and having total self-belief.[1]

A significant division between the rescuers was that some of them had reacted specifically to the horrors of the Holocaust. Oskar Schindler, Varian Fry and Jaap van Proosdij are three rescuers who fall into this category. Oskar and Varian were older than Jaap, who was only 21, and their earlier lives had not marked them out as people who went out of their way to help others. They performed amazing deeds for Jews in those desperate times, but altruism was not significant in their lives before or afterwards. Both Oskar and Varian are now dead, but Jaap van Proosdij admitted to me, 'I don't know whether I am an humanitarian',[2] saying he was more likely to help individuals or families than a nation of people in crisis.

Although Fry has been called the 'American Schindler', these two men came to their rescuees from different directions:

> Schindler was a sensualist and an opportunist who stumbled upon a humanitarian duty he could not ignore, although to begin with he probably did try to ignore it. Fry was a sensitive, even prissy individual, an aesthete and an epicure who was driven by idealistic motives to perform a humanitarian duty. Schindler's was the profiteering escapade that went awry once he discovered by chance that life was more important than money. Fry's was a deliberate mission that entailed a change of character (though he drew on resources he already possessed). Despite the differences between them, both men lived for a time at the very limit of their abilities, where they found their personalities at last fulfilled. What Thomas Keneally wrote of Oskar Schindler – 'The peace would never exalt him as had the war' – was also true for Fry.[3]

Many of the rescuers were known to be helpful to others all their lives. Charles Fawcett continued to help those in crisis, in spite of recurrent bouts of TB, until he was too frail. In the 1956 Hungarian revolution he rescued many Hungarians and later flew to the Belgian Congo and helped 250 Europeans escape. In the 1980s he was in Afghanistan filming Russian crimes against the Afghans. Henk Huffener also gave his time to help people after the war, assisting both Chileans and

West Indians in London in the 1970s. John Schoen's father was always having people turn up at his door wanting work, and Soeur St Cybard continually aided those in difficulties – she was like a social worker in the area. These were people who continually took responsibility for others who needed their help. They gave it willingly and unstintingly all their lives.

Many rescuers regarded their time in the war as the most significant in their lives. Carl Lutz, Varian Fry and Mary Jayne Gold, the wealthy socialite who funded Varian's work in Marseilles, all agreed on this:

> Those 13 months in Marseilles were the most important of his life and he was never again so fulfilled. Mary Jayne Gold died on 5 October 1997. One of her friends said at her funeral that she 'felt that only one year in her life really mattered and it was the year she spent in Marseille'. He added: 'She was a very shrewd woman whose heart was on the right side of issues and who at a crucial turning point in history understood what was called for.' That obituary could speak for Varian Fry too.[4]

Carl Lutz's stepdaughter wrote to me: 'My father always considered his time in Budapest and the rescue of innocent Jews as the most important part of his life.'[5] She subsequently told me: 'It was the main subject he talked about. He wrote lots of letters and reports but never wrote his memoirs.'[6] Jaap van Proosdij also said that the period when he was helping the Jews was the time when he felt he was most useful in his life.

Some of the rescuers were not particularly pro-Jewish but their aid was offered as being part of the Resistance or out of loyalty or neighbourliness. The Thiryn family and the Costagutis fell into this group. It has been said that you don't have to like someone to save them.

Many of the rescued kept close contact with their rescuers after the war. Betty Eppel went to see the Guicherds every year until they died and Suze Brown kept in close touch with the Schoens and visited them every year from America. Even after her death, her widower Arnold and daughters have kept in touch with the Schoens, although the people involved with the rescue are all now dead. Arnold told me how much Suze thought of the family and how she had been so traumatised that she had never spoken to her daughters about her experiences.[7] Margaret Kagan kept in touch with Vytautas as much as the Cold War allowed, and her cousin cradled her rescuer as she died years later. Hermann Maas kept in touch with the Rosenzweig children and continued his work through the ICCJ. The ties between these people were strong, not just because of the debt of saving their lives, but often because living together created powerful bonds – as with Betty Eppel, who experienced very strong love and affection from the Guicherds. Else Pintus, who never married and had no children, left her property to the Stenzels who hid her for two and a half years and saved her life. Irena Veisaite is still in touch with her rescuer's family and regards them as close family.

Some hidden children were traumatised by the need to return to parents they did not remember, as with Miriam Dunner, who remained closer to her foster mother Elizabeth than her own mother; and even after Elizabeth died, she continued to speak to her foster father Jelle every Sunday, until he too died eight months later. The Eppels did not want to go back with the father they hardly knew. When Josie Martin's parents turned up for her in August 1944: 'I took one look and I knew I didn't want to go with them. I even pretended I didn't know who they were.'[8] No one had counselling in those days and people were just expected to get on with their lives and be glad they were one of the 'lucky' ones. It appears that Josie's parents did not stay in touch with Soeur St Cybard, which Josie regrets to this day. Frank Auerbach too regrets not contacting Iris Origo, but he was only 8 at the time and it was never suggested to him. Manli Ho has not found many of the thousands her father saved.

If we look at the diplomats who saved thousands of people with a signature on pieces of paper, without exception all of them suffered in their subsequent careers – some with considerable financial loss. Dr Ho, Carl Lutz and de Sousa Mendes were all criticised for over-reaching their authority. Both Ho and de Sousa Mendes lost their pensions after decades of loyal service.

It is significant that many relatives I have been in touch with were unaware of much I had discovered. Louis Lacalle, grand-nephew of Soeur St Cybard, had no idea of her activities until I wrote to him. Paul Mower, son of Martha Mower, who was saved with her brother Paul, had little idea of how they had made contact with Hermann Maas. Benedetta Origo only found out about her mother's rescue of Jewish children after she died. It seems understandable that rescuers would perhaps not brag about their actions, but perhaps the rescued might have told their families more.

Nechama Tec, who attempted to establish the social determinants of rescuers, eventually concluded: 'These rescuers acted in ways that were natural to them' and she also noted that they came from all strata of society. Zygmunt Bauman juxtaposes Tec's conclusions with research on the high number of divorces amongst hijack victims, as documented in *Le Monde*. Previously perfectly happily married couples apparently found that the experience of being hijacked together revealed aspects of their spouse's personality that were unfavourable, and 'they saw their partners in a new light'. *Le Monde* concluded that in fact these two sides of the spouse's personality were Janus-like, but it was merely the experience of being hijacked that had revealed the other, 'which was always present but invisible'. Bauman makes a connection between this research and Tec's concluding observation:

> 'were it not for the Holocaust, most of these helpers might have continued on their independent paths, some pursuing charitable actions, some leading simple, unobtrusive lives. They were dormant heroes, often indistinguishable from those around them.' One of the most powerfully (and convincingly) argued conclusions of the study was the impossibility of 'spotting in advance' the signs, or symptoms, or indicators, of individual readiness for sacrifice, or of cowardice in the face of adversity; that is, to decide, outside the context that calls them into being or just 'wakes them up', the probability of their later manifestation.[9]

Varian Fry was precisely this type of person – a most unlikely rescuer. However, this inability to predict future behaviour also applies to the perpetrators. It is significant that in reviewing a new biography of Eichmann it was noted:

> Nothing in Eichmann's Protestant background in provincial Austria suggests why he became a mass murderer; his family was unexceptional, and

he experienced no difficulties in his chosen line of work as a salesman of
fuel oils, a job that familiarised him with distribution and transportation.[10]

Judge Moshe Bejski, who had been saved by Oskar Schindler, wrote
in 1974:

Unfortunately, no study has yet been carried out on the motives of those
who, despite the risk involved, did not bow to the edicts of the occupying authorities or conform to the behaviour of the general population
and extended help to Jews. In each case the motives are different, but
there is a common denominator among the 'Righteous' – the humanitarian motivation which dictates a charitable attitude toward one's fellow
man. Hostility toward the occupying authorities and opposition to the
cruel acts they perpetrated against the Jewish population were certainly
important, but even in these cases, the humanitarian motivation was
dominant. Very often religious conviction motivated individuals to help
Jews. This is paradoxical, as it is known, and it has been confirmed at this
conference, that the Church qua Church did almost nothing to induce
its adherents to extend help to the persecuted Jews. Nevertheless, quite a
few cases have come to our attention in which it was the individual's profound religious feeling that motivated him to fulfil the command: 'Thou
shalt love thy neighbor as thyself.' Of course personal acquaintance and
friendship between the rescuer and the rescued also constituted a motive
for extending help in time of trouble. We have already mentioned those
of the 'Righteous Among the Nations' for whom acts of rescue constituted an integral part of their underground activities.[11]

In the preceding chapters the stories of rescuers have been examined, some of whom fall into the categories discussed by Dr Bejski.
Whilst the rescuers were gathered in a somewhat random fashion
(see Introduction), in that they or the person they rescued presented
themselves to me, they come from various countries and from different strata in society. They also stated different motives for their actions.
Table 3 gives their background and demonstrates that rescuers were
not confined to any particular background, degree of education, political, religious or economic grouping.

We can therefore see that rescuers were motivated both by conditioning from the various influences on them and by an inherent sense of justice. This sense of justice and fair play appears in comments about many of the rescuers such as Jacob Klerk, who looked after Henri Obstfeld, and John Schoen's family, who saved Suze.

Perhaps the most significant aspect is the surprise most of them express when asked why they did what they did. Many, including the Guicherds and Vytautas Rinkevicius, said it was normal – anyone would have done it – yet the maths proves them wrong – most people didn't. If they had, there would have been no Holocaust and I would not have written this book.

DO SMALL GESTURES OF RESISTANCE AMOUNT TO RESCUE?

Studies of the Holocaust traditionally discuss four categories: perpetrators, bystanders, rescuers and victims. However, Hubert Locke, who describes himself as a black American Christian, has queried these categories as a vast oversimplification. To support his view he refers to the economic boycott, expected to last a week, announced on 1 April 1933. In fact, it fizzled out after one day because ordinary Germans refused to participate:

> There are countless stories of little old ladies who said, 'I've always shopped at that grocery store. I know it's owned by the Steins but I'm not going to pay any attention to the Brown Shirt thugs who are standing out front saying, "Don't buy Jewish goods".' People like this don't fit into any of the conventional categories: they were weren't perpetrators, they weren't victims and they certainly weren't bystanders. How are we to understand their motivation?[12]

Did these little old ladies end up hiding Jews? We don't know about them. We do know about Henry Walton's parents; we know about the Lovenheim book; we know about the people who were kind to Victor Klemperer and we *do* know that Mitzi did.

Victor Klemperer (1881–1960) was an academic who kept diaries of the Nazi years, which were published in 1999. Even though he had converted to Protestantism in 1912 and was married to an 'Aryan', he suffered the same gradual and serious deprivation as the other Jews. One of the Nazis' first acts of discrimination was to remove Jews from the civil service, which covered education and universities. However, Klemperer was a decorated war veteran and was therefore allowed to keep his post until April 1935. By then, displaced Jewish academics had flooded the international arena and he found it impossible to find work anywhere. His diaries record the continual 'mosquito bites'. '1,000 mosquito bites are worse than a blow to the head.'

He notes the loss of rights as follows: banned from library reading rooms (October 1936); forced to give up the telephone (December 1936); required to add 'Israel' or 'Sara' to given names (i.e. Klemperer must henceforth sign his name 'Victor Israel' – August 1938); restricted to shopping between 3 and 4 p.m. (August 1940); banned from owning a car (February 1941); 'the milkmaid ... is no longer allowed to deliver to Jews' houses' (March 1941); 'new calamity: ban on smoking for Jews' (August 1941); required to surrender typewriters ('That hit me hard, it is virtually irreplaceable' – October 1941); banned from use of public telephones (December 1941); banned from the buying of flowers (March 1942); banned from keeping pets ('This is the death sentence for Muschel', their tomcat – May 1942); forbidden to provide for the teaching of Jewish children either privately or communally (July 1942); banned from purchase or possession of newspapers (July 1942); prohibited from purchase of eggs or vegetables (July 1942); prohibited from purchase of meat and white bread (October 1942). 'Not a day without a new decree against Jews,' Klemperer writes.

Yet at the same time he also notes the small acts of heroism he comes across from ordinary Germans. People greeting Jews on the street, visiting them at home, giving them ration coupons for the purchase of bread, helping to carry potatoes, slipping them something extra in a food shop, whispering a friendly word;[13] small acts offering that small encouragement and hope.

Rabbi Hugo Gryn wrote of his father's words about hope when they were incarcerated in Auschwitz. The prisoners in their block saved their precious margarine ration to enable them to celebrate Chanukah by lighting a home-made menorah. Hugo created wicks with the threads from an abandoned cap. On the first night of the eight-day festival everyone in their block gathered around, including Protestants and Catholics, and Hugo as the youngest there tried to light the wicks but they only spluttered and refused to light. No one had remembered that margarine does not burn. Hugo was distraught as much by the waste of the precious calories and turned on his father:

> Patiently, he taught me one of the most lasting lessons of my life and I believe that he made my survival possible.
>
> 'Don't be angry,' he said to me. 'You know that this festival celebrates the victory of the spirit over tyranny and might. You and I have had to go once for over a week without proper food and another time almost three days without water, but you cannot live for three minutes without hope!'[14]

The current criteria for being recognised as a Righteous Among the Nations are very strict, involving having risked your life, but as we have seen many rescuers did a great deal without doing anything so risky. There is a whole gamut of help that ranges from leaving food on a doorstep at night to hiding someone for two and a half years like the Stenzels did with Else Pintus.

I came across the following text in 1997, written by Monia Avrahami, in the Beit Lohamei Haghetaot Museum, which is part of the Ghetto Fighters' Kibbutz. I have always found it very moving in describing the grades and levels of resistance and rescue:

> To smuggle a loaf of bread – was to resist
>
> To teach in secret – was to resist
>
> To cry out warning and shatter illusions – was to resist
>
> To forge documents – was to resist
>
> To smuggle people across borders – was to resist
>
> To chronicle events and conceal the records – was to resist
>
> To hold out a helping hand to the needy – was to resist
>
> To contact those under siege and smuggle weapons – was to resist

To fight with weapons in streets, mountains and forests – was to resist

To rebel in death camps – was to resist

To rise up in ghettos, among the crumbling walls, in the most desperate
revolt – was to resist. [15]

The main impact of the small gesture was that it gave people hope and
comfort, that they were not entirely alone in their dire plight. Rabbi Leo
Baeck wrote a remarkable story about a package he received when he
was in Theresienstadt: 'Its contents had been removed and it was really
only an empty cardboard box. But it gave me joy in the knowledge that
someone had thought of me in exile. I recognized the sender, a Christian
friend, by the handwriting, although he had used a fictitious name.'[16]

Ewa Berberyusz, a leading Polish journalist, born in 1929 in Warsaw,
did not act and regretted it. She has written with disarming honesty of
her failure to help Jews in the war, even though she was very young.
She describes how twice she failed to help a Jewish child from the
Ghetto when she had the opportunity. She adds that when she saw
someone giving food to such a child, she felt relief that someone was
doing the right thing, and when she saw her own mother doing it: 'my
morale soared again. It is interesting that we never talked about it at
all. Was it just fear? Or was it just shame that nothing more was being
done?' In her 1987 essay, 'Guilt by Neglect', she reflects:

If then, when chance brought me those two children, I had behaved
according to my conscience, would that have altered the fate of the Jews
in Poland? The answer 'yes' is not so unequivocally right, because my
desisting in these cases has to be multiplied by cases of similar behaviour by others. Possibly, even if more of us had turned out to be more
Christian, it would have made no difference to the statistics of the extermination, but maybe it would not have been such a lonely death?[17]

BYSTANDERS

Leo Baeck's comments on the economic boycott are significant and
damning – they were also reflective, as they were written twenty years

after the event. 'In truth, justice was boycotted. The Jewish business community overcame that day a long time ago; the concept of justice has not overcome that day'. He continued:

> Each retreat begins with a great cowardice. We have experienced it. The first of April 1933 speaks of that. The universities were silent, the courts were silent; the President of the Reich, who had taken the oath on the Constitution, was silent … This was the day of the greatest cowardice. All that followed would not have happened.

The passivity and indifference of the authorities that day gave Hitler permission to undertake his next step against the Jews. Baeck felt the individuals did not fail and 'The little people in Germany remained good'.[18]

Dr Frances Henry, a German-born anthropologist, returned to her birthplace in 1980. She conducted research in the small town which had 4,000 inhabitants in 1933, including 150 Jews. She protected her grandparents' hometown by using the pseudonym Sonderburg, and many people spoke to her frankly because she was 'Ostermann's granddaughter'. She added: 'If anything, their eagerness to talk to me was almost pathetic – as though they had never been able to discuss "those terrible times" with anyone before.'[19]

Henry discovered that before 1933, relations between the Jews and Germans were better than those between Catholics and Protestants.[20] Yet when the Nazis came to power in January 1933, suddenly everything altered and Jews, in particular, realised that life had changed. Joshua Abraham had for many years met up with his male neighbours twice a week to play cards. 'As soon as the Nazis came to power, I was no longer told when they were playing cards. Everything stopped. I would see them on the street and we pretended we didn't see each other. Not one of them spoke to me.'[21]

In time, some non-Jews benefited from the persecution of their Jewish neighbours – Jewish homes and businesses were for sale at considerably less than their true worth. However, as life became more difficult for the twelve Jews who remained in Sonderburg after 1939, their neighbours started bringing them food, letters and other necessities until they were all deported in 1942.[22] Dr Henry noted a variety of explanations for their behaviour:

- People did not realise what was happening to the Jews
- Some were genuine anti-Semites
- Many felt themselves to be poor and powerless
- They said they did not know what to do
- They felt they had to obey the Nazis, due to fear of what might happen to them, their husbands and children
- People who helped had close ties with the Jews
- Those with close ties to Jews did not necessarily help them

Dr Henry found the post-war reality was that the non-Jews were very warm to returning Jews:

> Henry had the impression that the townspeople wanted only to forget the Nazi period; they couldn't understand why this was impossible for Jews who had lived through Nazism. When the townspeople did discuss the Nazi era, 'the word *machtlos* [powerless] occurred over and over in our conversation'. They had been powerless, the non-Jews told Henry, paralyzed by fear and the threat of retribution (although, as Henry noted, there was very little actual retribution against people who did refuse to comply with Nazi policies). Most non-Jews expressed bewilderment, even today, at what had happened to their former neighbours: they 'were never sure why' the Jews had been persecuted and claimed that they still didn't understand it.

Willy Brandt wrote the foreword to Henry's book. He commented that in the normal course of events these Jews and non-Jews would have got along well enough:

> Under Nazism, the non-Jews of Sonderburg became bystanders to the Holocaust. These people, who had gotten along fine with their Jewish neighbours before 1933, had simply proceeded with their own lives after that date – not completely oblivious to what was happening to their Jewish neighbors, but oddly uninvolved, as though it had nothing

to do with them. Many continued to feel this way even after 1945, and this was the barrier that separated the citizens of Sonderburg long after the Shoah.[23]

Dr Henry wrote that her research 'shed light on some of the puzzling aspects of German behavior in the face of Nazism'. She concludes with what she calls a partial answer: 'Perhaps in the long run we must be content with the basic explanation that some people are more humanitarian than others.'[24] This opinion reinforces the views of Yehuda Bauer, who after examining the question of rescuers wrote: 'In the end, beyond political and religious convictions, it was basic morality that counted. There were places where it was easier to be a moral person, moral in the sense that when you were challenged with, "thy brother's blood is calling", you answered, "I am here".'[25]

The significant point is that Yehuda Bauer referred to 'thy brother', suggesting that no difference was made between the various peoples. He is suggesting that rescuers regard everyone as their brother. Men such as János Tóth certainly did not differentiate and, by his own admission, his action in saving Arnold Weinstock was so spontaneous that he had not considered the possible repercussions on himself and his family before defending Weinstock against a group of angry Hungarian Nazi soldiers.

WHY WERE BYSTANDERS IN THE MAJORITY?

When considering the proportion of bystanders to rescuers, it is important to realise that conditions for rescue varied in different countries. As Yehuda Bauer stated:

> It must be said right at the outset that it was much easier to be a friend of the Jews in Denmark or France, in Belgium or in Italy, than it was in Poland or in Lithuania, in the Ukraine or in Belorussia. Cases are known of Poles and their entire families executed for hiding Jews, their houses burnt, and their properties confiscated.[26]

Yet even Bauer, with his considerable academic experience and knowledge, showed reservation about generalisations on the subject of rescuers:

> Generalizations regarding the attitude of Gentiles to Jews during the Holocaust must be approached with the greatest diffidence. Of the generalizations that will hold water, one might mention these: in Poland, Lithuania, Latvia, and the Ukraine, in Croatia and Romania, the attitude of the overwhelming majority of the local population, including that of the majority churches, and excepting the left-wing political parties, ranged from hostile indifference to active hostility. Countries that saved most of their Jews were Bulgaria, Denmark, Belgium, and France. There is little in common between the democratic character of Protestant Denmark and the unfortunate traditions of Orthodox Bulgaria, yet the fate of the Jewish communities was similar, though the reasons for the rescue were not. There were vast differences between Walloon Belgium and a split French society, yet the percentage of Jews saved was similar. Minority churches tended to protect Jewish minorities.[27]

The courage taken to defy both the Nazis and the peer pressure of the community should never be underestimated. As many historians have written, the Nazis had good supporters and collaborators, and in some cases the Nazis were shocked at the latter's enthusiasm for the task:

> When the Germans invaded Lithuania, as in other occupied countries, deep-seated resentments against the Jews and murderous anti-Semitic hatreds were let loose. In Lithuania's second city of Kaunas, locals, encouraged by watching Germans, killed several dozen Jews they claimed were communists. The Jews were beaten to death with crowbars in a courtyard of an apartment block. Once the massacre was over, a local man picked up an accordion, stood on the bodies and began to play the Lithuanian national anthem. For him, the Jews' death was an occasion not just for satisfaction, but celebration.[28]

Poles had reason to be afraid to help the Jews. A poster from 14 December 1943, in the form of a 'Public Announcement' from the SS and the police in the district of Galicia, shows that of fifty-five people sentenced to death for assorted crimes, 'there were eight Christians who were sentenced to death for hiding Jews'.[29] However, using the principle of 'collective responsibility', the Nazis often punished the whole family, including children, or even the whole community. The lesson was often underlined by public executions, as in the case of the Baranek family. Wincenty Baranek, a prosperous but generous farmer, had hidden four Jews. On 15 March 1943 the Germans arrived at his farm at dawn. He hid his two sons aged 9 and 10, but they were discovered, and they were all shot in front of their neighbours, together with the four Jews they had attempted to hide. The two young boys had tried to escape, but had been restrained by a neighbour told to guard them.[30]

Some families were punished when groups of houses were destroyed by fire with the occupants inside. In the village of Stary Cieplow, four farms were surrounded by Germans, again at dawn. They plundered the cottages, taking the best items, then set fire to the houses with the occupants – thirty-three Poles and an unknown number of Jews – inside. According to an eyewitness, a young girl who ran out of one of the houses was shot and her body tossed onto the fire, after her new shiny, black boots had been pulled off. In Huta Pienacka, in the winter of 1944, the Germans learnt that the villagers occasionally gave food and shelter to about 100 Jews hiding in the forests. The Nazis surrounded the village and, with the help of the Ukrainian police, set fire to it and stopped anyone from leaving – even the animals were destroyed.[31]

It should be recalled that the Nazis fanned the existing anti-Semitism with their propaganda, using posters showing Jews as 'repulsive and dangerous criminals or as vampires sucking Polish blood … Public lectures were held asserting that Jews were immune to typhus but functioned as carriers of the disease and could pass it on to Aryans.'[32] Irene Opdyke was a Catholic Pole who hid twelve Jews in the house where she acted as housekeeper, even though her employer was an SS officer. She described her horror at returning to her hometown of Radom: 'And pasted on the walls were posters – cruel, mocking posters – caricaturing the Jews, who were liked to every depravity and sin. Every woe and affliction of the Polish people were laid at their feet. Loudspeakers on street corners blared warnings about the Jews in Polish and German.'[33]

It is fair to stress that the rescuers who responded to the plight of the Jews were in many cases going against the mores of their society and risked the condemnation of the authorities and their own social circle and family. That required true moral courage. Elia Rinkevicius' concerns for her child, when Vytautas told her about hiding the Kagans, seem perfectly understandable when we appreciate the risks they were running.

Michal Glowinski, born in 1934, is an established Polish writer little known in the West. In 1998 a book of essays, *Czarne Sezony* (*The Black Seasons*), about his Warsaw childhood during the Holocaust, appeared. 'Each of them is a record of real life experience, it comes from flashes of memory which do not include all events, do not encompass all my life in those times and history of my survival'.[34] A Polish literary critic, Jacek Leociak, describes the writing as 'an archipelago of memory'.[35] In one memorable essay he describes how even when there was no question of needing to hide a Jew, the presence of one, even a small boy, made a group of ordinary Polish women panic.

On this occasion, Michal's aunt Maria, his mother's younger sister, was entrusted with finding him somewhere to hide:

> she moved about on the Aryan Side most freely. She possessed what was then called 'good looks', which were not merely a privilege, but moreover a divine bestowal. Good looks meant that the person in hiding aroused less suspicion. People with good looks did not draw attention, they could blend into the crowd; it was easier for them to play the role of someone they were not. Maria's looks were exquisite; she was an attractive blonde who looked as though she had been born into a noble estate, rather than into a Jewish merchant's family. Anyone with less than intimate knowledge would never have discerned what origins lay behind her impeccable Slavic beauty. And so when I'd found myself homeless and no one knew what to do with me, it fell to Maria to deal with my very problematic situation.[36]

He described his experience in a pastry shop where Maria left him briefly to make a phone call. Within minutes he was being scrutinised by a group of ordinary Polish women who realised he was Jewish and began interrogating him: 'As usual in such situations, I would have most preferred to melt into the ground. I heard: "A Jew, there's no question, a Jew." – "She certainly isn't but him – he's a Jew." – "She's foisted him off onto us."'[37] It is ironical that Maria's blonde looks convinced them she was not Jewish:

> The women asked me various questions, to which by then I'd ceased to respond, rather muttering sometimes only 'yes' or 'no' ... Yet I heard not only the questions directed at me but also the comments the women expressed more quietly, to the side, as if only to themselves, but in such a way that I couldn't fail to hear. Most often they spit out the threatening word 'Jew', but also, most terrifying, they repeated: 'we have to call the police'. I was aware that this was equivalent to a death sentence ... Those women were not possessed by an uncontrollable hatred ... These were normal, ordinary, in their own way resourceful and decent women, hard-working, undoubtedly scrambling to take care of their families in the difficult conditions under the occupation. Neither would I exclude the possibility that they were exemplary mothers and wives, perhaps religious, possessing a whole array of virtues. They had found themselves in a situation that to them felt troublesome and threatening, and so they wanted to face it directly. They did not think, though, at what price. Perhaps that transcended their imaginations – although they must have known how it would end if they were to 'call them' – or perhaps it was simply not within the boundaries of the moral reflection accessible to them.[38]

Why were these women so worried about a little Jewish boy quietly eating his pastry in the darkest corner of the café? Why could they not ignore him and get on with their gossip? Why did they feel the need to call the police? Surely they knew this could mean death for him? They did not feel they could remain passive in this situation – why was this little Jewish boy such a threat to them?

INDIFFERENCE

Most bystanders were indifferent to the fate of the Jews – often denying they knew what was happening even when living close to a camp. This is always surprising from our perspective – exemplified by J.D. Salinger's (see pp. 201–2) comment to his little daughter: 'You never really get the smell of burning flesh out of your nose entirely, no matter how long you live.'[39]

Conversely, the victims were aware of life outside their restrictions, like Eva Heyman, who, while living in the Ghetto in Nagyvárad, Hungary, could hear her old icecream van go by on the other side of the fence.

Adina Szwajger recalled the burning of the Warsaw Ghetto at Easter 1943. She wrote: 'In Warsaw, on Krasinski square, outside the walls of a burning Ghetto in that awful Easter of 1943, the merry-go-round went round and jolly music played. And people enjoyed themselves.' She refers to the poem *Campo dei Fiori* written by Czelow Milosz and distributed by the Underground press in 1943. It refers to the burning alive in 1600 of the philosopher Giordano Bruno, in the Campo dei Fiori in Rome, whilst the locals were enjoying themselves in the square's tavernas:[40]

> Someone will read as moral
> That the people of Rome or Warsaw
> Haggle, laugh, make love
> As they pass by martyrs' pyres.
> Someone else will read
> Of the passing of things human,
> Of the oblivion
> Born before the flames have died.[41]

In a dream Adina sees the merry-go-round and behind the Ghetto wall 'my house is burning. Because that is where it stood. Right by the square.'[42]

The bystanders' indifference was because they did not care about the Jews or what happened to them. One Polish woman described her feelings for the Jews: 'That guilt of mine, which bordered on cruelty, was my indifference to the Jewish fate. I was completely indifferent to the human beings who were perishing in the Ghetto. They were "them" and not "us".'[43] This is the contrast between the bystanders and the rescuers; the rescuers did not differentiate between themselves and the Jews. That is why they were surprised to be asked about their motives.

In March 2001 Professor Richard D. Heffner published a series of interviews with the Nobel Peace Prize winner Elie Wiesel, himself a Holocaust survivor. The first interview, 'Am I my Brother's Keeper?', addressed the question of indifference. Heffner asked: 'You've spoken about those who put people in the death camps and brought about their deaths directly. You also speak about others who stood around indifferently. Do you feel that this is increasingly a theme in our times?' Elie Wiesel replied:

> Oh, more and more. I have the feeling that everything I do is a variation on the same theme. I'm simply trying to pull the alarm and say, 'Don't be indifferent'. Simply because I feel that indifference now is equal to evil. Evil, we know more or less what it is. But indifference to disease, indifference to famine, indifference to dictators, somehow it's here and we accept it. And I have always felt that the opposite of culture is not ignorance; it is indifference. And the opposite of faith is not atheism; again, it's indifference. And the opposite of morality is not immorality; it's again indifference. And we don't realize how indifferent we are simply because we cannot not be a little bit indifferent.[44]

The perpetrators and bystanders were indifferent – the rescuers were not.

DECIDING TO RESCUE

Gerda Haas, as a young woman with her parents in Germany, rescued a Jewess. She stressed to me there were only two types of rescuer: a) those who were approached by (or on behalf of) the fugitive; b) those who offered shelter to a persecuted person out of their own free will.

Gerda says she knew no one who refused to help when asked, but knew many who had suffered as a result, either by death or time in a concentration camp. She reveals that others were also hidden, such as a Catholic priest and a deserter from the German army. She claims: 'Practically in every third house in that village where I lived, was a fugitive hiding from the German authorities.'[45]

Henry Walton's parents, Siegmund Weltlinger and Grete (née Gumpel), remained in Berlin all through the war, where they were hidden by six different couples, whose names Henry doesn't know. But he knew they were all non-Jews who risked their lives and were prepared to share their meagre food rations. Whenever they thought there was a chance of discovery they were moved on to the next couple – 'always to loyal friends who would take them in at a moments notice'. Henry recalls the last one was a Mrs Hahn, who owned a grocer's shop and was therefore able to help the network with food. After the war his parents, who lived into their eighties, kept in touch with Mrs Hahn and helped her rebuild her business. 'They were friends we had known over many years. They hated what the Nazis were doing, and were intent on saving lives ... that was their only motivation.' Henry's parents were in hiding from 1942 until the end of the war. Henry says many people were murdered by the invading Russian troops, but because his father could speak a little Russian, he was able to save not only his wife but the people who had hidden them by saying they were all Jewish.[46] His parents were reluctant to talk about their traumatic time. He wrote to me: 'I just wanted you to know, there were loyal, and decent Germans, who were prepared to risk their lives, to save the lives of the "enemy" of the state.'[47] Henry Walton himself was able to escape to England from Germany as a young man, in June 1939, with the help of the Quakers.

Barbara Lovenheim's book *Survival in the Shadows* documents how seven Jews, from three families, went into hiding in Berlin in January 1943 and were discovered by the Red Army soldiers in April 1945. About fifty non-Jewish Germans ensured their survival without ID or ration cards. Barbara explains that she wrote the book 'as a reminder that not even the most despicable tyrant can fully eradicate goodness'.[48] Henry Walton's parents could have told a similar story.

Roman Halter has described how in March 1945, when he was 17, he and two other older Jewish men escaped from a death march and were taken in by a childless couple in Oberpoyritz near Dresden. He stayed with Kurt and Hertha Fuchs until May 1945 when, after seeing Russian troops, he dreamt about his grandfather who told him to go home. He immediately decided to return to his home in Poland to search out the rest of his family. In his hometown he discovered that he was one of only four Jews to survive from the pre-war Jewish community of 800. As he felt frightened and threatened in Poland, he went to Prague; there he found some Red Cross supplies which he decided to take to the Fuchs to thank them.

On his return he was appalled to find Hertha dressed in black. She said that five days after he had left, former local SS men had heard that the Fuchs had sheltered Jews. They had shot Mr Fuchs and one of the other Jews also being sheltered. The second Jew had survived to go to Israel. In 2002 Roman returned to see Mrs Fuchs with a television crew – she was 94. He asked her then why she had taken the three Jewish fugitives in when it had cost her so dear with the loss of her husband:

> She answered that both she and her husband felt they had to do it. 'You see although we are Germans, we were not Nazis; our minds were not poisoned by the twelve years of propaganda, and all the Nazi screeching against the Jews. It was our impulse to do this, to take you in and save you. You would do the same, I think, Roman.'

Roman has written:

> I replied that after the wonderful example she and Kurt had shown, I would like to think that I would do the same. But I know that it is easier to say yes than to do it. I often ask myself if I would have the courage, the sense of what is right and is wrong; the humanity to take in strangers and save them, when such an act was punishable by death for all. I would like to believe that I would.[49]

The veteran war reporter Max Hastings has written: 'Some of us feel too uncertain of how we ourselves would have behaved under occupation to pass merciless judgment on France's aesthetes for their dalliances with tyranny.'[50]

When we read about rescuers, we always assume we would not hesitate to do the same — but would we? Would we also risk the lives of our children or, like Vytautas' wife, protest about the danger they were being put in. Personally, in my own life, I have found myself involved in a discussion of this subject twice, not instigated by me on either occasion. Both times were when I lived in a Worcestershire village, and was conspicuous as the mother of the only Jewish family. On one occasion Vicky, a very devout Christian woman, volunteered that she and her husband would have, or even *would*, hide me and my sons. Sadly, she died aged 45 of breast cancer. On the other occasion, a woman, whose children were of similar ages and good chums of my three young sons, casually remarked that she would not risk her kids to protect me and mine. It is perhaps a perfectly reasonable comment that any mother might make, but I know I felt stunned and numbed. Rightly or wrongly, I never felt the same about her again.

Philip Gourevitch, the child of Holocaust survivors, and a staff writer on the *New Yorker*, has commentated on the Holocaust and the 1994 Rwandan massacres. He admits he was very critical of the creation of the Washington Holocaust Museum.[51] He declares that nobody knows how they would respond in a similar crisis:

> You cannot know. People like to go to the Holocaust Museum and say, that's who I relate to, the guy who did right. Either they relate somehow to the victim and feel bad about themselves and sorry for themselves, or they relate to the good guy. Very few go in there and say, oh yeah I probably would have been just like an ordinary conformist Nazi murderer, right? But probably the great majority of people who go through that museum would have been, because that's what the great majority of people in Europe were. They were either bystanders, collaborators, or in some other way morally reprehensible positions which are all too understandable.[52]

J.D. Salinger, author of *Catcher in the Rye*, was a liberator of Dachau concentration camp, which had a profound impact on him. Margaret

Salinger quotes him as saying: 'anyone could turn out to be a Nazi – your neighbor, your babysitter, the man at the post office – anyone. And anyone could be a hero; you never knew until it happened who would be a hero and who would be a coward or traitor.'[53]

An American professor posted some 'mischievous questions about the Holocaust', of which the third was about the paucity of rescuers given the risks:

> And now, turning inward, if we ask ourselves who among our relatives or friends – not strangers, which the Jews often were in the misfortunes of war, but people close to us – if we ask who in this circle of ours we could rely on for such help if the penalty were probable death for the person and possibly also for his family: how large would this number be? To what extent could we honestly include ourselves in this?[54]

It is important, however, to remember the context in which these events occurred. It is misleading for us to nonchalantly glance backwards from the safety of 2010. Ian Kershaw reminds us that we are studying extraordinary times:

> For an outsider, a non-German who never experienced Nazism, it is perhaps too easy to criticize, to expect standards of behaviour which it was well impossible to attain in the circumstances. I have consciously strived to avoid making over-simplistic, moralizing judgements. And where I have been critical, I have still tried above all to understand sympathetically the position of ordinary people living under such a regime, to recognize the art of the possible.[55]

He describes his book as being about the 'muddled majority, neither full-hearted Nazis nor outright opponents':

> But I would claim it accords much more than most depictions of Nazi society with the unclear attitudes and inconsistent behaviour of ordinary Germans during the Nazi tyranny. I should like to think that had I been around at the time I would have been a convinced anti-Nazi engaged in the underground resistance fight. However, I know really that I would

have been as confused and felt as helpless as most of the people I am writing about.[56]

Christopher Browning, an eminent Holocaust historian, has written about the behaviour of Reserve Police Battalion 101 from Hamburg, whose task was to shoot Jews in Poland in 1942 – he was able to see the papers regarding 210 men out of less than 500 sent to Poland in June 1942. He shows that the battalion over the period of July 1942 to November 1943 was responsible for shooting a minimum of 38,000 Jews and deporting a minimum of 45,200 to Treblinka in the period August 1942 to May 1943.[57] Readers should be aware that it has been calculated that 50 per cent of the victims of the Holocaust died in the six main extermination camps; 25 per cent in the ghettos, labour and other camps, and death marches; and the remaining 25 per cent were shot.[58] Browning wrote:

Never before had I encountered the issue of choice so dramatically framed by the course of events and so openly discussed by at least some of the perpetrators. Never before had I seen the monstrous deeds of the Holocaust so starkly juxtaposed with the human faces of the killers.[59]

I found much of what was done extremely upsetting and have chosen not to reproduce it. There are also descriptions of the infamous 'Jew Hunts' in rural areas where any discovered Jews were made to lie on the ground naked and were shot in the neck:

I must recognize that in the same situation, I could have been either a killer or an evader – both were human – if I want to understand and explain the behavior of both as best I can. This recognition does indeed mean an attempt to empathize. What I do not accept, however, are the old clichés that to explain is to excuse, to under-stand is to forgive. Explaining is not excusing; understanding is not forgiving.[60]

He concluded with difficulty as the story made him uneasy:

This story of ordinary men is not the story of all men. The reserve policemen faced choices, and most of them committed terrible deeds. But those who killed cannot be absolved by the notion that anyone in the same situation would have done as they did. For even among them, some refused to kill and others stopped killing. Human responsibility is ultimately an individual matter.[61]

As the letter from the regional German civil administrator Carl Slutsk demonstrates, not all Germans chose to be involved in such barbarity and opted out. Even on the Reserve Police Battalion's first task dealing with the 1,800 Jews of Józefów there was no compulsion. Their commander, Major Wilhelm Trapp, was struggling with his emotions when he told his men they had to take the men of working age to a work camp, but 'The remaining Jews – the women, children and elderly – were to be shot on the spot by the battalion. Having explained what awaited his men, Trapp then made an extraordinary offer: if any of the older men among them did not feel up to the task that lay before him he could step out.'[62]

However, in time, the use of alcohol and becoming accustomed to their task desensitised the men. Browning considers the influence of peer pressure on men who opted out and the others who volunteered readily.

Another study referred to the dehumanising of the Jews, desensitising the perpetrator. A rescuer called Otto described how he asked a guard in a camp whether he had used his gun to kill anyone. The guard said: 'Once I had to shoot six Jews. I did not like it but when you get such an order, you have to be hard.' He added: 'You know, they were not human anymore.' Otto speculated that the conditions of filth and starvation in the camps, where the Jews had no names or dignity, made them 'skin-colored skeletons'. The guard was right; 'It is much easier to kill non-humans than humans'.[63]

INSTITUTIONAL EFFORTS

We can now read about individuals who tried to change the course of history and persuade powerful bodies to speak out against the atrocities – of course we now know they were unsuccessful, but they tried. We can only speculate on what would have happened had their efforts met with success.

Such cowardice contrasts with the courage found in the actions of James Grover McDonald, an American diplomat who was the High Commissioner for Refugees at the League of Nations 1933–35, and who protested about the situation of the Jews in the mid-1930s. His papers were recently presented to the United States Holocaust Memorial Museum by his daughters, Barbara McDonald Stewart and Janet McDonald Barrett, in April 2004. His importance is twofold – partly because his long diplomatic career led him to meet most of the key players on the world stage over a long period, but also because he noted every meeting in his diaries, which he kept assiduously from 1922 to 1936 and then again from 1946 to 1951. He dictated his entries to his secretary and so the collection consists of over 10,000 typed pages and 5,000 pages of correspondence. *The Times* reported McDonald's note of the views of Cosmo Lang, the Archbishop of Canterbury (1928–42), whom he met just before the Second World War. Lang had suggested that the Jews themselves 'might be responsible for the excesses of the Nazis'. In a similar vein, Nancy Astor, the leader of the 'Cliveden Set' which had favoured appeasement of Hitler, asked him: 'Did I not after all believe that there must be something in the Jews themselves which had brought them persecution throughout all the ages?' She suggested it was really their fault. McDonald noted: 'To this I took violent exception.'[64] His views on Roosevelt were generous as he described him as being keen to do more, but with the Depression and high US unemployment it was difficult for him to open the doors to many immigrants.

He became aware of the reality of Nazi policy very early. On Tuesday 4 April 1933 his diary records a meeting with two Nazi officials, ostensibly to discuss their economic programme. After fifteen minutes' discussion they:

> drifted back to the subject of the Jews, which seems to be an obsession with so many of the Nazis ... The casual expressions used by both men in speaking of the Jews were such as to make one cringe, because one

would not speak so of even a most degenerate people. When I indicated my disbelief in their racial theories, they said what other Nazis had said, 'But surely you, a perfect type of Aryan, could not be unsympathetic with our views' ... I had the impression that they really do set unbelievable store by such physical characteristics as long heads and light hair.[65]

McDonald would not have been surprised at Pope Pius XII's subsequent controversial behaviour, because when he met him in 1933, when he was Cardinal Pacelli, the cardinal was more concerned with the plight of Bavarian Catholics than German Jews. What was not recorded in *The Times'* article was that McDonald resigned from his post as High Commissioner for Refugees (Jewish and Other) Coming from Germany at the League of Nations on 27 December 1935 because of the League's failure to respond adequately to the situation of the Jews in Germany.

He had written in his diary on 25 November:

I then explained to him [Viscount Robert Cecil, a League of Nations founder] what I had in mind in connection with my letter of resignation [as High Commissioner] to the Secretary General, that I intended in that to speak with complete frankness about affairs in Germany which are making for the destruction of the whole of the Jewish people and in addition a certain number of non-Aryans.[66]

His letter of resignation was published the day he delivered it and runs to six manuscript-sized pages, explaining his concerns over what was happening to 'non-Aryans' in Germany. In addition, there was a thirty-four-page annex which McDonald described as 'containing an analysis of the measures in Germany against "Non-Aryans", and of their effects in creating refugees'.[67] The annex is quite remarkable in detailing the Germans' gradual deprivation of rights of German citizens who were regarded as members of the 'non-Aryan race', and giving details of all the legislation. There are also two tables showing how one's Jewishness would be determined from baptised Jewish parents and from a mixed marriage. According to these tables, the fourth generation from baptised parents would be Aryan but the third generation was Aryan from a mixed marriage.[68]

James McDonald's resignation sparked an immediate response by several international organisations, in the form of a petition to the XVIIth Plenary Assembly of the League of Nations supporting McDonald's request that the League use its moral authority to demand a modification of the German government's policy towards non-Aryans.[69] But as we know from history, this had little effect.

In 1943 he wrote a paper, which was published by the Jewish Agency, in which he described the dire condition of Europe's Jews. He wrote:

> [It was] estimated that already two million of the seven million Jews in Germany and the Nazi-controlled territories had perished. No pretence of humanity or legality any longer hides the savage slaughter by mass killings, starvation, forced overwork and overcrowding, with the resultant toll of disease and epidemic, whereby the Nazis are making large portions of Europe 'Jewless'.[70]

McDonald eventually became America's first Ambassador to Israel in 1948. In the preface to his memoirs, he wrote that his acceptance of the earlier post and his interest in Jewish affairs arose from his experience as Chairman of the Foreign Policy Association in the early 1930s:

> I had spent much time in Europe, talked much, read more, listened still more. I had met Hitler; and I had become convinced that the battle against the Jew was the first skirmish in a war on Christianity, on all religion, indeed on all humanity. And I, a Middle Western American of Scotch and German ancestry, a teacher and student by profession and inclination, found myself increasingly engaged in an active career which gave me the privilege of fighting a good fight. The right of the Jew not only to life but to his own life is in its way a symbol of every man's right.[71]

There is some irony in McDonald's reference to the Nazis' attack on the Jews being a prelude to an attack on Christianity, all religion and ultimately humanity itself. Firstly, it has resonance with Pastor

Niemoller's famous poem in which 'they' come first for the Jews, then the Communists, the Trade Unionists, and when 'they' came for him there was no one left to speak for him. Secondly, amongst the mere ten international organisations who were signatories of the petition supporting McDonald's letter of resignation was the International Federation of Trade Unions, whose president at the time was Sir Walter Citrine.[72]

McDonald made his choices and presented his case, but no one took much notice. However, William Temple (1881–1944), Archbishop of Canterbury (1942–44), made an impassioned speech pleading for help for the persecuted Jews; much opposed to his predecessor Cosmo Lang's views. He brought a resolution to the House of Lords on 23 March 1943 saying:

> That in view of the massacres and starvation of Jews and others in enemy and enemy-occupied countries, this House desires to assure His Majesty's Government of its fullest support for immediate measures, on the largest and most generous scale compatible with the requirements of military operations and security, for providing help and temporary asylum to persons in danger of massacre who are able to leave enemy and enemy-occupied countries.[73]

He spoke eloquently for some considerable time and was well informed on conditions for Jews, quoting several different sources. He begged the House to avoid procrastination as an exploratory conference in Ottawa had already been months in the planning. He stressed:

> The Jews are being slaughtered at the rate of tens of thousands a day on many days, but there is a proposal for a preliminary exploration to be made with a view to referring the whole matter after that to the Inter-Governmental Committee on Refugees. My Lords, let us at least urge that when that Conference meets it should meet not only for exploration but for decision …
>
> We at this moment have upon us a tremendous responsibility. We stand at the bar of history, of humanity and of God.[74]

Even prior to his appointment he had joined with Chief Rabbi Hertz (1872–1946) to help establish the Council of Christians and Jews (CCJ).[75] Unfortunately, his passion and eloquence in the House of Lords seemed only to lead to the Bermuda Conference of 19–29 April 1943. This consisted of discussions between US and UK officials, with no Jewish representation, 'there amid the Eater lilies' the officials decided there was little they could do to help the Jews:

> Today, we may look back and wonder how different history might have been if other church leaders, in America and England, had followed Archbishop Temple's lead. Or if his predecessor, Cosmo Lang, had spoken out for the rescue of Jewish refugees in the 1930s, before the Nazi persecution turned to mass murder.[76]

We may here also recall the controversial role of Pope Pius XI (Pope 1922–39). His failure to speak out was apparent to Edith Stein, who although born into an orthodox Jewish family in 1891, converted to Catholicism in 1922 and entered a Carmelite convent in Cologne in 1934. It was well known that she had written to Pope Pius XI in 1933; however the letter, dated 12 April 1933, was only recently discovered in papers in the Vatican archives. They were part of the mass of secret pre-war files opened by the Vatican on 15 February 2003. A Jewish-Catholic team of academics had asked to see the letter some three years before, but permission was denied at that time.[77]

Edith had held a post at the German Institute of Scientific Pedagogy in Münster, but the anti-Jewish legislation led to her being dismissed.[78] At Easter 1933, her anxieties about the Jews' plight led Edith to wish to speak to Pope Pius XI personally at a private audience. When this did not prove possible, she wrote to him describing the impact of the Nazi boycott on Jewish businesses. She told him that it had destroyed many people's livelihoods and led to many suicides:

> While the greater part of the responsibility [for their deaths] falls on those who pushed them to such gestures, it also falls on those who kept silent.

> Not only the Jews, but thousands of faithful Catholics in Germany –
> and I think throughout the world – wait and hope that the Church will
> make its voice heard against such abuse of the name of Christ …
>
> All of us who are watching the current situation in Germany as faith-
> ful children of the Church fear the worst for the image of the Church
> itself if the silence is further prolonged. We are also convinced that this
> silence cannot, in the long term, obtain peace from the current German
> government.[79]

In her diary, Edith noted that she received a reply from the Vatican
sending the Pope's blessings to her and praying that God would protect
the Church enabling it to respond.[80] In a memoir dated 18 December
1938 she wrote:

> I know that my letter was delivered to the Holy Father unopened; some
> time thereafter I received his blessing for my self and for my relatives.
> Nothing else happened. Later on I often wondered whether this letter
> might have come to his mind once in a while. For in the years that
> followed, that which I had predicted for the future of the Catholics in
> Germany came true step by step.[81]

Edith was arrested by the Gestapo in Holland, as a result of Hitler's
order for the arrest of all non-Aryan Roman Catholics dated 26 July
1942. She was sent to Auschwitz where she went to the gas chamber on
9 August 1942, as a 'reprisal against a Dutch Catholic Church official's
condemnation of Nazi-anti-Semitism'.[82] She was beatified by Pope
John Paul II in 1986 and on 11 October 1998 she was canonised as a
martyr-saint. This caused controversy amongst Jews because the Nazis
killed her precisely because she was not Aryan.[83]

When it comes to choices by bodies in the UK, there were different
reactions in England in the pre-war period amongst the most educated
in the land. However, bodies do not have their own minds – they are
led by individuals and those individuals decide on policy.

As the Nazis' persecution increased, the British government had
to consider how to deal with all the visitors arriving at its ports who
admitted to being refugees. The arrival of many refugees led the

Cabinet to review its position. Medawar and Pyke examined Cabinet papers and noted that on 12 April 1933 the Cabinet had reviewed the question of the Jewish exiles. It decided to:

> 'Try and secure for this country prominent Jews who were being expelled from Germany and who had achieved distinction whether in pure science, applied science, such as medicine or technical industry, music or art.' This, the Cabinet considered, would 'not only obtain for this country the advantage of their knowledge and experience, but would also create a very favourable impression in the world, particularly if our hospitality were offered with some warmth'.[84]

This resonates with the work of Varian Fry, who was sent out with a list of 200 names of prominent artists and intellectuals but ended up saving thousands of people – mostly quite unknown and insignificant. Instead of winning praise he was castigated on his return to the US for breaching his instructions and there was a major row with the Emergency Rescue Committee (ERC). It seems that both the ERC in America and Britain's Cabinet were only interested in the prominent and the famous. When Varian was expelled from Marseilles, the chief of police told him it was because 'you have protected Jews and anti-Nazis'.[85] When he returned to America, he was expelled from the ERC for helping anti-fascists who were mostly Jewish. This was covered in the original version of his book *Surrender on Demand* in 1941, although a modified version was published in 1945. As late as December 1942 his most famous article, 'The Massacre of the Jews', pleaded that immigration should be increased and the procedure for issuing visas improved.[86]

Whilst the British Medical Association (BMA) was not very sympathetic to its fellow refugee physicians in the pre-war years, Lord Dawson of Penn, President of the Royal College of Physicians, told Home Secretary Sir John Gilmour in 1933 that 'the number that could be usefully absorbed or teach us anything could be counted on the fingers of one hand'. He was convinced that those doctors seeking admission were merely economic migrants.[87]

It is generally known that the medical profession became very agitated by the attempts to permit Austrian doctors to come to England following the Anschluss in 1938, when Germany took over Austria. Viscount Templewood, who was descended from Quakers on his father's side, wrote of his time as Home Secretary (1937–39) and his sympathy for the desperate Jews. However, his attempts to help caused suspicion – was he letting in German spies or 'endangering professional and Trade Union standards by admitting cheap labour'? In his memoirs he wrote:

> More than once I received an unpleasant shock to my humanitarian sentiments. When, for instance, I attempted to open the door to Austrian doctors and surgeons, I was met by the obstinate resistance of the medical profession. Unmoved by the world-wide reputation of the doctors of Vienna, its representatives, adhering to the strict doctrine of the more rigid trade unionists, assured me that British medicine had nothing to gain from new blood, and much to lose from foreign dilution. It was only after long discussions that I was able to circumvent the opposition and arrange for a strictly limited number of doctors and surgeons to enter the country and practise their profession. I would gladly have admitted the Austrian medical schools en bloc. The help that many of these doctors subsequently gave to our war effort, whether in the treatment of wounds, nervous troubles and paralysis or in the production of penicillin, was soon to prove how great was the country's gain.[88]

Nevertheless, he had to be more circumspect when he answered questions in the House of Commons. On 7 July 1938 he was asked about the numbers of refugee doctors, dentists and oculists permitted to practise after being registered with British medical and dental registers since 1933. The answer was 185 and 93 respectively.[89] A week later, the question was raised again and the Home Secretary was discretion itself; reading his answers in the debate one would never have known his true feelings. He referred to co-operation with the medical profession, the refugee committees and the Home Office to reconcile the needs of the refugees and the fears of the doctors 'of flooding the profession here with doctors who are not required in the country'. Perhaps he should have been more open with his views.

The lack of understanding of the refugees' true plight is exemplified by the final question to the Home Secretary that day. Mr William Thorn, MP for West Ham Plaistow, asked: 'Does not the right hon. Gentleman think that if an application were made to the German Government, they would allow these doctors to stop in their own country?'[90]

It appears that dentists were more fortunate than doctors, since those holding German diplomas were allowed to practise without undergoing extra training.[91]

A positive reaction to the plight of the persecuted European academics came from the Academic Assistance Council (AAC), which was created mainly at the instigation of Sir William Beveridge. He was then Director of the London School of Economics (LSE) and was encouraged by a Hungarian nuclear physicist, Dr Leo Szilard, who wanted to set up a 'University in Exile'. Beveridge himself was a witness to the early dismissals of Jewish academics when he visited Vienna in March 1933 with his colleague from the LSE, Professor Lionel Robbins:

> This distinguished pair of British academics read in a newspaper, whilst sitting in a café, about the suspension of 12 important Jewish scientists from German Universities. Beveridge realised that all this knowledge and experience had to be saved, and that the dignity of the German academics must be upheld for the benefit of the entire learned world.[92]

Szilard was staying in Vienna temporarily in a hotel, and being somewhat nosy he checked the hotel register and found Beveridge was residing there too. Szilard decided Beveridge, a true member of the British establishment, could be his ally over this issue and contacted him. Beveridge duly promised to do something on his return to London. Beveridge himself has described his concern on reading that leading professors were being dismissed by the Nazis 'on racial or political grounds'. He detailed the fear being created when he travelled back to England from Vienna with a German professor he knew slightly, not yet proscribed:

> He was in a state of panic all the way because in the next compartment was a youth, little more than a boy, whom he took for a Nazi agent,

detailed to keep watch on him and hand him to the police. My friend's fears may have been imaginary, but his panic was real, and mind-and spirit-destroying.[93]

The letter to *The Times*, with its forty-one signatories, was his first move.[94] He invited the distinguished 1908 Nobel Prize-winning chemist, Lord Rutherford (1871–1937), to become chairman of the council. Although in poor health, and against the advice of both his doctor and, perhaps more importantly, his wife, Rutherford agreed. He was the immediate past president of the Royal Society and head of the famous Cavendish Laboratory in Cambridge – originally funded by a former chancellor of Cambridge University: William Cavendish, 7th Duke of Devonshire (1808–91). William's descendant, Andrew Cavendish, the 11th Duke of Devonshire (1920–2004), was a good friend of the Jews as recorded in the *Jewish Chronicle*'s obituary, 28 May 2004. The Duke told me that it was his father who gave him such respect for Jews. The 10th Duke had been instrumental in supporting Zionism in the years before the 1917 Balfour Declaration, and Chaim Weizmann was a regular visitor in their London home. He wrote of the excitement in the house when a visit was due: 'My father had an enormous admiration for the contribution the Jewish community had made to our national life. He was at great pains to make me share his regard and enthusiasm for the Jewish community.'[95] He said his father was always sorry there was no Jewish blood in the Cavendishes as there was in the Cecils.[96] In reply to a question I asked him, he wrote his father had 'a considerable number of friends who shared his passionate views on justice for the Jewish people'.[97]

Beveridge chose a younger and more energetic Nobel Prize winner, Professor A.V. Hill, to be the AAC's vice-chairman. His partner in receiving the 1922 Nobel Prize was Otto Meyerhof, who, together with his wife Hedwig and son Walter, were helped to escape from Marseilles by Varian Fry in 1941. Walter Meyerhof (1922–2006) was born the year his father won the Nobel Prize for Medicine. When he retired in 1992, Walter set up the Varian Fry Foundation to honour his family's rescuer. It must be remembered that in the early days there was no understanding of the Nazis murdering the Jews. As A.V. Hill wrote to Beveridge in 1934: 'It is not that these academics will perish as human beings, but that as scholars and scientists they will be heard of no more, since they will have to take up something else in order to live.'

His concerns were merely that 'knowledge and learning were threatened by petty-minded and vindictive edicts of a racial nature, and that much important scientific work was in danger of being lost because dedicated people with fine minds were being denied the chance to work. That they were generously given that chance in this country should always be remembered as a glorious moment for decency and humanity. As we know only too well, those who had not left Germany before the outbreak of War in 1939 did in fact perish.'[98]

A.E. Housman (1859–1936) was one of the forty-one signatories of the letter in *The Times* in May 1933. I have tried to establish how active he was without much success. I found three letters from him – two sending apologies for not attending meetings (on 1 June 1933 and 21 February 1936) and one dated 7 May 1934 complaining to the general secretary that he had been listed in the annual report as a Fellow of the British Academy![99]

However, I find poignancy in his participation when considering some of his most famous lines from *A Shropshire Lad*, verse XL:

Into my heart on air that kills
From yon far country blows:
What are those blue remembered hills
What spires, what farms are those?

That is the land of lost content,
I see it shining plain,
The happy highways where I went
And cannot come again.

These could have been written by any exiled refugee, remembering his homeland with nostalgia, at any time. But I feel it has a particular intensity in this context. He remembers the landscape of home and a lost happiness which he can no longer visit. Only a year or so before she died, my Aunt Ibi, the last of my mother's three sisters to pass away, spoke to me in Toronto about her family and suddenly said: 'I wish I could go home!' She had had a really tough life. I often wonder exactly what she meant – I don't think she meant she just wanted to go back to Hungary; I think she wanted to go back to that secure time of being within her family, with parents and sisters and all the extended family before it was so tragically disrupted.

By August 1933 the AAC had raised £10,000 from British academics and the Jewish Central British Fund (CBF – later World Jewish Relief). Albert Einstein had spoken at the Albert Hall in October 1933 to help raise money and subsequently a special fund was set up at LSE where staff donated 1–3 per cent of their salary for persecuted German colleagues. These funds were used to provide for refugees who could not find work; married scholars were given £250 a year whilst the single had £180. In 1936 the AAC became the Society for the Protection of Science and Learning (SPSL), and later the Council for Assisting Refugee Academics (CARA).[100]

These grants were generous, bearing in mind that the 10,000 children who came on the Kindertransport by September 1939 were divided into 'Guaranteed' and 'Non-Guaranteed'. The Guaranteed were those for whom relatives or friends undertook to pay, as we have already seen Iris Origo did for six Jewish children. The 'Non-Guaranteed' were those sponsored by an organisation or local communities.[101]

THE HOLOCAUST AND RWANDA AND DARFUR

We can speculate on what has changed in international affairs since McDonald's attempts to arouse world opinion in the 1930s were so unsuccessful. The League of Nations has been replaced by the United Nations but world mayhem and massacres continue. Sir David Frost interviewed Bill Clinton in July 2004 for the BBC and asked him what he wished he could change about his presidency. Clinton said:

> I wish I had moved in Rwanda quickly. I wish I had gone in there quicker, not just waited 'til the camps were set up. We might have been

able to save, probably not even half those who were lost, but still a large number of people.

I really regret that. I care a lot about Africa and I don't think that these … wars are inevitable and these kinds of murders are inevitable. And I've spent a great deal of time in the last ten years trying to make it up to Africa in general and the Rwandans in particular – so I regret that deeply.[102]

The Rwandans saw the UN stand aside in 1994 and Tom Ndahiro of the Human Rights Commission told the BBC that Yugoslavia was treated differently to Darfur and Rwanda – western countries do not move unless their national interests are at stake. Perhaps indifferent is the word he meant.[103]

The Rwandan genocide also produced its own rescuers – Sara Karuhimbi hid over twenty people, but does not believe she did anything special and cannot understand why anyone would not do the same. Paul Rusesabagina's story was told in the film *Hotel Rwanda*.[104] Paul was a hotel manager in Kigali, and when the manager of the Hotel des Mille Colline, the best in town, left the country, Paul, a Hutu married to a Tutsi woman, was moved in to manage it. When the Hutus started killing the Tutsis, more than 1,000 Tutsis and moderate Hutus took refuge in the hotel and he protected them by using the alcohol on site to influence the militia that he invited in.[105] Also, he and the influential guests phoned everyone they could, including the White House, the French foreign ministry, the Belgian king and Sabena HQ. Paul was a true hero but his modest words echo very closely those of Holocaust rescuers:

So in a sense he did not want to be thought of as exceptionally great or as a hero in any sense because the only standard by which he was exceptional was by comparison with the abysmal measure of the murderer. And so he did not want to accept that you were an exceptional man for not having become a murderer. He wanted to think they were exceptional for having become murderers. But he was very clear about it. He was shocked by how many people he knew had crossed the line and co-operated with the genocidal order without much resistance. And as he always said, 'They could have done as I did if they had wanted to'. [106]

In 2005 Holocaust Memorial Day (27 January) was marked in Kigali, Rwanda. At the newly erected memorial to the victims of the Rwandan genocide there is an exhibition about the Holocaust. Teddy Mugabo, who lost her grandparents and many other relatives in 1994, told BBC reporter Robert Walker about the similarities between the Nazis and the Hutus. She said: 'It shows how the Nazis started segregating people and it shows the way they measured the nose and eyes to show that they are different people. In Rwanda when they were killing Tutsis they did the same thing. They measured the nose. They were measuring the eyes, heights and it is very similar.'

Additionally, in both genocides the victims were dehumanised by their enemies, who called them vermin and cockroaches. This is a classic tool:

> Dehumanisation occurs when members of one group – usually the dominant group – deny the humanity of another. This can be done by equating people to animals, insects, vermin or diseases. In Rwanda Tutsis were often referred to as cockroaches and Nazi propaganda equated Jews to (among other things) 'poisonous mushrooms', spiders and snakes with poisonous fangs. Propaganda images used, particularly by the Nazis, exaggerate physical features to further dehumanise members of the target group. [107]

A Rwandan survivor, Beata Uwazaninka, has stated:

> I stayed in Kigali and things were tense: in the first week there was a grenade at the bus station. They said it was the 'cockroaches', meaning the Tutsis, but in reality it was Interahamwe who used to play around with grenades on the road. Some people were killed and all the Tutsis felt less secure. The week before the genocide began, they announced in Kinyarwanda on Radio Mille Collines that something big was going to happen the next week (*Mube maso rubanda nyamwishi kuko icyumwerugitaha hazaba akantu!*). That's what led to the genocide of 1994. [108]

Yad Vashem, recognising the significance of the Rwandan genocide, held an innovative seminar in November 2005. Entitled *The Genocide in Rwanda: Have we Learned Anything from the Holocaust?,* the seminar was a turning point in Yad Vashem's history because it was the first time a non-Holocaust-related issue was dealt with at its international school for Holocaust studies. The seminar was the initiative of a group of Tutsi survivors who sought help from Yad Vashem in planning their own remembrance, and it was conducted with the help of a Belgian and Rwandan based Tutsi NGO and the French Shoah Memorial. Yolande Mukagasana, director of Nyamirambo Point d'Appui, was one of the first survivors of the Rwandan genocide to document the event. She lost her husband, brothers and sisters, and her three children in the massacres, and has devoted her life to caring for orphans and helping her savaged country reconstruct itself. She said: 'You suffered before we did, and you have important lessons to teach us ... We need you in order to rebuild.'[109]

Yolande had contacted Yad Vashem and asked if 'members of different organizations, involved in memorializing the Rwandan genocide, could come to Yad Vashem to learn about Holocaust remembrance in Israel, as well as educational activities related to the Holocaust and its consequences worldwide, that might serve as a model for similar efforts on the part of the Tutsi tribe'. The most moving part of the event was when Rwandan survivors met Holocaust survivors and the latter came to listen. This encouraged the Tutsis to talk about their experiences, perhaps for the first time. Yolande said: 'The meeting with the Holocaust survivors helped me more than anything to cope with the trauma I experienced. Other people, even psychologists, know how to pity. These meetings helped me understand what I really feel.'[110]

Avner Shalev, chairman of Yad Vashem, commented that survivors and the international community, which had failed to prevent both the Holocaust and the most recent Rwandan genocide, were obliged to create a system of values for human existence to prevent such catastrophes.

However, even as the survivors of these two genocides seek comfort from each other, another catastrophe has unravelled before the world's televisions since 2003 – Darfur. But the world has prevaricated, as it did to James McDonald's warnings and as it did with Rwanda. Elie Wiesel has been speaking out about the situation in Sudan since 2004. Whose voice has greater credibility and authority than this survivor of Auschwitz, when he says:

> The brutal tragedy is still continuing in Sudan's Darfur region. Now its horrors are shown on television screens and on front pages of influential publications. Congressional delegations, special envoys and humanitarian agencies send back or bring back horror-filled reports from the scene. A million human beings, young and old, have been uprooted, deported. Scores of women are being raped every day; children are dying of disease, hunger and violence …
>
> What pains and hurts me most now is the simultaneity of events. While we sit here and discuss how to behave morally, both individually and collectively, over there, in Darfur and elsewhere in Sudan, human beings kill and die. [111]

Yosef 'Tommy' Lapid (1931–2008), a fellow survivor of the Budapest Ghetto – whom I met briefly in the Knesset in 2004 when he was still Minister of Justice – has also spoken about Darfur. On Yom Hashoah[112], 22 April 2007, 'Tommy' Lapid spoke about the relationship between Darfur and the Holocaust. He asked why there was no world outcry over the genocide being perpetrated in Darfur, Sudan:

> Humanity has seen genocide since time immemorial. After the Holocaust, too: we've been witness to the genocide in Biafra, in Cambodia, in Rwanda. We have to raise an outcry against the genocide now being perpetrated in Darfur, Sudan. Meanwhile, the world sits with its arms folded, sending a few sacks of flour – not so much to feed the hungry as to salve its consciences. [113]

Oona King, who combines two ethnicities, wrote about the impact of the Rwandan genocide on the war in the neighbouring Congo, and on the family of one woman, Monique. After the genocide had been under way for forty-eight hours, 36-year-old Monique was told by a friend that she would be killed. Monique listened and fled.

Her 12-year-old niece Geraldine was raped that night and as a result of contracting Aids took years to die. Monique lost twenty-seven members of her close family in 1994. Additionally, her grandfather had been murdered in 1963, her aunt was raped and murdered in 1973 and her father was attacked and interrogated in 1990, which caused him to die of a heart attack. 'Monique's family provides a gruesome snapshot of 30 years of cyclical bloodshed that paved the way for genocide.' Oona listened to Monique's story and wrote: 'No matter how incomprehensible the scale of catastrophe, Monique reminds me that individuals make a difference. It was an individual that saved her.'[114]

James and Stephen Smith, who came from a Methodist family, created the Holocaust Centre in the midst of rural Nottinghamshire in 1995, after being overwhelmed by what they learnt about the Holocaust on a visit to Yad Vashem in 1991. Whilst they planned the project to commemorate the Holocaust and explain it to non-Jews, the tragedy of Rwanda unravelled. They did not initially see the connection between Rwanda and what they were doing:

> It was only towards the end of the genocide that we realised we had missed something huge in our lifetime. Our criticism that the world did know and did nothing to help, now applied to us.
>
> Meanwhile in Srebrenica, a massacre was happening right on our doorstep, right on the cusp of our opening. We had the embarrassment of opening a centre which was meant to be a warning from history while genocide was again under way in Europe.[115]

The Smiths' work on the Holocaust led to them being invited to help create the Kigali Rwandan memorial, which was opened in 2004, and the creation of the Aegis Trust, which is intended to prevent further genocides and confront extremism. The Smiths' work on the Holocaust led directly to their work in all the new disaster areas.

This leads us back to consider the wise words of Rabbi Hugo Gryn:

> Those who survive a tragedy such as the Holocaust cannot keep silent, but must do everything in their power to testify to the fact that

life is the gift of God, and that it is sacred. I recreated a family. I have devoted my energy to the building up of my people. I also became and remain a kind of ethical nuisance. Wherever there is oppression or hunger or brutalization, regardless of colour or creed, I consider it is morally my territory and their cause is my cause. Bigots, racists and fanatics are my personal enemies and I intend to do battle with them until they become civilized, decent people, if needs be for the rest of my life.[116]

TODAY'S INDIFFERENCE TO SUFFERING

We all know that even in normal everyday life we have to make moral choices. Sometimes people feel overwhelmed by the problem and their own insignificance – if no one does anything nothing will change.

Many of us were impressed by Londoners' response to the dreadful bombings in July 2005, by the revival of what Tennessee Williams called 'the kindness of strangers'. But just later that month we were reading about the murder of Richard Whelan. Do people now remember how or why he died? He was the young man of 28 who, on 29 July 2005, was attacked and stabbed by a man who had been tossing chips at people, including Whelan's girlfriend, on top of a No 43 bus in north London. After the attack, no one on that bus seemed prepared to help his girlfriend or the bleeding and mortally wounded young man who collapsed on the bus. Only one young woman came forward to help and she phoned 999. When she asked other passengers for help they refused and melted away into the streets. She wrote about the experience in the *Guardian* under the pseudonym Tara McCartney, and described how people disappeared off the bus and refused even to give their clothes to cover Whelan. There was no danger, the assailant had long left. 'I heard a girl say, as he was being taken away in the ambulance, that she hadn't wanted to give him any of her clothes. I said, "What, in case they got messy?" Her face said yes.' There had been a man who Tara thought got on the bus just to have a look. He was wearing a proper jacket. She asked him if she could have the jacket to put over him. He just said no. Tara could not save Whelan but she did her best for him and comforted him in his final moments. She did what was right. Why did the others fade away? There were no Nazis threatening them.[117]

Only recently we were shocked to read about the tragic deaths of Fiona Pilkington and her disabled daughter Frankie. Their lives had been made so miserable by the taunting behaviour of local youths that one night, in October 2007, the vulnerable single mother, who not only suffered from depression but also had borderline learning problems herself, put her severely disabled 18-year-old daughter Francesca, with a mental age of 4, into the car. She gave her the family's pet rabbit to hold for reassurance. She drove to the A47, poured petrol over the car and set fire to it. Later that night their severely burnt bodies were discovered. How can such a woman be driven to such desperate measures in England in 2007? The inquest in September 2009 found that Fiona had contacted the police thirty-three times in the seven years she was being victimised. Nothing was done to help her and her daughter with the appalling behaviour of the bullying youths, some of whom were as young as 10.[118]

The phrase attributed to Edmund Burke has become a cliché: 'It is necessary only for the good man to do nothing for evil to triumph.' But less well known is another Burke quotation: 'When bad men combine, the good must associate; else they will fall, one by one, an unpitied sacrifice in a contemptible struggle.'[119] The good have to act – they cannot be indifferent to evil. It may involve putting your head over the parapet and you may get shot at.

We have to fight the negativity of indifference – the Nazis were able to succeed with the Holocaust because most people were indifferent to the fate of the Jews and the others. In the same way, most of the people on the bus were indifferent to Richard Whelan's plight.

When we consider Elie Wiesel's views about perpetrators and indifference, as discussed on page 160, we may think of man-made humanitarian crises such as those of Darfur or the Congo as we hear these words. We watch the catastrophes on our plasma television screens as we eat our sushi or Thai supper. We may contribute a few pounds for Children in Need, Live Aid, the Tsunami … whatever – between mouthfuls. It is not difficult if you have a healthy bank account. We don't really inconvenience ourselves and we don't risk much – we don't risk anything at all – certainly not our own safety.

We remember the story of the Good Samaritan in the Bible. Those who went to school in the 1950s, like me, know all about Sir Philip Sidney and his courageous words, 'Thy necessity is greater than mine'. We may not remember the circumstances – that he was mortally wounded in 1586 at the battlefield of Zutphen, but yet passed his water bottle to a fellow dying soldier over 400 years ago. None of us now know where Zutphen was and what the battle was about, but we remember Philip Sidney because of his act of generosity and moral courage.

Roughly eighty years later, in September 1665 – close to my home in Sheffield, in the village of Eyam – the tailor George Viccars received a parcel of cloth he had ordered from London. Unbeknown to him it had been infected with the Plague in London, and within a few days the tailor was dead. The Plague spread through the village speedily killing many people. Villagers panicked and wanted to flee to Sheffield. But they listened to their young rector, William Mompesson, and the villagers courageously sealed themselves off from the rest of the world for about twelve months, keeping the Plague within the village boundaries and preventing its spread outside. Out of a population of 350, 257 died, including the rector's young wife. Their moral and physical courage is still commemorated today almost 350 years later.

How do we make these moral decisions? A fellow Hungarian Holocaust survivor, Eugene Heimler, wrote about a local journalist (previously right-wing) who made up his mind to print posters with the slogan 'National Socialism is Death' whilst shaving. He quite literally had a conversation with himself:

He stood in front of the mirror, he said, and suddenly saw his face in a way in which he had never seen it before. He said it was the face of a traitor. The face asked him, 'What are you going to do about this? What are you going to do about the injustice that is on its way?' By the time he had finished shaving he was ready with the answer. When everyone had gone home that night he used his own paper's presses to print the posters and then went out and put them up himself.[121]

We all have to look at ourselves in the mirror – we speak of 'not being able to face ourselves'. Heimler commented: 'there is something symbolic in this episode: a man's seeing his face in the mirror and the reflection's speaking to him from the glass.' Presumably perpetrators don't have this problem – we know of them returning home, as loving husbands and indulgent fathers, after a day of persecution and cruelty. The Holocaust taught an extraordinary lesson:

> It suddenly transpired that the most horrifying evil in human memory did not result from the dissipation of order, but from an impeccable, faultless and unchallengeable rule of order. It was not the work of an obstreperous and uncontrollable mob, but of men in uniforms, obedient and disciplined, following the rules and meticulous about the spirit and letter of their briefing. It became known very soon that these men, whenever they took their uniforms off, were in no way evil. They behaved very much like all of us. They had wives they loved, children they cosseted, friends they helped and comforted in case of distress. It seemed unbelievable that once in uniform the same people shot, gassed or presided over the shooting and gassing of thousands of other people, including women who were someone's beloved wives, and babies who were someone's cosseted children.[122]

Following the 1961 trial of Adolf Eichmann, a Yale University psychologist devised a series of experiments which bear his name. Stanley Milgram considered Eichmann's defence to be that he was simply following orders when he ordered the deaths of so many Jews. In his 1974 book *Obedience to Authority*, Milgram asked: 'Could it be that Eichmann and his million accomplices in the Holocaust were just following orders? Could we call them all accomplices?' His famous experiments demonstrated a very disturbing relationship between power and authority. Milgram felt the Holocaust and his experiments demonstrated 'often it is not so much the kind of person a man is as the kind of situation in which he finds himself that determines how he will act'.[123]

Whilst these controversial experiments were being considered, America was rocked by the story of the thirty-eight bystanders to the murder of 28-year-old Kitty Genovese in New York in 1964. The case fascinated social psychologists who attempted to explain the bystanders' behaviour, who allegedly were aware of the attack but failed to respond or contact the police.[124] Two in particular, Bibb Latané and John Darley, conducted further experiments into what became known as the 'bystander effect'. They demonstrated that the greater the numbers of people present, the less likely people are to help in an emergency.[125]

This is a field of considerable research for psychologists, such as Charles Garfield at San Francisco University, who says: 'The bystander is a modern archetype, from the Holocaust to the genocide in Rwanda to the current environmental crisis. Why do some people respond to these crises while others don't?' Kristen Monroe, a political scientist, has defined the term 'John Donne's People' based on his writings, *Devotions XVII*:

> No man is an island, Intire of itself; every man is a peece of the Continent,
> A part of the Maine ... Any man's death diminishes me, Because I am
> involved in Mankinde; and therefore never send to know for whom the
> bell tolls; it tolls for thee.

Her language is very specialised, but she concludes that the rescuers and heroes she interviewed had a clear view of their shared humanity which led to instinctive altruism. She quotes Otto, a German–Czech rescuer: 'I never made a moral decision to rescue Jews. I just got mad. I felt I had to do it. I came across many things that demanded my compassion.' She concluded: 'What does explain the actions of all our selfless individuals is a common perception of themselves as individuals strongly linked to others through a shared humanity.' This attitude is so integral to their make up that they have no choice in how they react. 'They are John Donne's people. All life concerns them. Any death diminishes them. Because they are part of mankind.'[126]

This concurs with my own view. Whatever reasons the rescuers I have written about gave for their actions, I believe in the end they were all humanitarians. We all may have to respond to the persecuted, wounded, hunted, sick and frightened in our midst. We never know what will happen – when we will have to respond. When a fellow human being is attacked, will we regard him as our brother or sister, and, as Yehuda Bauer said, shout 'I am here'?[127]

Would you be a rescuer or a bystander?

POSTSCRIPT TO THE PAPERBACK EDITION

This postscript is an opportunity to provide an update on some of the stories in the book for which I have discovered further information. As I write, I look back on the thirteen months since I submitted my manuscript to The History Press with some astonishment at what has happened in that short time. Thanks to an enthusiastic response from readers, the initial hardback print run of 2,000 went to two further reprints, making a total of 4,000. The eBook version has been launched, and my English version is now being translated into Brazilian Portuguese. My small book has ventured into the world like my little grandson – the first timorous footsteps becoming more confident with success.

The thirteen months have been busy and varied. I appeared on UK TV on Channel 4 being interviewed by Fern Britton and was interviewed on BBC radio. I have given my PowerPoint presentation to hundreds of people and the excitement of signing copies has not worn off, neither has the joy of seeing people carrying the book. I travelled to the USA to give presentations at the UN bookshop in New York, the Washington Holocaust Museum and Georgetown University, among other places.

During my trip to America I visited Providence, Rhode Island, and stayed with Arleen Kennedy (b. 1959) whose mother, Suze van der Bijl, was the little Dutch girl hidden by the Schoens (see pp. 116–23 and Plate 31). Suze was taken to America in 1953 by her Aunt Klara. I had the pleasure of staying with Arleen and her husband Ted, and of meeting their youngest son, Jason, and Klara's son Marcel Aardewerk and his wife Elaine. Marcel gave me a copy of an unpublished memoir written by his mother, Klara, in 1979. By the wonders of Skype, I also spoke to Suze's rescuer's daughter, Tiny van Rijswijk (b. 1929) and her son Ed. Tiny told me about meeting Suze for the first time, one day in June 1944 when she came home from school and saw a little girl in 'a light rose dress with a white collar' standing by her mother. She recalls Suze cried a lot for her parents. After the war, Suze came to visit the family every holiday and was a bridesmaid at Tiny's wedding in 1953, just before immigrating to America. Her first visit back to Holland was in 1964 with Arleen, who was 5.[1]

In her memoir, Klara described how her husband, Maurits Wynschenk, with whom she had run a fish shop in Amsterdam, was arrested and sent to Westerbork in September 1942. Left at home, in December 1942 Klara gave birth to her second son, Jo. Her husband wrote to her almost every day from the camp and told her the conditions were very difficult with no milk or hot water to wash nappies. He suggested it would be best to put the children into hiding with the Underground, for if she brought them with her, they would die. In early 1943 both her children were placed with foster parents – baby Jo was only eight weeks old and Donnie was 3. Klara wrote:

> My neighbour knew someone who worked for the underground and told me that he would bring me in touch with them. Jo, my baby, was exactly eight weeks old when my neighbour's wife took him with her in a baby carriage. I took the baby from my breast and made some regular milk bottles and a suitcase with his baby clothes, diapers, oil, perfume, soap, everything a baby needs. It was just terrible to give my eight week old baby to someone I didn't even know.[2]

The two boys were sent to two different childless couples who were, according to Klara's memoir, very caring towards them. She commented:

> It was extremely dangerous for Christian people to take in a Jewish child and they did so at the risk of losing their own lives or at least to be

sent to a concentration camp. I will never be able to thank those people enough for what they did for me personally and for all the Jewish people in Holland.[3]

Naturally I asked Arleen about the impact of her mother's experiences in the Holocaust. She subsequently wrote about her gratitude to Ed van Rijswijk for discovering that her mother's family were sent to Sobibor, a death camp in the Ukraine, where they were all killed within three days of their arrival. She said she was 'always haunted by the thoughts of what happened to them. I was comforted to know they did not languish and suffer in camps before their deaths.' Arleen voiced every mother's emotional reaction about giving their child away to save its life:

I will always be grateful to my grandparents for having the courage and strength to give up my mother to the Underground to save her life. I often wonder if I could have given up my sons given the same situation ... Even though I did not marry a Jew, I raised my children as Jews because I did not want my family's Jewish heritage to end because of the Holocaust.[4]

Additionally, Klara writes in her memoir about her sister Ali (Alida – see p. 121):

My sister, Ali, would have liked her children to go in hiding, but the two oldest said: 'mamma, wherever you go we are going to help you.' Thus only the little one, four years old, was hidden and saved by the underground. After the war when I came back from the concentration camp, she was six years old and I took her in my house as my own daughter.[5]

This child was Suze, Arleen's mother, and I was excited to read this because it had never been clear how Suze came to be separated from the rest of her family. My first informant, John Schoen, had believed Suze was at a neighbour's house when her family were rounded up (see p. 117). Klara's memoir resolved this important issue.

Klara herself was sent to Westerbork in the 'rassias' of 20 June 1943, where she was reunited with her husband after ten months, although they were in separate barracks.[6] She worked in the kitchens and eventually they were given the 'luxury' of a double room, which was very rare. On 4 September 1944 they were sent to Theresienstadt in cattle trucks with no seats – once they arrived they were housed by country of origin so all the Dutch people were together. Six weeks later they were sent to Auschwitz in cattle trucks again and in January 1945 Klara was sent to Mauthausen, where she managed to survive until 5 May when the Americans arrived.[7] After the war Maurits did not come back, but both her sons were returned to her safely. She married another survivor, Gerrit Aardewerk, and had another son, Marcel, in 1947. In 1953 they immigrated to America 'being afraid that the Russians were to take over Holland'. She concludes: 'we went with four children with three surnames – 2 Wynschenks, 1 Van der Bijl and 1 Aardewerk.'[8] Klara died on 1 January 2000.

On 24 November 2010 I was speaking about the book at the Friends Meeting House on Euston Road, London, when a member of the audience who was flicking through a copy of the book gasped in surprise: 'Good Heavens! There's a picture of my grandfather in this book!' We spoke afterwards and he explained that Siegmund Weltlinger (see Plate 36) was his grandfather and Henry Walton (see p. 199) his uncle. His name is David Clark and he was able to flesh out the limited information Henry Walton sent me in 2000.

Following Kristallnacht on 9 November 1938, 35,000 Jewish men were arrested, and those from Berlin ended up in Sachsenhausen camp. Henry Walton's father, David Clark's grandfather, Siegmund Weltlinger, was there until just before Christmas 1938, when he was released on account of his army service during the First World War. David wrote: 'He must have been about 53 at the time, he came back from Sachsenhausen a different man, thin, visibly aged, almost beyond recognition, after only 6 weeks in the camp.'[9] Whilst in the camp Siegmund witnessed a savage beating, which he later described for a Holocaust Research Project.[10] David recalls his grandfather telling him about it and the impact the incident had on him when he was a teenager. It made Siegmund realise 'that the Nazis really meant business and would stop at nothing, absolutely nothing'.[11] He came home determined to make sure his children would be safe by getting them on the Kindertransport. In January 1939, David's mother Resi, then aged 17, was sent off and came to London. She was followed in May 1939 by her brother Henry, aged 14, who was sent to Manchester by the Quakers. He was shocked to find he could not continue his schooling because of his age, and was instead put to work in a factory.[12]

On 16 September 2010 a plaque was unveiled in Berlin to Dorothy and George Möhring, who from August 1943 until April 1945 hid Siegmund Weltlinger and his wife in their small, two-roomed apartment at 25 Kissingen Strasse. Professor Dr Johannes Tuchel, head of the German Resistance Memorial Centre Foundation in Berlin, made a speech at the unveiling of the plaque and outlined the story of the rescue. Dr Tuchel opened by referring to the 160,000 German Jews killed by the Nazis and observing: 'Most Germans watched as their German neighbours were deported; most Germans did nothing when their neighbours and their friends, until then, were deported and went to meet an uncertain fate.'[13] An estimated 12,000 German Jews went into hiding and of these about 5,000 survived, including over 1,700 in Berlin. It is now clear that each hidden person had a network of at least ten non-Jewish people supporting them in various ways. Dr Tuchel then spoke about the Weltlingers: Siegmund was born in 1886 in Hamburg into a family of artists. He became a bank clerk and completed one year of military service in 1905. In 1908 he moved to Berlin and became a bank employee. By 1914 he was a financial journalist and became chief editor of *Stock Exchanges Archives*. He then became a soldier during the First World War and was moved to the army's finance department in Brussels. After the war he returned to managing his journal in Berlin and in 1919 he married a former bank manager's daughter, Margaret Gumpel. In 1925 he became a stockbroker at the Berlin Stock Exchange. He was doing well until the events of 1938 led to his arrest.[14]

Once his children had been sent to England, he became involved in the Berlin Jewish Community as a leading administrator. In February 1943 he was due to be deported with other Jews but he decided to go underground. When speaking about his experiences in 1954, in a speech he made to mark the 21st anniversary of Hitler's rise to power on 30 January 1933,[15] he noted that he and his wife were first hidden by Professor Elsa Schiller in Berlin-Friedenau. They were there from 26 February 1943 until 27 August 1943, when:

> There was one morning, a house search by the Gestapo, and in our nightgowns, we were hidden behind a bookcase; by a miracle of wonder, were not discovered. Now we fled to friends to the Pankow district, friends who had once said to us that they would find a refuge for us and help if it was necessary. They were very pious people, followers of Christian Science, who saw it as their duty to accept the persecuted.[16]

The two couples lived in the Möhrings' two-bedroomed flat with the Möhrings' daughter, Jutta. The Weltlingers had the kitchen as their bedroom. The privations both parties suffered during that long period together can only be imagined. They had to leave briefly to go to Joanna Reingold in Berliner-Heiner until they were liberated on 8 May 1945. Tragically, George Möhring died on 11 May 1945; his widow lived in East Berlin after the war. Weltlinger spoke on her behalf when she wanted to move to West Berlin. He said 'at great risk to herself, [she] deprived herself of some of her badges and Ration cards, throughout all that time we were in hiding, in order to help provide for us'. Accordingly she was honoured, with Jutta, by the Mayor of Berlin, Willy Brandt, in 1962. She died as a result of a traffic accident in 1967.

Siegmund explained the Möhrings' motivation to help them:

> They had trust in their God – never having slightest fear for themselves of being discovered and arrested. Every day they read the Bible. This helped me a lot at the time and in that time I began to seriously consider religious issues with them … We never left the small rooms, not even during air raids, because within the apartment block lived some committed Nazis.[17]

After marvelling at the courage of the Möhrings, Professor Tuchel concluded his speech: 'and so I return to my thoughts – again, there-remains the bitter taste of how few Germans rescued persecuted Jews and how many Germans either looked away or who supported mass murder.'

The story of the Thiryn family in Belgium, given to me by Claire Keen-Thiryn, has expanded in two ways since the publication of the book. One was, bizarrely, down to the vagaries of the Jubilee Line on the London Underground, whose malfunction kept me at home when I had planned to visit an exhibition. As a result, quite by chance, I saw a TV programme, *Secret War 2*, which showed a black and white photograph of a man I recognised as Prosper de Zitter, the Belgian traitor who had betrayed Louis Thiryn. That programme revealed that Major Hardy Amies (1909–2003), the couturier who designed clothes for the Queen from 1950, had been involved in the hunt for de Zitter in Belgium during the war.

Major Hardy Amies was a senior member of the Special Operations Executive (SOE) in Belgium and was keen to eliminate de Zitter, who had betrayed too many members of the Resistance and escaping members of the RAF to the Gestapo. The SOE had been set up by Churchill to undertake sabotage in occupied Europe. I have seen documents signed by Amies at The National Archives planning to add de Zitter to the list of targets for assassination. In fact, de Zitter managed to evade his fate until 1947. This is a fascinating area of research which I will be pursuing.

In addition, there was a second line of expansion on the story. Eugene Black from Hungary lives in Leeds and regularly speaks to groups about his experiences in the Holocaust. He survived three camps: Buchenwald, Dora and Bergen-Belsen. When I read that he had been in Dora-Mittelbau, situated east of Berlin, I contacted his daughter Lilian to check his opinion on what I had written about Dora-Mittelbau in connection with Louis Thiryn (see pp. 142–3). Lilian explained that Eugene was sent to Dora in May 1944 from Buchenwald with 1,000 Hungarian Jews. He was given the worst work clearing rocks from newly created tunnels: 'They worked in the most inhumane conditions and it was the worst slave labour camp.' The work on the V1 and V2 rockets was much better and reserved for non-Jewish prisoners. Eugene also agreed with my comments about von Braun (see p. 142): '... we lost everything, our homes, our families, our country and when we were liberated we had nothing. Von Braun knew what was going on and he was helped to make a new life – he was a war criminal.'

Of particular relevance to the subject of this book, Lilian explained that Dora was part of a trio of camps with Ellrich and Harzhungen. Eugene had developed double pneumonia and was sent to Harzhungen where his life was saved by a German doctor, who was not a prisoner, although his name is unknown. She added:

> Finally the most awful thing about Dora, Ellrich and Harzhungen is that these camps are so near to where people lived and they saw what was happening and no-one lifted a finger to help – in fact when father was in Harzhungen he had to march through the town/village and the children and women used to throw stones at them and spit at them.

Sadly, Lilian said her father's only help was from the German doctor – everyone else stood by.[18]

Sending my manuscript off in January 2010 was inevitably a terrible rush. Frustratingly new material on Else Pintus came just a few weeks afterwards and, as the book shows, I did not even know the Stenzels' first names. However, my original informant, Doris Stiefel, wrote to me on 1 April 2010 telling me that they were called Josef and Klementyna.[19] She had been sent a book published in Polish and German which gave details of Else's family and the Stenzels.[20] As before, I am indebted to Doris for translating parts of the book to provide further information on the Pintus family. Max Pintus was the elder brother of Doris' grandfather, Moritz Pintus.

Max Pintus was born in 1850 in Prockau (now Prokowo) in the Karthaus area in West Prussia. He died in 1919, having lived all his life in Karthaus where he was buried in Chmielno. He had eight children of whom Else Pintus, born in 1893, was the youngest (see pp. 157–62). Max was a 'highly regarded merchant' and was a member of the synagogue in Karthaus where he was a member of the board. In 1890 the

congregation consisted of 133 members. Doris has translated the following from the book:

> Besides a farmstead at nearby Lake Reckow, the Max Pintus family
> owned a house in the center of the village of Chmielno, where he ran
> a grocery store and a tavern. Old man Pintus was known for having
> respect for Kashubian and Christian traditions. Klementyna Stenzel
> would tell her children that the Pintus couple was more knowledge-
> able about Catholic festivities than the other residents of Chmielno. On
> Sundays, Max Pintus would send the people from his pub off to church.
> The Pintus house burned down in the early 30s. The siblings, Heinz,
> Anna and Else, moved into the Stenzel house where the two sisters ran
> a dry goods store. Heinz earned a living as a watchmaker. They also
> got some rental income from their lake property. Several years prior
> to the war the siblings moved to Karthaus [Kartuzy]. The two former
> neighbor families from Chmielno continued to visit each other on a
> regular basis. [21]

This paragraph is interesting for several reasons. It puts flesh on the
relationship between the Pintus and Stenzel families, showing they
were much more involved than I previously understood. Secondly, it
shows how assimilated the Pintus family was, and how respectful Max
Pintus was of his Catholic neighbours. Thirdly, it introduces the area of
Kashubia which I had never heard of before.

In response to my request for more information about Kashubia, Dr
Borzyskowska wrote:

> Kaszuby (Polish), Kaschubei (German), Kashubia (English) is a histori-
> cal region in the north of Poland, on the Baltic Sea, on the historical
> German-Polish borderland. The region is populated by the Kashubians,
> ethnic slavic minority. [From] 1772–1918 the region belonged to Prussia,
> since 1871 had been a German Province West Prussia. After 1918 a central
> part of Kashubia came to the recreated Poland, Gdansk/Danzig. The
> most of the Jewish population was assimilated to the German culture
> and this way they migrated from polish part of the region after 1918. A
> part of them, like Else Pintus stood in Poland, maybe because they had

already had regional identity. The father of Else Pintus – Max Pintus – was a known person in the region, one of the members of Society for Kashubian Culture (founded 1904) and he had published articles about Kashubian culture.[22]

Doris added in her notes:

> ... in Chmielno as in Kartuzy it was said that the Pintus [family] were good people who spoke all the pommerellischen languages, Kashubian, Polish and German fluently. Supposedly they spoke German amongst themselves but that in their home in Chmielno, Kashubian may have predominated. Indeed Max Pintus was also actively involved with Kashubian culture. He served on the Board and as treasurer of the Society for Kashubian Folklore, founded in 1907. His collection of local Chmielno sayings, customs and practices (including one about a wedding) were published under his name in the Society's publication of 1910.[23]

In concluding this additional material on Else's family, I had some queries about her siblings. Of the eight children I knew that the eldest, Hedwig, died in the Holocaust; Otto was killed in the First World War; Paul escaped to Shanghai; Albert died in the Holocaust and Gustav was hidden by his non-Jewish girlfriend, whom he subsequently married.[24] Doris explained that the remaining three had stayed in Chmielno – Anna, Heinz and Else. Anna died in 1933 before the Nazi era, leaving Else and Heinz who lived together. Heinz worked for himself as a watchmaker with his own business in Karthaus.[25] He was taken by the Nazis within days of their invasion of Poland on 1 September 1939, and he died at Stutthof concentration camp, in Danzig. Apparently, Stutthof was established immediately after the invasion of Poland and two weeks later several hundred leading Danzig Jews were deported there; 'Within a week most of them had died as a result of deliberate brutality'.[26]

Finally, during a visit to Belbroughton, the Worcestershire village in which I lived for sixteen years, an old friend told me about a friend of hers, Lore Godden *née* Steinhardt (1924–91), who had come from

Germany and whose family was rescued by the Rothschild family. Lore's son, Jeremy Godden, has compiled a fascinating family history. Due to lack of space here I will not be able to reiterate it in full, but the particular aspect I wanted to note is the war record of Jeremy's grandfather, Hugo Steinhardt, who fought in the First World War. Jeremy commented on the German Jews' desire to be considered good Germans (confirming what I wrote on pp. 134–6). Hugo's brother Robert was one of the 12,000 Jews who died fighting for Germany. Hugo was sent home wounded from the Western Front and later honoured with the Iron Cross.[27] Like other similarly honoured soldiers, he discovered its true value when on 26 June 1933 he received a letter from the State of Hessen dismissing him from his teaching post in a state school. There is some irony in this, since it wasn't until January 1935 that he received a document acknowledging his war record.[28]

Unfortunately, Hugo was amongst the men sent to Buchenwald after Kristallnacht in November 1938, where he suffered dreadfully. Like Siegmund Weltlinger, his relatively early release was put down to his war record. For the Steinhardts, too, this was their wake-up call. The family wrote desperately to everyone they could think of asking for help. And whilst President Roosevelt was unable to help, the Rothschild family responded to the letter addressed to 'Lord Rothschild, London' and saved the family and thirty-one boys from the Jewish home Hugo had been running since 1937. They became 'the Cedar Boys' because the large mock-Tudor house allocated to them at the Rothschilds' home, Waddesdon, was called 'The Cedars'.[29]

Having lived with many of the stories in the book for many years, I found it exciting to discover more information about these courageous people – both the rescuers and the rescued. I am delighted to have had the opportunity to add this information to the original text for the paperback edition, and also to thank all the readers for their support and the warmth of their response to my book.

Agnes Grunwald-Spier
May 2011

RIGHTEOUS AMONG
THE NATIONS & YAD VASHEM

Yad Vashem was created by the Knesset in 1953 as the Jewish people's living memorial to the 6 million Jewish victims of the Holocaust. It was intended to be a world centre for four main aspects: documentation, research, education and commemoration of the Holocaust. Yad Vashem is today a dynamic and vital place of intergenerational and international encounter. At the same time, one of its principal roles is to demonstrate the gratitude of the State of Israel and the Jewish people to those non-Jews who helped rescue Jews in that darkest time. Since 1963 the authority has run its worldwide Righteous Among the Nations scheme. This is run by a public commission headed by a Supreme Court judge.

Moshe Bejski, who as we have already seen was on Schindler's list, emigrated to Israel after the war and became a judge. He told no one of his wartime experiences until, in 1961, he gave evidence to the Eichmann trial in Jerusalem. As a result he became involved with commemoration and subsequently joined the Commission of the Righteous. He soon became president and wrestled with the moral dilemma of who should be awarded the 'Righteous' title and who denied. He ensured that his own rescuer was honoured but this was problematic as there was a philosophical divide over which rescuers were considered worthy.

Apparently there was an issue over honouring Schindler because of his lifestyle. The original chair of the Righteous Commission, Judge Moshe Landau, was looking for heroes with no flaws, who had saved Jews and had a virtuous lifestyle. Bejski, with his close relationship to Schindler, knew him 'warts and all', and was looking for ordinary flawed people. He said to Schindler's detractors that had he not been the type of man he was, he would not have had the verve to achieve his outrageous rescue. He defended other 'dubious' rescuers – a prostitute who served Nazi officers but hid Jews and the SS officer George Duckwitz, the trade attaché in the German Embassy in Copenhagen. As soon as he heard of the plan to deport the Danish Jews he told the Danish authorities, even though he was a Nazi.[1] However, Dr Paldiel, former Director of the Department of the Righteous, has argued that Avner was incorrect in his article when he claimed Landau was looking for the perfect Righteous. He claims Landau's objections to Schindler 'stemmed from Schindler's forceful takeover of two Jewish firms in Krakow during the initial period of the Nazi occupation, and even threatening force to bring this about'.[2]

Gabriele Nissim, an Italian journalist, spent three years visiting Bejski, who died in March 2007 aged 86, while writing his book *Divine Grace*. He told me about Bejski's theory of the 'inherent consistency of the rescuer's gesture, which has to be triggered by a genuinely humanitarian spirit'.[3]

The Yad Vashem website gives very full details about the award of the title 'Righteous Among the Nations'. The awards could be deemed somewhat arbitrary, in as much as they are dependent on survivors telling Yad Vashem about the rescuer and providing the appropriate documentation. It is a tragic fact that, inevitably, it is only the participants in successful rescues who can become involved in the process. There were undoubtedly many, many courageous rescuers whose attempts failed and consequently they and their charges were discovered and paid with their lives.

Most Righteous were recognised as a result of requests made by the Jews they rescued. But sometimes survivors could not overcome the difficulties of dealing with the painful past and didn't take any action. Others were not aware of the programme or were unable to apply, particularly those who lived behind the Iron Curtain during the years of communism in Eastern Europe. In other cases, the survivors may have died before they could make the request. Titles and medals, however, are still being awarded even now, sixty-five years after the end of the war, as with Soeur St Cybard, recognised in November 2009.

Appendix II

TABLES

TABLE 1: DETAILS OF RESCUERS AND INFORMANTS

KEY:

1. Face-to-face interview; notes made during interview, typed afterwards and corroborated with interviewee.
2. Unpublished memoirs or memoirs and letters; followed up with correspondence or telephone. Notes made and filed.
3. Video; follow-up as in 2.
4. Correspondence by letter or e-mail; follow-up as in 2.
5. Book or newspaper articles; follow-up as in 2.

Rescuers	Informant	Informant's place of residence	Status	Primary Data Source
Bracey, Bertha	Pat Webb and Joan Bamford (deceased)	UK	Both nieces of rescuer	1
van Dyk, Jelle and Elizabeth	Miriam Dunner	London	Rescued	1
Keen-Thiryn, Claire	Self	Blackburn*	Rescuer	1
Ladigiené, Stefanija	Irena Veisaite	Vilnius, Lithuania	Rescued	1

Rescuers	Informant	Informant's place of residence	Status	Primary Data Source
Lutz, Carl	Agnes Hirschi	Bern, Switzerland	Step-daughter of rescuer	1
Petras, Charles	Hilde Holger and daughter Primavera	London	Daughter	1
Schindler, Oskar	Judge Bejski	Tel Aviv	Rescued	1
Borciñska, Pani	Margarita Turkov	Oregon, USA	Rescued	2
Fawcett, Charles	Self	London	Rescuer	2
Maas, Hermann	Ron Mower	Hertfordshire	Wife was rescued	2
Petras, Charles (Karl)	Primavera Boman	London	Daughter of rescued	2
van Proosdij, Jaap	Self	Pretoria, South Africa	Rescuer	2
Rinkevicius, Vytautas	Lady Margaret Kagan	Huddersfield	Rescued	2
Stenzel family (first names not known)	Doris Stiefel	Seattle, USA	Second cousin to Else Pintus who was hidden	2
Strauch, Richard	Lea Goodman	London	Rescued	2
Tóth, János	Naomi Szinai	London	Rescued	2
Guicherd, Victor and Josephine	Betty Eppel	Jerusalem	Rescued	3
Barczynski, Józef	Olympia Barczynska	Leeds	Niece	4

Rescuers	Informant	Informant's place of residence	Status	Primary Data Source
Costaguti, Achille and Guilia	Milton Gendel	Rome	Friend of rescuing family	4
Ho, Feng Shan	Manli Ho	San Francisco, USA	Daughter of rescuer	4
Huffener, Henk	Self	Guildford	Rescuer	4 – visited him
Klerk, Jacob and Hendrika	Henri Obstfeld	London	Rescued	4
Saidler, Maria 'Mitzi'	Otto Fleming	Sheffield	Mitzi was Otto's parents' cook in Vienna	4
St Cybard, Soeur	Josie Martin	California, USA	Rescued	4
Van der Velde family	Willi Buntinx	Brussels, Belgium	Son of rescued	4
Weltinger, Siegmund and Grete **	Henry Walton	Cheshire	Son of rescued	4
Hahn-Beer, Edith	Angela Schluter	London	Daughter of rescuer	5
Maistriau, Robert	Rose Marie Guilfoyle	Brussels, Belgium	Interviewed him in French on my behalf	5
Origo, Iris	Benedetta Origo	Tuscany, Italy	Daughter of rescuer	5
Rácz, Vali	Monica Porter	London	Daughter of rescuer	5
Schoen, Joost and Anna	John Schoen	Wales	Son of rescuers	5
de Sousa Mendes, Dr Aristides	John Paul Abranches	California, USA	Son of rescuer	5

Rescuers	Informant	Informant's place of residence	Status	Primary Data Source
Commentators non-rescuers:				
Devonshire, Duke of	Self	Chatsworth, Derbyshire	Views on anti-Semitism in UK	1
van Rijswijk, Ed	Self	Amsterdam	Information on Dutch Resistance saving Jewish children	4
Sanders, Ria	Self	Poole, Dorset	Lived through WWII in Netherlands	4

*   Was in Blackburn when information was provided. Now in Belgium.

** Rescued – rescuers not known.

TABLE 2: RIGHTEOUS AMONG THE NATIONS AND NATIONAL POPULATIONS

Country	No of Righteous[1]	National Population 1939[2]	Notes
Poland	6,195	34,775,700	
Netherlands	5,009	8,729,000	
France	3,158	40,000,000	
Ukraine	2,272	41,340,000	
Belgium	1,537	8,386,600	
Lithuania	772	3,037,100	
Hungary	743	9,129,000	
Belarus	608	5,568,000	
Slovakia	498	3,577,000	
Italy	484	44,394,400	
Germany	476	69,622,500	
Greece	306	7,221,900	
Russia	164	108,377,000	
Yugoslavia (Serbia)	131	7,583,000	1960 figure*
Latvia	123	1,994,500	
Czech Republic	108	9,679,400	1960 figure*
Croatia	102	4,140,000	1960 figure*
Austria	87	6,652,700	
Moldova	79	2,468,000	1940 figure*
Albania	69	1,073,000	
Romania	60	19,933,800	
Norway	45	2,944,900	

Country	No of Righteous[1]	National Population 1939[2]	Notes
Switzerland	45	4,210,000	
Bosnia	40	3,240,000	1960 figure*
Denmark	22**	3,795,000	
Bulgaria	19	6,458,000	
Great Britain	14	47,760,000	
Armenia	13	1,281,600	
Sweden	10	6,341,300	
Macedonia	9	1,392,000	1960 figure*
Slovenia	6	1,331,000	
Spain	4	25,637,000	
Estonia	3	1,134,000	
USA	3	131,028,000	
Brazil	2	40,289,000	
China	2	517,568,000	
Chile	1	4,914,000	
Georgia	1	3,542,000	
Japan	1	71,380,000	
Luxembourg	1	295,000	
Montenegro	1	400,000	1948 figure*
Portugal	1	7,627,000	
Turkey	1	17,370,000	
Vietnam	1	20,268,000	

[1] Figures from Yad Vashem, Department for the Righteous Among the Nations, 1 January 2010 – www1.yadvashem.org/righteous_new/statistics.html.

[2] Figures from Population Statistics – www.library.uu.nl (accessed 2004); www.populstat.info (Vietnam, Chile, Georgia); http://www.tacitus.nu/historical-atlas/population (Montenegro).

* 1939 figure N/A.
** Danish Underground asked for participants in their rescues to be listed as one.

TABLE 3: DETAILS OF RESCUERS AND RESCUED

Column 1. Rescuer	2. Name of informant – relationship to rescuer	3. Rescuer's country of origin	4. Country where rescue occurred	5. Age of rescuer at time	6. Rescued	7. Sole rescuer
Barczynski, Józef	Olympia Barczynska – niece	Poland	Poland	39–45	250 people	No
Borciñska, Pani	Margarita Turkov – hidden	Poland	Poland	Not known	Small girl of 8	Family – see column 10
Bracey, Bertha	Joan Bamford and Pat Webb – both nieces	England	Germany	45	Kindertransport children: about 10,000	No – member of the Quakers
Afan de Rivera Costaguti, Achille and Giulia	Milton Gendel – friend	Italy	Italy – Rome	Not known	Families – 18 people from 4 families	Couple and their servants
Denner, Christl	Angela Schluter – daughter of rescued	Austria	Austria	18	Edith Hahn-Beer	Yes
van Dyk, Jelle and Elizabeth	Miriam Dunner – rescued	Holland	Holland	Both 30 in 1942	16 months	Couple
Fawcett, Charles	Self	USA	Vichy France	22	Various – women of marriageable age	No
Guicherd, Victor and Josephine	Betty Eppel – rescued	France	France	30–40	7 and 5	Couple
Ho, Feng Shan	Manli Ho – daughter	China	Austria	30s	About 12,000	Yes

8. Photos	9. How contact was made with informant	10. Religion or other major motivation	11. Year of Righteous Award if given	12. Notes, including date of death if appropriate
; Nos -18	HSFA Leeds	Very strong sense of justice – brought up to care for others – childhood experience of displacement	1993	Józef died Sept. 1980. Would not accept recognition as a Righteous Gentile in his lifetime, because he said he had only done his duty
	I read about her in the Journal of the Child Survivors' Association	Her rescuer was paid both by Jewish organisation and the Polish Underground		She was not kind to Margarita, who was quite traumatised by the experience
; No 1	Through a Sheffield Quaker who knew a relative of Bertha's living in Sheffield	Very devout Quaker and also had mystical interests		Bertha died in 1989 aged 95
	Through Iris Origo's daughter who put me in touch with Milton Gendel	Humanitarianism and neighbourliness. Not really pro-Jewish. It was the right thing to do	2002	Kept good relations after the war, Achille as a volunteer in the fascist militia. Both died some time ago
	Through letter	Sheer humanitarianism – she was only 18 and never hesitated to help	1985	Stayed good friends until Christl died in 1992. Edith died in 2009
	Through a mutual contact	Very religious Protestants		Traumatised by return to family. Jelle 1912–93 and Elizabeth 1912–92. Miriam died in 2006
Nos 2–4	Through work on MA	Brought up Episcopalian – still has strong faith		Married 6 Jewish women to rescue them from the camps. Helped people after the war. Charles died in 2008
Video; 19–22	Article in *Jewish Chronicle*	Compassion and love	1979	Her parents came from Poland many years ago. Her rescuers were a poor farming couple
No 26	Through media coverage and personal contacts	Suffered as a child, which together with his education made him a humanitarian	2000	Died in 1997 aged 96

Column 1.	2.	3.	4.	5.	6.	7.
Rescuer	Name of informant – relationship to rescuer	Rescuer's country of origin	Country where rescue occurred	Age of rescuer at time	Rescued	Sol rescu
Huffener, Henk	Self	Holland	Holland	18	All ages	No – w family
Keen-Thiryn, Claire	Self	Belgium	Belgium	19	1 girl of 13 or 14; elderly couple	No – w family a Mme H
Klerk, Jacob and Hendrika	Henri Obstfeld – rescued	Holland	Holland	50s	2½-year-old boy	Couple
Ladigienė, Stefanija	Irena Veisaite – rescued	Lithuania	Lithuania	32	14 or 15	No – parents friends made th contact
Lutz, Carl	Agnes Hirschi – stepdaughter	Switzerland	Hungary	49	60,000	No – w Gertrud and oth colleag
Maas, Hermann	Ron Mower – his wife was rescued	Germany	Germany	67	Too many	No
Maistriau, Robert	Rose-Marie Guilfoyle	Belgium	Belgium	22	231	2 others
Petras, Charles (Karl)	Primavera Boman-Behram	Austria	India/Austria	Not known	Not known	No
van Proosdij, Jaap	Self	Holland	Holland	22	240	No
Rácz, Vali	Monica Porter – daughter	Hungary	Hungary	33	5 or 6	No
Rinkevicius, Vytautas	Lady Margaret Kagan – rescued	Lithuania	Lithuania	37	With husband and mother-in-law	No – ot colleag

8. Photos	9. How contact was made with informant	10. Religion or other major motivation	11. Year of Righteous Award if given	12. Notes, including date of death if appropriate
)	Article in *The Times*	Family involved in the Resistance	1998	Still helped people after the war. Henk died in 2006
)	London Jewish Cultural Centre	Members of the Resistance and her brother died as a slave labourer		Very establishment family – father an officer in Belgian army. Helping Jews was part of resisting the Nazis
s; Nos –34	AJR journal	Freemasons and Baptist. Sense of justice	1999	Organised through the Freemasons
)	Attended RFTF 2000	Roman Catholic – very humane and embarrassed at Lithuania's behaviour	1992	Stefanija died in 1967 in Irena's arms
s; Nos 10	Through a Board of Deputies' contact	Methodist – mother's influence to help people and very disturbed by what he saw	1964 with Gertrude	Diplomat – died 1975 aged 80. In correspondence and met his stepdaughter Agnes Hirschi. Recognised as Righteous Gentile
s; No 11	AJR journal	Lutheran pastor	1964	Worked with Quakers in England to get people out of Germany. Died in 1970
	Saw book on him and press coverage	Very anti-German and wanted to resist	1994	Died 26 Sept. 2008
s; No 35	Hilde Holger responded to the AJR journal but died before I could see her	Friendship I assume – no clear information		He died in 1951. Hilde died in 2001
	South African contact	Protestant – his father was a very strong influence	1997	Said his parents brought him up with high ethical standards
; Nos –13	Article in *Jewish Chronicle*	Catholic, strongly influenced by a working life spent with Jews	1991	Correspondence with her daughter Monica Porter. Vali died in 1997. Very compassionate for those that needed help
: Nos –30	Through cousin Irena Veisaite who attended RFTF 2000	Roman Catholic – very decent man	1976	Vytautas died in 1988

Column 1. Rescuer	2. Name of informant – relationship to rescuer	3. Rescuer's country of origin	4. Country where rescue occurred	5. Age of rescuer at time	6. Rescued	7. Sole rescue
Saidler, Maria 'Mitzi'	Rescuer	Austria	Austria	40	Middle-aged couple	Yes
Schoen, Joost and Anna	John Schoen – son	Holland	Holland	21	5-year-old girl called Suze	No – with parents
de Sousa Mendes, Dr Aristides	John Paul Abranches – son	Portugal	France	55	30,000	Yes
St Cybard, Soeur	Josie Martin – rescued	France	France	49	5-year-old Josie	Yes
Stenzel family (first names not known)	Doris Stiefel – 2nd cousin to Else Pintus who they hid	Poland	Poland	50s	Else Pintus	Family
Strauch, Richard	Lea Goodman – rescued	Poland	Poland	Not Known	Quite a few	No – ran factory w. camp
Tóth, János	Naomi Szinai – rescued	Hungary	Hungary	Not known	18	Not relev.
Weltinger, Siegmund and Grete (rescued)	Henry Walton – son	Germany	Germany	Not known – probably same as rescued	Probably in their 40s – had a grown-up son	6 differe. couples
Unknown Nazi official and Van der Velde family	Willi Buntinx – son	Not known, presumably Belgium	Belgium	Parents of young family – mother was pregnant at the time with their 8th child	6-year-old Gisele	Yes

8. Photos	9. How contact was made with informant	10. Religion or other major motivation	11. Year of Righteous Award if given	12. Notes, including date of death if appropriate
; Nos –25	Otto Fleming was a Sheffield friend	Loyalty to employers and decency	1978	Mitzi was cook to Otto Fleming's parents. She offered to hide them and when they refused, she hid someone else. Otto died in 2007
; Nos –32	CCJ Journal	Not religious – always helping people. Objected to Nazi policy on Jews and invasion		Involved in the Underground – girl rescued was Suze aged 5. Subsequently went to USA and died May 1999. She visited Anna Schoen in Holland every year
	LJCC Visas Exhibition	Devout Catholic	1966	He died 3 April 1954. Contact was his son John Paul Abranches who died in 2009
, Nos –16	Jewish Chronicle article	Religious, good woman	2009	Soeur St Cybard died in 1968
; No 6	Through Gerda Haas who wrote to me about rescuers – AJR Journal	Loyalty – she had lent the Stenzels money		Else died in 1975. They hid her for 2¼ years. Decent people, not pro-Nazi but would probably not have helped another Jew
	AJR Journal	Opportunist like Schindler		Had to pay to be in the camp but it offered protection – run by Richard Strauch
	Found papers in Wiener Library	Loyalty and good person	1999	Unable to discover Tóth's dates
; No 36	AJR Journal	Decent people wanted to help		Henry escaped in 1939, came to England with help of Quakers. Parents lived into their 80s in Germany
	Visit to Brussels and conversation with bilingual secretary at EU about Robert Maistriau	Decency and neighbourliness. Christian family		Gisele is still alive but traumatised and Willi had never spoken of this.

NOTES

INTRODUCTION & RESCUERS WITH RELIGIOUS MOTIVES

1. George Eliot, *Middlemarch* (London: Penguin, 1994), p. 838.
2. 'The Ethics of the Fathers', Chapter II, verses 20–21, in *The Authorised Daily Prayer Book*, trans. Rev. S. Singer (London: Eyre and Spottiswood, 1962), p. 258.
3. Varian Fry, *Surrender on Demand* (Boulder: Johnson Books, 1997), p. xii.
4. Ibid., p. xiii.
5. Ibid.
6. Ibid.
7. Mary Jayne Gold, *Crossroads Marseilles 1940* (New York: Doubleday, 1980), p. xvi.
8. www1.yadvashem.org/yv/en/about/index.asp
9. Yad Vashem's Department for the Righteous among Nations, 1 January 2010.
10. Marilyn Henry, 'Who, exactly, is a Righteous Gentile?' in *Jerusalem Post Internet Edition*, 29 April 1998, www.jpost.com/com/Archive/29.Apr.1998/Features/Article-6.html, accessed 13 December 2002.
11. Walter Meyerhof, Prospectus for the Varian Fry Foundation, Stanford University, August 1997, p. 1.
12. Walter Meyerhof, notes of meeting with writer in London, 22 September 1997.
13. See p. 54.
14. See p. 34.
15. See p. 120.
16. Quakers' Humanitarian Efforts Assisted Thousands of Refugees, p. 3, 18 February 2002, www.holocaust-heroes.com/quakers.html, accessed 18 December 2002.
17. Hans A. Schmitt, *Quakers and Nazis: Inner Light in Outer Darkness* (Columbia: University of Missouri Press, 1997), p. 1.
18. Brenda Bailey, 'Bertha's Work for German Jewish Refugees', unpublished lecture given at Armscote General Meeting on 8 August 1993, pp. 4–5.

19.   Alma Cureton, Bertha's niece, in telephone conversation with the author, 7 January 2003.

20.   Brenda Bailey, *A Quaker Couple in Nazi Germany: Leonhard Friedrich Survives Buchenwald* (York: The Ebor Press, 1994), p. 42.

21.   Bertha L. Bracey, 'Germany: April, 1933' in *Quaker World Service*, Vol. 7, No 5 (1 May 1933) pp. 9–10.

22.   Bailey, *A Quaker Couple in Nazi Germany*, p. 7.

23.   Ibid., p. 9.

24.   Ibid., p. 10.

25.   Naomi Shepherd, *A Refuge from Darkness: Wilfrid Israel and the Rescue of the Jews* (New York: Pantheon Books, 1984), p. 73.

26.   Michael Smith, *Foley: The Spy who Saved 10,000 Jews* (London: Hodder & Stoughton, 1999), pp. 63–4.

27.   Shepherd, *A Refuge from Darkness*, p. 90.

28.   Ibid., pp. 146–7.

29.   Ibid., p. 148.

30.   Bertha L. Bracey, Work of the Society of Friend for Refugees from the Hitler Regime in Central Europe, typed note signed by Miss Bracey but undated, found in File G15 of The Wiener Library.

31.   Hensley Henson, Introduction to *The Yellow Book* (London: Victor Gollancz Ltd, 1936), p. 8.

32.   Papers concerning the Treatment of German Nationals in Germany 1938–39, Command 6120 (London: HMSO, 1939), pp. 3–4.

33.   Andrew Sharf, 'The British Press and the Holocaust' in *Yad Vashem Studies V* (Jerusalem: Yad Vashem, 1963), pp. 169–91, 179.

34.   Alex Bryan, 'Bertha L. Bracey: Friend of the Oppressed' in *Friends' Quarterly* (January 1991), pp. 238–9.

35.   Victor J. Burch, 'A Testimony to the Grace of God in the Life of Bertha Lilian Bracey', on behalf of Banbury & Evesham Monthly Meeting, 15 April 1989, pp. 1–4.

36.   Ibid., p. 4.

37.   Ibid., p. 2.

38.   Bryan, 'Bertha L. Bracey: Friend of the Oppressed', pp. 233–41, p. 240.

39.   Pat Webb (Bertha's great-niece), letter to author, dated 13 January 2003.

40.   Alma Cureton (Bertha's niece) to Pat Webb, letter given to author, 12 August 2002.

41.   Norman Coxon to Bertha Bracey, letter dated 1 April 1988, lent to author by Pat Webb.

42.   Burch, 'A Testimony to the Grace of God in the Life of Bertha Lilian Bracey', p. 4.

43.   Christopher Robbins, unpublished draft biography of Charles Fawcett, pp. 7–8.

44.   Charles F. Fawcett, conversation with the author, 17 June 2002, at his Chelsea home.

45.   Robbins, unpublished draft biography of Charles Fawcett, p. 9.

46.   Charles Fawcett, obituary in *The Daily Telegraph*, 9 February 2008.

47.   April Fawcett, e-mail to author, 23 November 2009.

48. Philippe Olivier, 'The Fate of Professional French Jewish Musicians under the Vichy Regime', on The Orel Foundation website, www.orelfoundation.org/index.php/journal/journalArticle/the_fate_of_professional_french_jewish_musicians_under_the_vichy_regime/#112909_19, accessed 1 January 2010.

49. Sheila Isenberg, *A Hero of Our Own: the Story of Varian Fry*, p. 33.

50. Official Josephine Baker website: www.cmgww.com/stars/baker/about/biography.html, accessed 1 January 2010.

51. Isenberg, *A Hero of Our Own*, pp. 32–3.

52. Fry, *Surrender on Demand*, pp. 37–8.

53. Gold, *Crossroads Marseilles 1940*, p. 163.

54. Ibid., p. 164.

55. Ibid., pp. 173, 256.

56. Andy Marino, *American Pimpernel: the Man who Saved the Artists on Hitler's Death List* (London: Random House, 1999), pp. 234–5.

57. Fry, *Surrender on Demand*, p. 131.

58. Charles Fawcett, interview with the author at his home, 15 November 1997, p. 4.

59. Marino, *American Pimpernel*, pp. 232–3.

60. Ibid., p. 239.

61. Gold, *Crossroads Marseilles 1940*, p. 258.

62. Agnes Spier, *Affected by Atrocity: The impact and motives of Varian Fry, Charles Fawcett and the Emergency Rescue Committee*, unpublished MA dissertation at Sheffield University, October 1998, p. 59. Notes of conversation with Charles Fawcett on 21 February 1998 at The Gay Hussar, London.

63. Marino, *American Pimpernel*, p. 140.

64. Robbins, unpublished draft biography of Charles Fawcett, pp. 25–6.

65. Undated letter from Charles Fawcett to the author, received 4 September 1998.

66. Letter from Charles Fawcett to the author, dated 29 September 1997.

67. 'A Book of Tribute to Varian Fry', United States Holocaust Memorial Council, 10 April 1991, p. 11.

68. April Fawcett, e-mail, 23 February 2011.

69. April Fawcett, e-mail, 23 November 2009.

70. Eric Margolis, 'A real gentleman adventurer', *The Toronto Sun*, 2 November 1995.

71. Andy Marino, 'You couldn't make it up' in *Telegraph Magazine*, November 1999, pp. 28, 30, 31.

72. Letter from Lord Salisbury to April Fawcett, dated 21 May 2008.

73. Obituary in the *Telegraph*, February 2008.

74. Letter from Tony Blair to April Fawcett, 2008.

75. Agnes Hirschi (Carl Lutz's stepdaughter), notes of author's meeting in London, 14 April 2002.

76. Theo Tschuy, *Dangerous Diplomacy: the Story of Carl Lutz, Rescuer of 62,000 Hungarian Jews* (Grand Rapids: Eerdmans, 2000), p. 27.

77. Ibid., p. 29.

78. Ibid., p. 33.

79. Ibid., p. 34.

80. Yehuda Bauer, *Jews for Sale? Nazi-Jewish Negotiations, 1939–1945* (Yale: Yale University Press, 1994), p. 162.

81. Ibid., p. 158.

82. Obituary of Professor Tibor Barna (1919–2009), economist, *The Times*, 12 August 2009. I recall my mother telling me that many young men she knew could not get into Hungarian universities and went to Germany instead.

83. Tschuy, *Dangerous Diplomacy*, pp. 116–7.

84. Ibid., p. 117.

85. Bernard Wasserstein, *Britain and the Jews of Europe 1939–1945* (London: JPR, 1999), p. 271.

86. Ian Kershaw, *Popular Opinion and Political Dissent in the Third Reich: Bavaria 1933–1945* (Oxford: OUP, 1988), pp. 158–9.

87. Bauer, *Jews for Sale?* pp. 181–2.

88. Tschuy, *Dangerous Diplomacy*, p. 107.

89. Agnes Hirschi, e-mail to author, 30 October 2002.

90. Charles R. Lutz, 'The Rescue Work of a Swiss in World War II' in *Neue Zuercher Zeitung* (NZZ), No 2464, 30 June 1961, pp. 5–8.

91. Bauer, *Jews for Sale?* p. 235.

92. Lutz in *NZZ*, p. 8.

93. Agnes Hirschi, e-mail to author, 15 March 2001.

94. Ruth Rothenberg, 'Belated honour for Swiss diplomat who saved Jews' in *Jewish Chronicle*, 7 April 2000.

95. Alfred Werner, 'A Saintly German Pastor' in *Congress Weekly* (published by Zionist Congress in USA), 27 October 1952, Vol. 19, No 26, pp. 5–7.

96. Schmitt, *Quakers and Nazis*, p. 41.

97. Ibid., p. 41.

98. Christine King, 'Jehovah's Witnesses During the Holocaust' in *Perspectives: Journal of the Holocaust Centre, Beth Shalom*, Autumn 2002, pp. 36–7.

99. Ibid., p. 37.

100. Cited in Schmitt, *Quakers and Nazis*, pp. 41–2.

101. Reginald Pringle, 'Paul Rosenzweig', unpublished memoir written in 1990. Forwarded to the author by Pringle's brother-in-law Ron Mower, p. 1.

102. Ron Mower, letter to author, received 7 August 2000.

103. Pringle, 'Paul Rosenzweig', p. 18.

104. Ibid., p. 20.

105. Mower, letter to author, 7 August 2000.

106. Pringle, 'Paul Rosenzweig', p. 39.

107. Ibid., p. 41.

108. Ibid., p. 42.

109. Ibid., p. 43.

110. Ibid., p. 44.

111. Ibid., p. 45.

112. A Mezuzah is a sign of a Jewish home and a sign of God's presence and the sanctification of the dwelling place. It is a small case which contains a piece of parchment on which specific prayers have been written. Fixing a Mezuzah is a Biblical law from Deuteronomy 6:9: 'And thou shalt write them upon the posts of thy house, and on thy gates.'

113. 'In dark days a brave friend to the Jews' in *Rheim-Neckar Heiliggeist* Newsletter, 8 November 1995.

114. Richard Gutteridge, *Open the Mouth for the Dumb!: The German Evangelical Church and the Jews 1879–1950* (Oxford: Basil Blackwell, 1976), pp. 214–5.

115. Kenneth Slack, *George Bell* (London: SCM Press Ltd, 1971), p. 56.

116. Ibid., pp. 58–9.

117. Ronald C.D. Jasper, *George Bell: Bishop of Chichester* (London: OUP, 1967), p. 141.

118. Bailey, *A Quaker Couple in Nazi Germany*, p. 82.

119. Schmitt, *Quakers and Nazis*, p. 182.

120. H.D. Leuner, *When Compassion was a Crime: Germany's Silent Heroes 1933–1945* (London: Oswald Wolff, 1966), p. 114.

121. Werner, 'A Saintly German Pastor', p. 7.

122. William W. Simpson and Ruth Wehl, *The Story of the International Council of Christians and Jews* (London: CCJ, 1988), p. 23.

123. Ibid., p. 21.

124. Hermann Maas, translation of a letter to Martha dated 14 August 1947, copied to author by Ron Mower.

125. Rheim-Neckar Newsletter.

126. Quoted by her husband, Ron Mower, in a telephone conversation with the author, 19 December 2002.

127. Rheim-Neckar Newsletter.

128. Monica Porter, *Deadly Carousel: A Singer's Story of the Second World War* (London: Quartet, 1990), p. 8.

129. Ibid., pp. 10–2.

130. Ibid., p. 16.

131. Ibid.

132. Ibid., p. 17.

133. Vali Rácz, obituary in *The Daily Telegraph*, 27 February 1997.

134. Porter, *Deadly Carousel*, pp. 19–20.

135. Ibid., p. 25.

136. Ibid., p. 27.

137. Ibid., p. 28.

138. Ibid., pp. 29, 142.

139. Monica Porter, e-mail to author, 30 October 2002.

140. Porter, *Deadly Carousel*, p. 10.

141. Monica Porter, e-mail to author, 15 November 2002.

142. Porter, *Deadly Carousel*, p. 185.

143. Vali Rácz, obituary in *The Daily Telegraph*, 27 February 1997.

144. 'Parents and Heroes', *Home Truths* on BBC Radio 4, September 2002, www.bbc.co.uk/radio4/hometruths/0240heros.shtml, accessed 28 December 2009.

145. Monica Porter, e-mail to author, 22 December 2009.

146. Jane Marks, *The Hidden Children: the Secret Survivors of the Holocaust* (Bantam: London, 1997), p. 251.

147. Tom Tugend, 'French village honours "hidden child" survivor of Holocaust' in *Jewish Chronicle*, 24 November 2000.

148. Marks, *The Hidden Children*, p. 252.

149. Ibid., pp. 252–3.

150. Josie Martin, e-mail to author, 11 March 2001.

151. Janine Morant-Mestradie, privately produced memoir of the Institution Saint-André in Angoulême, dated June 2001, pp. 5–7. Translated from the French by Prof. Hamish Ritchie.

152. Tom Tugend, *Jewish Chronicle* article, 24 November 2000.

153. Josie Martin, e-mail to author, 11 March 2001.

154. Marks, *The Hidden Children*, p. 258.

155. Josie Levy Martin, *Never Tell your Name* (1st Books Library, 2002), p. 197.

156. Bernadette Landréa, letter to author, 18 November 2003. Bernadette has translated Josie Martin's book into French, *Ne Dis Jamais Ton Nom*.

157. Louis Lacalle, letter to Madame Landréa, 10 December 2003. Madame Landréa translated the author's letter into French and then Louis' reply into English. I am deeply indebted to her.

158. Lacalle, letter to Madame Landréa, 10 December 2003.

159. Bernadette Landréa, letter to author, 29 December 2003.

160. Martin, *Never Tell your Name*, p. iii.

161. Ibid., p. 199.

162. Martin, e-mail to author, 27 November 2009.

163. Martin, e-mail to author, 25 November 2009.

164. John Paul Abranches, letter to author, 12 August 2002, p. 1. He was the ninth son of Aristides, born in 1932 in Belgium. He was international chairman of the committee to commemorate his father, and he worked tirelessly to get his father's work recognised.

165. Maria Julia Cirurgiao & Michael D. Hull, 'Aristides de Sousa Mendes (1885–1954)' in *Lay Witness* published by Catholics United for Faith (CUF) in October 1998, p. 3.

166. José-Alain Fralon, *A Good Man in Evil Times* (London: Viking, 2000), p. 46.

167. Abranches, letter to author, 12 August 2002, p. 2.

168. Eric Silver, *The Book of the Just: the Silent Heroes who Saved Jews from Hitler* (London: Weidenfeld & Nicolson, 1992), p. 52.

169. Fralon, *A Good Man in Evil Times*, p. 57.

170. Ibid., p. 47.

171. Cirurgiao & Hull, 'Aristides de Sousa Mendes (1885–1954)', p. 6.

172. Fralon, *A Good Man in Evil Times*, p. 48.

173. Cesar Mendes, 'Memories of Cesar Mendes', undated memoir from the 1960s, p. 2.

174. Ibid., p. 1.

175. Cirurgiao & Hull, 'Aristides de Sousa Mendes (1885–1954)', p. 7.

176. Fralon, *A Good Man in Evil Times*, p. 60.

177. Ibid., p. 62.

178. Ibid., pp. 73–4.

179. John Paul Abranches, letter to author, 12 August 2002, p. 2.

180. Fralon, *A Good Man in Evil Times*, p. 118.

181. 'A Protest' dated 10 December 1945, sent to the author by JPA, 12 August 2002.

182. John Paul Abranches, letter to author, 15 May 2003.

183. Henrie Zvi Deutsch, 'The Many Marvelous Mitzvot of Aristides de Souse Mendes', on the website of the Portuguese Sephardic History Group, www.saudedes.org/500yrs2.htm, accessed 27 December 2002.

184. Ibid.

185. Silver, *The Book of the Just*, pp. 52–3.

186. Sebastian Mendes, e-mails to the author, 21 December 2009.

187. JPA, 12 August 2002.

188. Miriam Dunner, interview with the author, 18 November 2001, at Miriam's home.

189. Abraham Dunner, telephone conversation with the author, 20 December 2009.

190. Max Arpel Lezer, 'Shame on this Dutch Law' in *Mishpocha*, Summer 2002, Newsletter of the World Federation of Jewish Child Survivors of the Holocaust, and e-mail to the author, 10 March 2003.

RESCUERS WITH HUMANITARIAN MOTIVES

1.   Olympia Barczynska, letter to author, 31 August 2000. Olympia is Józef's niece.

2.   Olympia Barczynska, *Józef Robert Barczynski*, biographical notes dated 2 March 2001 sent to the author, p. 2.

3.   Ibid., p. 2.

4.   Olympia Barczynska, telephone conversation with the author, 11 March 2001.

5.   Barczynska, biographical notes, p. 2.

6.   Barczynska, letter to author, 31 August 2000, p. 3.

7.   Ibid., p. 4, and e-mail of 6 January 2010.

8.   Barczynska, biographical notes, p. 2.

9.   File No 5846 on Józef Barczynski at Yad Vashem.

10. Barczynska, e-mail to the author, 6 January 2010.

11. Milton Gendel, e-mail to the author, 29 December 2003.

12. Vivo Vivanti, 'The Righteous are not Forgotten' in *Shalom* (the Journal of the Jewish Community of Rome), No 12, December 2002, p. vi of insert. Translated by Phil Jacobs of Nottingham, January 2003.

13. File No 9707 from Yad Vashem's Commission for Selecting Righteous Among the Nations, 2002.

14. Ibid.

15. Ibid.

16. Ibid.

17. Duchess Clotilde Capece Galeota, e-mail to the author, 6 November 2002.

18. Milton Gendel, e-mail to the author, 27 February 2003.

19. Vivanti, 'The Righteous are not Forgotten', December 2002.

20. Ibid.

21. Edith Hahn-Beer, *The Nazi Officer's Wife* (London: Little Brown, 2000), p. 151. Apparently, Plattner did this several times so he must have thought it was the right thing to do. He was responsible for checking the papers proving racial

background of anyone who wanted to get married: telephone conversation with Edith's daughter, Angela Schluter, 4 July 2003.

22. Angela Schluter, e-mail to the author, 17 August 2003, and telephone conversation of 12 January 2010.
23. Hahn-Beer, *The Nazi Officer's Wife*, p. 153.
24. Angela Schluter, telephone conversation with the author, 12 January 2010.
25. Edith Hahn-Beer, obituary in the *Jewish Chronicle*, 7 May 2009.
26. Angela Schluter, telephone conversation with the author, 4 July 2003.
27. Lewis Smith, 'Last dream of Jewish survivor who fell in love with a Nazi', *The Times*,
    24 May 2004, p. 11.
28. The information for this section comes mostly from Video No 639204 of the Survivors of the Shoah Visual History Foundation, recorded on 13 May 1998 in Jerusalem by Betty Eppel.
29. David Eppel, 'Key to Righteousness' in *Jewish Chronicle*, 28 July 2000.
30. Ibid.
31. Betty Eppel, e-mail to the author, 10 February 2004.
32. Victor Guicherd, letter to Yad Vashem, *c.* 1980. Translated from French by David Eppel.
33. Betty Eppel, notes of telephone conversation with the author, 6 March 2004.
34. Eppel, 'Key to Righteousness', 28 July 2000.
35. Betty Eppel, e-mail to the author, 24 February 2004.
36. Betty Eppel, notes of telephone conversation with the author, 1 March 2004.
37. Ibid., 19 December 2009.
38. Manli Ho, 'Dr Feng Shan Ho', unpublished memoir, 2001, p. 1.
39. Gail Lichtman, 'The People's Hero', *Jerusalem Post*, 1 March 2004, p. 2.
40. Mark O'Neil, 'The Angel of Austria's Jews', *South China Morning Post*, 2000.
41. Ibid.
42. Manli Ho, unpublished memoir, p. 2.
43. Marion Koebner, 'Charles Peter Carter', AJR Information, Vol. LV, No 12, December 2000, p. 2.
44. Otto Fleming, e-mail to the author, 1 July 2004.
45. Otto Fleming, telephone conversation with the author, 1 July 2004.
46. Lotte Marcus, 'Letter to ex-Viennese Shanghailanders', 8 August 2003, p. 2, www.chgs.umn.edu/Visual__Artistic_Resources/Diplomat_Rescuers, accessed 5 September 2004.
47. Manli Ho, unpublished memoir, p. 3.
48. Ibid.
49. Marcus, 'Letter to ex-Viennese Shanghailanders', p. 2.
50. Manli Ho, unpublished memoir, p. 4.
51. Ibid., p. 5.
52. Anthea Lawson, 'Ho the hero in line for Israeli award', *The Times*, 10 February 2000.
53. Manli Ho, e-mail to the author, 22 June 2004, based on a speech entitled 'Remembering my Father, Dr Ho Feng Shan', p. 1.
54. Ibid., p. 2.
55. Manli Ho, unpublished memoir, p. 5.

56. Manli Ho, e-mail to the author, 22 June 2004, p. 1.

57. Lichtman, 'The People's Hero', p. 1.

58. Manli Ho, e-mail to the author, 22 June 2004, p. 2.

59. Manli Ho, unpublished memoir, p. 5.

60. Manli Ho, 'Remembering my father, Dr Ho Feng Shan' in *China Daily*, 26 September 2007.

61. Lichtman, 'The People's Hero', p. 2.

62. Ellen Cassedy, 'We are all Here: Facing History in Lithuania', pp. 77–85, Bridges Association 2007, www.judaicvilnius.com/repository/dockumentai/cassedy_bridges.pdf?, accessed 27 December 2009.

63. Most of this narrative is based on the writer's interview with Irena Veisaite in Huddersfield on 23 December 2000.

64. Michail Erenburg and Viktorija Sakaité, *Hands Bringing Life and Bread*, Vol. 1 (Vilnius: 1997), p. 61. * Irena has corrected this translation to read 'love to your fellow man', e-mail to the author, 6 November 2001. ** Paneriai is a town 9–10km from Vilnius, where all the Jews from Vilnius were killed by the Nazis. There is a Holocaust memorial there now.

65. Irena Veisaite, letter to the author, 23 July 2003.

66. A *gymnasium* in Europe is the equivalent of a sixth-form college or grammar school for 14–18 year olds in preparation for university. It comes from ancient Greece where the term was used for both intellectual and physical education. In Britain it is used exclusively for physical activity.

67. Irena Veisaite, interview with the author, 23 December 2000.

68. Cassedy, 'We are all Here: Facing History in Lithuania', p. 78.

69. www.humanrights.gov.sc/stockholmforum/2001/page1272.html, accessed 26 December 2009.

70. Cassedy, 'We are all Here: Facing History in Lithuania', p. 79.

71. Ibid., p. 80.

72. Erenburg and Sakaité, *Hands Bringing Life and Bread*, p. 61.

73. Iris Origo, *Images and Shadows: Part of a Life* (London: John Murray, 1998), p. 88.

74. Richard Owen, 'To the Tuscan manor born' in *The Times* (Register), 25 July 2002.

75. Origo, *Images and Shadows*, p. 226.

76. Ibid., pp. 228–9.

77. Ibid., p. 227.

78. Amy Gottlieb, *Men of Vision: Anglo-Jewry's Aid to Victims of the Nazi Regime 1933–1945* (London: Weidenfeld & Nicolson, 1998), p. 99.

79. Walter Block, 'Anna Essinger and Bunce Court School' in *Gathered Stories: Commemorating the Kindertransport* (Friends House, 2008).

80. Frank Auerbach, letter to author, 30 November 2009.

81. Robert Hughes, *Frank Auerbach* (London: Thames and Hudson, 1990), p. 17. A 'stetl' is meant to be 'shtetl' – the Yiddish word for a small town in Eastern Europe predominantly occupied by Orthodox Jews. These towns were destroyed by the Holocaust. The inhabitants are often contrasted with the urbane, assimilated Jews who predominated in Central Europe.

82. Hughes, *Frank Auerbach*, p. 18.

83. Origo, *Images and Shadows*, p. 228.

84. Harris and Oppenheimer, *Into the Arms of Strangers* (London: Bloomsbury, 2000), p. 277.

85. Louise London, *Whitehall and the Jews, 1933–1948: British Immigration and the Holocaust* (Cambridge: CUP, 2000).

86. Iris Origo, *War in Val d'Orcia: An Italian War Diary, 1943–1944* (London: Allison and Busby, 1999), p. 25.

87. Origo, *Images and Shadows*, p. 241.

88. Origo, *War in Val d'Orcia*, p. 100.

89. Ibid., p. 101.

90. Benedetta Origo, e-mail to the author, 1 August 2002.

91. Ibid., 28 September 2002.

92. Ibid., 30 September 2002.

93. Caroline Moorehead, *Iris Origo: Marchesa of Val D'Orcia* (London: John Murray, 2000), pp. 215–16.

94. Lady Margaret Kagan, http://collections.ushmm.org/artifact/image/b00/00/b0000246.pdf, accessed 23 December 2009.

95. Lady Margaret Kagan, 'Remembering Vytautas', unpublished memoir written in the 1990s, given to the author in June 2001, p. 4.

96. Ibid., p. 7.

97. Ibid., pp. 7–8.

98. Stephen Goodell, 'The Story of Avraham Tory and his Kovno Ghetto Diary', www.eilagordinlevitan.com.

99. Kagan, telephone conversation with the author, 1 November 2001.

100. Kagan, b0000246.pdf, p. 2.

101. Kagan, 'Remembering Vytautas', p. 10.

102. Ibid., p. 12.

103. Ibid., p. 13.

104. Ibid.

105. Ibid., p. 14.

106. Ibid., p. 15.

107. Kagan, b0000246.pdf.

108. Kagan, pp. 19–20.

109. Tam Dalyell, obituary for Lord Kagan in *The Independent*, 19 January 1995.

110. Kagan, letter to the author, 3 July 2001.

111. Jaap van Proosdij, unpublished memoir dated February 1996, sent to the author in March 2001, p. 6.

112. Jaap van Proosdij, interview with South African journalist Paula Siler, 4 December 1998, p. 1.

113. Jaap van Proosdij, telephone conversation with the author, 17 December 2009.

114. Jaap van Proosdij, letter to the author, 28 December 2003.

115. Lucy Dawidowicz, *The War Against the Jews 1933–45* (London: Penguin, 1990), p. 438.

116. Martin Gilbert, *Holocaust Atlas*, p. 106.

117. Peta Krost, 'At last, saviour of 240 Jews gets recognition', interview in *Saturday Star* (South African newspaper), 7 March 1998.

118. Van Proosdij, interview with Paula Siler, p. 1.

119. Ibid., p. 2.
120. Ibid., pp. 2–3.
121. Ibid., p. 3.
122. Prof. Shirley Kossick, 'Pretoria's Own Righteous Gentile' in *Pretoria Jewish Chronicle*, August 1994, p. 5.
123. Krost, 'At last, saviour of 240 Jews gets recognition', 7 March 1998.
124. Ibid.
125. Ibid.
126. Van Proosdij, letter to the author, 23 December 2003.
127. Krost, 'At last, saviour of 240 Jews gets recognition', 7 March 1998.
128. Van Proosdij, interview with Paula Siler, p. 2.
129. Van Proosdij, letter to the author, 25 March 2001.
130. Van Proosdij, letter to the author, 4 July 2001.
131. Krost, 'At last, saviour of 240 Jews gets recognition', 7 March 1998.
132. Van Proosdij, interview with Paula Siler, p. 1.
133. Van Proosdij, letter to the author, 12 January 2004.
134. Van Proosdij, interview with Paula Siler, p. 1.
135. Jewish Agency Press Release, 27 May 2003, www.jafi.org.il/press/2003/may/may27.htm.
136. John Schoen, letter to the author, 20 January 2001.
137. John Schoen, telephone conversation with the author, 14 March 2001.
138. Ibid., 17 January 2001.
139. John Schoen's notes about Suze, sent to the author with a letter, 20 May 2001.
140. Ed van Rijswijk, notes of 1 January and e-mail of 2 January 2010.
141. Dutch Famine of 1944, http://everything2.com/title/Dutch+Famine+of+1944, accessed 2 January 2010.
142. Ria Sanders, notes of 2 April and letter of 8 April 2002 sent to the author.
143. Richard Evans, 'I want Spielberg to tell how we hid little Suze from Nazis' in *Wales on Sunday*, 12 September 1999, p. 8.
144. John's notes, 20 May 2001, p. 1.
145. Richard Evans, 'I want Spielberg to tell how we hid little Suze from Nazis', p. 8.
146. Conversation with Josie Martin in London, 17 November 2003.
147. John Schoen, telephone conversation with the author, 14 March 2001.
148. John's notes, 20 May 2001.
149. John Schoen, 'Life Under the Nazis' in the *Cardiff Post*, 15 May 1986.
150. Ed van Rijswijk, notes of 1 January 2010.
151. Richard Evans, 'I want Spielberg to tell how we hid little Suze from Nazis', p. 9.
152. Arnold Brown, telephone conversation with the author, 22 November 2001.
153. Peter Schoen, notes to the author and e-mail dated 2 January 2010.
154. Peter Schoen, telephone conversation with the author, 17 December 2009.
155. Van Rijswijk, notes of 1 January 2010.
156. Van Rijswijk, e-mail to the author, 2 January 2010.
157. Ibid., 8 January 2010.
158. Bert Jan Flim, *Saving the Children: History of the Organized Effort to Rescue Jewish Children in the Netherlands 1942–1945* (Bethesda, Maryland: CDL Press),

pp. 40–2; sent by Ed van Rijswijk, 8 January 2010. Bert Flim's family was involved in these Resistance groups.

159. Arleen Kennedy, e-mail to the author, 4 January 2010 (14:46).
160. Van Rijswijk, notes of 1 January 2010.
161. Arleen Kennedy, e-mails of 4 January 2010 (14:46, 15:14 and 16:08).

RESCUERS WITH OTHER MOTIVES

1.   Michelle Quinn, 'The Artists' Schindler' in *San Jose Mercury News*, G-1, 29 March 1999, p. 10.
2.   Grace Bradberry, 'Surrey's own Oskar Schindler' in *The Times*, 1 March 1999, p. 15.
3.   Teresa Watanabe, 'Japan's Schindler' in *The Los Angeles Times*, 1994.
4.   *Chinese People's Daily*, 10 September 2001.
5.   Dominic Kennedy, 'British Schindler saved 1,000 Jews from Nazis' in *The Times*, 5 April 2002, p. 6.
6.   Dr Bal-Kaduri, '1,100 Jews Rescued by a German' in *Yad Vashem Bulletin*, December 1957, No 2, pp. 12–3.
7.   Linley Boniface, 'Saved from Death by Schindler's List' in *Hampstead & Highgate Express*, 5 May 1995, p. 50.
8.   Judith Simons, obituary for Victor Dortheimer 1918–2000, *Jewish Chronicle*, 26 May 2000.
9.   Ron Fisher, *A Schindler Survivor – The Story of Victor Dortheimer*, Carlton TV, 1995.
10. Svitavy in Czech, Zwittau in German.
11. Herbert Steinhouse, 'The Man Who Saved a Thousand Lives', 1949, in *Oskar Schindler and His List* (Forest Dale, Vermont: Eriksson, 1995), ed. Thomas Fensch, p. 13.
12. Ibid., p. 35.
13. Luitgard N. Wundheiler, 'Oskar Schindler's Moral Development During the Holocaust' in *Humboldt Journal of Social Relations*, Vol. 13, Nos 1 & 2, 1985–86, pp. 335–56, 340.
14. Eric Silver, *The Book of the Just: The silent heroes who saved Jews from Hitler* (London: Weidenfeld and Nicolson, 1992), pp. 147–8.
15. Wundheiler, 'Oskar Schindler's Moral Development During the Holocaust', p. 333.
16. Ibid., pp. 340–1.
17. Dina Rabinovitch, 'Schindler's Wife' in *Guardian Weekend*, 5 February 1994.
18. Robin O'Neil, 'Schindler – An Unlikely Hero – the Man from Svitavy', Introduction, p. ix, unpublished MA dissertation on Schindler, 1996, University College London, Dept for Hebrew and Jewish Studies. O'Neil cites his interview with Dr Moshe Bejski in Tel Aviv, 1995.
19. Emilie Schindler, *Where Light and Shadow Meet: A Memoir* (New York: Norton, 1996), p. 46.
20. Emilie Schindler's obituary, *The Independent*, 7 October 2001.
21. Schindler, *Where Light and Shadow Meet*, p. 58.
22. Ibid., p. ix.

23. Ibid.

24. Ibid., p. 162.

25. Allan Hall, 'Widow fights to retrieve Schindler's original list' in *The Times*, 27 April 2001.

26. Dina Rabinovitch, 'Schindler's Wife' in *Guardian Weekly*, 5 February 1994.

27. Steinhouse, 'The Man Who Saved a Thousand Lives', pp. 17–8.

28. Rachel Fixsen, 'Spielberg's Hero Died Alone and Forgotten', Reuters News Service, 10 February 1994 in *Oskar Schindler and his List*, pp. 250–1.

29. Testimony of Yitzhak Stern, May 1962, www1.yadvashem.org/righteous_new/germany/germany_shindler_testimony_1print.html.

30. Martin Gilbert, *The Boys* (London: 1996), Glossary, p. 482.

31. Dr Moshe Bejski, notes of telephone conversation with author in Jerusalem, 3 January 2004.

32. Bradberry, 'Surrey's own Oskar Schindler', 1 March 1999.

33. Henk Huffener, telephone conversation with the author, 1 July 2002.

34. Huffener, unpublished memoir written for the author, dated 10–11 May 1999.

35. Bradberry, 'Surrey's own Oskar Schindler', 1 March 1999.

36. Huffener, letter to the author, 2 July 2002.

37. Brenda Bailey, *A Quaker Couple in Nazi Germany* (York: William Sessions, 1994), p. 36.

38. Henk Huffener, letter to the author, 21 October 2002.

39. Ibid.

40. Ibid., 29 December 2002.

41. Speech by the Ambassador of Israel on presenting Henk Huffener the award of Righteous Among the Nations at the Israeli Embassy, London, 3 February 1999.

42. Bradberry, 'Surrey's own Oskar Schindler', 1 March 1999.

43. Carol Ann Lee, *The Hidden Life of Otto Frank* (London: Viking, 2002), p. 15; and Naomi Shepherd, *Wilfrid Israel: Germany's Secret Ambassador* (London: Weidenfeld and Nicolson, 1984), p. 26.

44. Erna Paris, *Long Shadows: Truth, Lies and History* (London: Bloomsbury, 2001), p. 72.

45. Theo Richmond, 'How German Can you Get?' in *The Sunday Times Culture* magazine, 9 March 2003.

46. Victoria J. Barnett, *Bystanders: Conscience and Complicity During the Holocaust* (Westport: Greenwood Press, 1999), p. 99.

47. Else Pintus, 'The Diary of Else Pintus: The Story of a Holocaust Survivor, 1947', unpublished diary translated by Doris Stiefel (*née* Pintus), June 1998, and sent to the author, p. 33.

48. Barbara Lovenheim, *Survival in the Shadows: Seven Hidden Jews in Hitler's Berlin* (London: Peter Owen, 2002), pp. 24–6. Photo and citation between pp. 124–5.

49. Jew Count, http://en.allexperts.com/e/j/je/jew_count.htm, accessed 3 January 2010.

50. Citation from Yad Vashem, sent by e-mail, 16 December 2009.

51. Huffener, letter to the author, 6 June 1999, p. 14b.

52. Ibid.

53. Ibid., 14 April 2000, pp. 3–4.
54. Ibid., 6 June 1999, p. 14b.
55. Tanya Harrod, obituary of Maria Sax Ledger, *The Independent*, 11 April 2006.
56. *Cipher Caput* by Treatment, 1993, www.delerium.co.uk/bands/treatment/deleco26.html.
57. Philip Hardaker, e-mail to the author, 10 January 2010.
58. Hardaker, telephone conversation with the author, 11 January 2010.
59. HE Dror Zeigerman, speech honouring Henk Huffener in the Israeli Embassy, 3 February 1999.
60. Bradberry, 'Surrey's own Oskar Schindler', 1 March 1999.
61. Claire Keen-Thiryn, e-mail to the author, 23 March 2001.
62. Keen-Thiryn, interview with the author in Bolton, 21 April 2001, p. 1.
63. Ibid.
64. Ibid., p. 2.
65. John Clinch, *Escape & Evasion Belgium WW2*, www.belgiumww2.info, section 7, accessed 28 December 2009.
66. Ibid.
67. Guido Zembsch-Schreve, *Pierre Lalande: Special Agent* (London: Pen & Sword Books Ltd, 1998), p. 297.
68. Leaflet about exhibition to commemorate fiftieth anniversary of the liberation of Dora, provided by Claire Keen-Thiryn.
69. Obituary of Guido Zembsch-Schreve, a member of the Special Operations Executive (SOE), in *The Times*, 3 April 2003.
70. Keen-Thiryn, e-mail to the author, 3 May 2001.
71. Freddie Knoller, 'A History of the Dora Camp' in *Perspectives*, Autumn 2004, p. 35.
72. *Une base intéressante de 1944 (prisonniers politiques) – Forums Généalogie* – www.genealogie.com/v4/forums/recherches-genealogiques-benelux, accessed 28 December 2009.
73. Evert Kwaadgras, e-mail to the author, 16 January 2004. Mr Kwaadgras is the archivist, librarian and curator of the Dutch Freemasons' Grand Lodge of the Netherlands, based in The Hague.
74. Henri Obstfeld, e-mail to the author, 6 May 2001.
75. Henri Obstfeld, 'A Bridge Too Far' in *Zachor: Child Survivors Speak* (London: Elliott & Thompson, 2005), pp. 89–96 (89–90).
76. Obstfeld, e-mail to the author, 25 April 2001.
77. Ibid., 6 May 2001.
78. Ibid., 1 December 2009.
79. Ibid., 28 December 2003 (10:34).
80. Ibid.
81. Ibid., (18:24).
82. Ibid., 25 April 2001.
83. Obstfeld, *Zachor*, p. 95.
84. Obstfeld, e-mail to the author, 6 May 2001.
85. Ibid., 16 April 2001.
86. Lena Berggren, 'Elof Eriksson (1883–1965): A Case-study of Anti-Semitism in Sweden', *Patterns of Prejudice*, Vol. 34, No 1, January 2000, pp. 39–48 (46).

87. Museum of Tolerance, Multimedia Learning Center, http://motlc.wiesenthal. com/text/x07/xr0776.html, accessed 26 December 2003.

88. Matthew Scanlan, 'The KGB's Masonic Files Returned to France' in *Freemasonry Today*, Issue 18, October 2001.

89. I am grateful to Evert Kwaadgras for the information provided on Freemasons; e-mail of 16 January 2004.

90. Evert Kwaadgras, e-mail to the author, 16 January 2004.

91. Ibid., 12 January 2004.

92. Ibid., 16 January 2004.

93. Obstfeld, e-mail to the author, 16 December 2009.

94. Ibid., 14 September 2002.

95. Ibid., 1 December 2009.

96. Marion Schreiber, *Silent Rebels* (London: Atlantic Books, 2003), Appendix, pp. 269–308.

97. Ian Black, 'The Heroes of Mechelen', the *Guardian*, 19 June 2003.

98. Schreiber, *Silent Rebels*, pp. 242–4.

99. Hephzibah Anderson, 'Survivors of heroic raid on train 801' in *Jewish Chronicle*, 20 June 2003.

100. Rose-Marie Guilfoyle, e-mail to the author, 3 August 2004. I am grateful to Ms Guilfoyle who interviewed M. Maistriau on my behalf because she is bilingual and he spoke no English. He was apparently very pleased at my interest in his story.

101. Paul Spiegel, Foreword in Schreiber's *Silent Rebels*, p. ix. Paul Spiegel was the President of the Central Council of Jews in Germany, and was himself saved by being hidden as a small boy by a Belgian family. He died on 30 April 2004 aged 68.

102. Steve Jelbert, e-mail to the author, 24 July 2003.

103. Steve Jelbert, 'A great escape' in *The Times* Play Section, 19 July 2003 (review of *Silent Rebels*).

104. Jelbert, e-mail to the author, 25 July 2003.

105. Schreiber, *Silent Rebels*, p. 89.

106. Ibid., p. 90.

107. Black, 'The Heroes of Mechelen', 19 June 2003.

108. Schreiber, *Silent Rebels*, p. 4.

109. Robert McCrum, 'What ho, Adolf', *The Observer Review*, 18 November 2001, p. 2.

110. Spiegel, Foreword in Schreiber's *Silent Rebels*, p. ix.

111. Simon Kuper, *Ajax, the Dutch, the War: Football in Europe During the Second World War* (London: Orion, 2003), p. 137.

112. Hannah Arendt, *Eichmann in Jerusalem* (London: Penguin, 1994), pp. 169–70.

113. Rose Marie Guilfoyle, e-mails to the author, 6, 7 and 10 September 2004.

114. Robert Maistriau, meeting with Rose Marie Guilfoyle in Brussels, 2 August 2004.

115. 'Belgium bids farewell to resistance hero who saved Jews', Haaretz, 2 October 2008.

116. 'Aryanised' is the term for the compulsory taking over of Jewish property by non-Jews.

117. Otto Fleming, notes on Mitzi, 21 May 1997.

118. Otto Fleming, telephone conversation with the author, 12 March 2001.
119. Dorothy Fleming, e-mail to the author, 12 December 2009.
120. Otto Fleming, 'A Jewish Family in Hietzing', unpublished memoir, December 2002.
121. Ibid., pp. 7–8.
122. Ibid., p. 9.
123. Dorothy Fleming, e-mail to the author, 26 December 2009 (12:46).
124. Ibid., (13:01).
125. Otto Fleming, telephone conversation with the author, 25 May 1997.
126. The area was part of Germany until 1918, when it became Polish.
127. Doris Stiefel, e-mail to the author, 19 March 2001.
128. Else Pintus, 'The Diary of Else Pintus: The Story of a Holocaust Survivor', 1947, unpublished diary translated by Doris Stiefel (née Pintus), June 1998, and sent to the author, p. 43.
129. Ibid., pp. 43–4.
130. Ibid., p. 44.
131. Judith Marton, *The Diary of Eva Heyman* (New York: Yad Vashem, 1988), p. 20.
132. Ibid., pp. 94–5.
133. Adina Blady Szwajger, *I Remember Nothing More* (London: Collins Harvill, 1990), p. 164.
134. Pintus, 'The Diary of Else Pintus', p. 45.
135. Ibid., p. 49.
136. Ibid., p. 52.
137. Ibid., p. 58.
138. Else Pintus, letter to Erich Pintus dated 26 September 1949, sent by Doris Stiefel; translated from the original by Prof. Hamish Ritchie.
139. Zsoka Mayer, 'The History of the Mayer Family', unpublished memoir written by Naomi Szinai's sister in 1997, p. 1. Sent to the author by Naomi in June 2003. (Elizabeth was known as Zsoka.)
140. Ibid., p. 3.
141. Naomi Szinai, 'My Moment of Truth: A Summernight's Journey', 1997, unpublished memoir found in the Wiener Library (K4b (1)H), p. 1.
142. Naomi Szinai, telephone conversation with the author, 9 March 2003.
143. Szinai, 'My Moment of Truth', p. 2.
144. Ibid., p. 4.
145. Ibid., p. 5.
146. Ibid., pp. 7–8.
147. Mayer, 'The History of the Mayer Family', p. 4.
148. Mr and Mrs Bela Grunfeld, declaration to Yad Vashem in Tel Aviv, 26 December 1967. Translated from Hungarian by Dr Tom Keve.
149. Grunfeld declaration.
150. János Tóth, undated memoir sent by Yad Vashem, 18 February 2004, File No 8588. Translated from Hungarian by Dr Tom Keve.
151. Ibid.
152. Ibid.
153. Dvora Weis, e-mail to author, 2 March 2004, from Department of the Righteous, Yad Vashem.

154. Hilde Holger, letter to the author, 22 August 2000.

155. Julia Pascal, obituary of Hilde Holger, the *Guardian*, 26 September 2006.

156. Hilde Holger, 'Hilde Holger History Notes', unpublished memoir written around 1990, p. 9. I am grateful to Primavera Boman-Behram, Hilde's daughter, for sharing this material with me in 2009.

157. Ibid.

158. Ibid., p. 10.

159. Primavera told me her cousin Mimi Schwartz told her the number was twenty-five, but Hilde has written fourteen.

160. Dr Margit Franz, e-mail to the author, 6 December 2009 (21:39).

161. www.mkgandhi.org/articles/ginterview.htm. Dehra Dun's most famous inmate was Heinrich Harrer, who after several attempts finally escaped in 1944. He recounted his time at the camp in *Seven Years in Tibet* (Rupert Hart-Davis, 1953) and *Beyond Seven Years in Tibet: my life before, during and after* (Labyrynth Press, 2007).

162. 'Cultural Activities of Delhi I.F.L. Centre', *The Evening News*, 13 February 1951.

163. Franz, e-mail to the author, 6 December 2009 (21:48).

164. Pascal, obituary of Hilde Holger, 26 September 2001.

165. Margarita Turkov, 'When Darkness Prevailed: A Holocaust Memoir', unpublished memoir dated 2003, sent to the author from Oregon, Pt 2, p. 26.

166. Ibid., pp. 1, 4.

167. Ibid., pp. 6–7.

168. Ibid., p. 10.

169. Ibid., p. 11.

170. Ibid., pp. 12–13.

171. Ibid., p. 14.

172. Ibid., p. 17.

173. Ibid., p. 37.

174. Margarita Turkov, e-mail to the author, 11 December 2003.

175. Ibid., 9 December 2003.

176. Lea Goodman, autobiographical letter to her niece Laura, May 1992, p. 1.

177. Lea Goodman, 'In Slovakia and in Poland' in *Zachor*, pp. 75–7.

178. Goodman, autobiographical letter to her niece, May 1992, p. 4.

179. Ibid., p. 3.

180. Robert Rozett, 'From Poland to Hungary, Rescue Attempts 1943–44', Yad Vashem Studies, Vol. 24, 1995, pp. 177–93, cited in Goodman, autobiographical letter, May 1992, p. 5.

181. Goodman, letter to the author, received 8 January 2010.

CONCLUSIONS

1.   Monica Porter, e-mail to the author, 17 November 2002.

2.   Jaap van Proosdij, letter to the author, 12 January 2004.

3.   Andy Marino, *American Pimpernel: The man who saved the artists on Hitler's death list* (London: Hutchinson, 1999), p. 337.

4.   Agnes Spier, *Affected by Atrocity*, p. 87.

5.   Agnes Hirschi, e-mail to the author, 15 March 2001.

6.   Agnes Hirschi, notes of meeting with the author in London, 14 April 2002.

7.   Arnold Brown, notes of telephone conversation with the author,
     22 November 2001.

8.   Jane Marks, *The Hidden Children: The Secret Survivors of the Holocaust* (London:
     Bantam, 1993), p. 253.

9.   Zygmunt Bauman, *Modernity and the Holocaust* (Cambridge: Polity Press, 1991),
     pp. 5–7.

10. Michael Burleigh, 'The Chill of Evil' book review, *Sunday Times Culture* magazine,
     25 July 2004.

11. Dr Moshe Bejski, 'The Righteous Among the Nations', in *Rescue Attempts
     during the Holocaust*, ed. Y. Gutman and E. Zuroff (Jerusalem: 1977), based on
     Proceedings of the Second Yad Vashem International Historical Conference,
     April 1974, pp. 634–5.

12. Hubert Locke, 'My Professional and Spiritual Journey', *Perspectives*, Autumn
     2003, p. 22.

13. Thomas Powers, 'The everyday life of tyranny' in *The London Review of Books*,
     Vol. 20, No 18, 21 September 2000, pp. 3–7.

14. Hugo Gryn, *Chasing Shadows: Memories of a Vanished World* (London: Viking,
     2000), pp. 236–7.

15. Monia Avrahmi, *Flames in the Ashes*, written in 1985 for the film. Monia
     worked at the museum.

16. H.D. Leuner, *When Compassion was a Crime: Germany's Silent Heroes 1933–45*
     (London: Wolff, 1966), p. 71.

17. Ewa Berberyusz, 'Guilt by Neglect' in *My Brother's Keeper? Recent Polish
     Debates on the Holocaust*, ed. Antony Polonsky (London: Routledge, 1990),
     pp. 69–71 (70).

18. Leonard Baker, *Days of Sorrow and Pain: Leo Baeck and the Berlin Jews* (New
     York: OUP, 1981), pp. 156–7.

19. Dr Frances Henry, 'Were All Bystanders Indifferent or Malevolent?' in
     Dimensions: A Journal of Holocaust Studies, Fall 1985, Vol. 1, No 2, pp. 7–10 (8).

20. Victoria J. Barnett, *Bystanders; Conscience and Complicity During the Holocaust*
     (Westport: Greenwood Press, 1999), p. 2.

21. Ibid., p. 3.

22. Ibid., p. 4.

23. Ibid., p. 5.

24. Henry, 'Were All Bystanders Indifferent or Malevolent?', p. 10.

25. Yehuda Bauer, *The Holocaust in Historical Perspective* (London: Sheldon Press,
     1978), pp. 91–2.

26. Bauer, 'Jew and Gentile: The Holocaust and After' in *The Holocaust in Historical
     Perspective*.

27. Ibid., pp. 77–8.

28. Adam LeBor and Roger Boyes, *Surviving Hitler: Choices, Corruption and
     Compromise in the Third Reich* (London: Simon & Schuster, 2000), p. 306.

29. Nechama Tec, *When Light Pierced the Darkness; Christian Rescue of Jews in Nazi-
     Occupied Poland* (Oxford: OUP, 1987), p. 65.

30. Ibid., pp. 64–6.

31. Ibid., pp. 66–8.

32. Michal Grynberg (ed.), *Words to Outlive Us: Eyewitness Accounts from the Warsaw Ghetto* (London: Granta, 2003), p. 19.

33. Irene Gut Opdyke, *In My Hands: Memories of a Holocaust Rescuer* (New York: Knopf, 1999), p. 83.

34. Piotr Wilczek, 'Michal Glowinski, Czarne Sezony', *Chicago Review*, 2000, 3/4, Vol. 46, pp. 383–5 (383).

35. Marci Shore, translator's Preface to *The Black Seasons*, sent to the author by e-mail, 8 July 2004, p. 1.

36. Michal Glowinski, *The Black Seasons*, trans. Marci Shore, p. 77. (I am grateful to Marci for sending me the complete translated manuscript prior to publication in December 2004.)

37. Ibid., p. 79.

38. Michal Glowinski, 'A Quarter-Hour Passed in a Pastry Shop', cited in Jan T. Gross' *Neighbours* (Woodstock: PUP, 2001), pp. 135, 241.

39. Margaret A. Salinger, *Dream Catcher* (New York: Washington Square Press, 2000), p. 55.

40. Adina Blady Szwajger, *I Remember Nothing More* (London: Collins Harvill, 1990), p. 164.

41. Czeslaw Milosz, *Campo dei Fiori*, 1943, in *Holocaust Poetry* (London: Fount, 1995), p. 168, verse 5. This Polish poet received the Nobel Prize for Literature in 1980.

42. Szwajger, *I Remember Nothing More*, p. 87.

43. Barnett, *Bystanders*, p. 112.

44. Elie Wiesel and Richard D. Heffner, *Conversations with Elie Wiesel* (New York: Schocken Books, 2001), p. 14.

45. Gerda Haas, letter to the author, 29 April 2000.

46. Henry Walton, letter to the author, 20 August 2000.

47. Ibid., 10 August 2000.

48. Barbara Lovenheim, *Survival in the Shadows: Seven Hidden Jews in Hitler's Berlin* (London: Peter Owen, 2002), p. 19.

49. Roman Halter, 'The Kindness of Strangers' in *Perspectives: Journal of the Holocaust Centre*, Beth Shalom, Autumn 2003, pp. 10–11.

50. Max Hastings, 'The Shameful Peace: How French Artists and Intellectuals Survived the Nazi Occupation' in *The Sunday Times*, 23 November 2008.

51. Philip Gourevitch, 'Behold now Behemoth: The Holocaust Memorial Museum: one more American Theme Park', *Harper's Magazine*, July 1993.

52. 'Reporting the Story of a Genocide', conversation with Philip Gourevitch, Institute of International Studies, UC Berkeley, 11 February 2000, p. 6.

53. Salinger, *Dream Catcher*, p. 45.

54. Berel Lang, 'Uncovering Certain Mischievous Questions About the Holocaust', Ina Levine Scholar-in-Residence Annual Lecture, 12 March 2002, p. 11.

55. Ian Kershaw, *Popular Opinion & Political Dissent in the Third Reich: Bavaria 1933–1945* (Oxford: Clarendon Press, 1988), p. vii.

56. Ibid., p. viii.

57. Christopher Browning, Tables 1 & 2, *Ordinary Men*, pp. 191–2.

58. Raul Hilberg, *The Destruction of the European Jews* (New York: 1985), cited by Browning, p. 194.

59. Browning, *Ordinary Men*, p. xvi.

60. Ibid., p. xx.

61. Ibid., p. 188.

62. Ibid., p. 2.

63. Kristen Renwick Monroe, *John Donne's People*, pp. 427–8.

64. Nicholas Wapshott, 'Archbishop of Canterbury blamed the Jews for excesses of the Nazis' in *The Times*, 23 April 2004, p. 11.

65. Arthur Berger, Papers of Ambassador James G. McDonald, Record Rise of Nazism to Creation of Israel, Washington Holocaust Museum Press Release, 22 April 2004, p. 2; www.ushmm.org/museum/press/archive/collections/mcdondiary/htm, accessed 2 May 2004.

66. Ibid.

67. James G. McDonald, Letter of Resignation to the Secretary General of the League of Nations (London: 1935).

68. Ibid., p. 5.

69. 'Petition in Support of James Grover McDonald's Letter of Resignation', undated printed booklet in British Library, ref: 20087 b.38.

70. James G. McDonald, *Palestine to the Rescue* (London: Jewish Agency, 1943), p. 3. Document in the British Library, ref: 4035.aa.15.

71. James G. McDonald, *My Mission in Israel 1948–1951* (London: Gollancz, 1951), p. xi.

72. Ibid., p. iii.

73. House of Lords, *Hansard*, Column 811–21, 858–60.

74. House of Lords, Columns 820–1.

75. CCJ website, www.ccj.org.uk/history.html, accessed 3 January 2010.

76. David Wyman, 'Remembering William Temple' in *Jerusalem Post*, 20 February 2006.

77. 'Stein plea to Pius XI' in *Jewish Chronicle*, 28 February 2003.

78. John Cornwell, *Hitler's Pope: The Secret History of Pius XII* (London: Penguin, 1999), p. 140.

79. Susanne M. Batzdorff, *Edith Stein: Selected Writings* (Illinois: 1990), pp. 16–7. Ms Batzdorff is Edith Stein's niece.

80. 'Stein plea to Pius XI', 28 February 2003.

81. Batzdorff, *Edith Stein*, p. 17.

82. Epstein and Rosen, *Dictionary of the Holocaust* (Westport: Greenwood Press, 1997).

83. Abraham H. Foxman and Rabbi Leon Klenicki, *The Canonization of Edith Stein: An Unnecessary Problem*, www.adl.org/opinion/edith_stein.asp, October 1998, pp. 1–3 (3).

84. Jean Medawar and David Pyke, *Hitler's Gift: Scientists Who Fled Nazi Germany* (London: Piatkus, 2002), pp. 53–4.

85. Fry, *Surrender on Demand*, p. 224.

86. Varian Fry, 'The Massacre of the Jews' in *The New Republic*, 21 December 1942.

87. Amy Z. Gottlieb, *Men of Vision: Anglo-Jewry's Aid to Victims of the Nazi regime 1933–1945* (London: Weidenfeld & Nicolson, 1998), p. 44.

88. Viscount Templewood, *Nine Troubled Years* (London: 1954), p. 240.

89. Hansard, 7 July 1938 – Written Answers (Commons), http://hansard.millbank-systems.com/written_answers/1938/jul/07/refugees, accessed 5 January 2010.

90. Hansard, 14 July 1938. William Thorn (1857–1946) had been an MP since 1906.

91. Gottlieb, *Men of Vision*, p. 45.

92. Dr Ralph Kohn, *Nazi Persecution – Britain's gift: A personal reflection* (London: The Royal Society and Cara, May 2009), pp. 6, 7.

93. Lord Beveridge, *A Defence of Free Learning* (London: OUP, 1959), p. 1.

94. R.M. Cooper, *Refugee Scholars: Conversations with Tess Simpson* (Leeds: Moorland Books, 1992), p. 33.

95. Duke of Devonshire, letter to the author, 7 April 2000.

96. Notes of the author's meeting with the Duke of Devonshire in his study at Chatsworth, 25 October 2000.

97. Duke of Devonshire, letter to the author, 13 April 2000.

98. CARA booklet, p. 4.

99. Archie Burnett (ed.) *The Letters of A.E. Housman* (Oxford: Clarendon Press, 2007), 2 vols.

100. CARA booklet, pp. 13, 15.

101. Norman Bentwich, *They Found Refuge* (London: The Cresset Press, 1956), p. 67.

102. BBC *Breakfast with Frost*, Sir David Frost interviewed Bill Clinton on Sunday 18 July 2004.

103. Robert Walker, 'Rwanda Remembers the Holocaust', BBC News, 27 January 2005.

104. Sula and Paul's stories are on the Holocaust Memorial Day Trust's website: www.hmd.org.uk.

105. Stefan Lovgren, '"Hotel Rwanda" Portrays Hero Who Fought Genocide', National Geographic News, 9 December 2004, http://news.nationalgeo-graphic.com/news/pf/44550124.html.

106. Philip Gourevitch, 'Reporting the Story of a Genocide', at Berkeley University, 11 February 2000, http://globetrotter.berkeley.edu/people/Gourevitch/gourevitch-con4.html.

107. Holocaust Memorial Day Trust website: www.hmd.org.uk.

108. Ibid.

109. Etgar Lefkovits, 'Rwandan genocide survivors look to Israel' in *Jerusalem Post*, 3 November 2005.

110. Yifat Bachrach-Ron, 'Shaping Remembrance: Seminar for Survivors of the Rwandan Genocide' in *Yad Vashem Quarterly Magazine*, Vol. 40, Winter 2006.

111. Elie Wiesel, speech at the Darfur Emergency Summit, 14 July 2004 in New York (www.ajws.org), cited in *Darfur: A Jewish Response* (London: The Pears Foundation, 2007), pp. 11–2.

112. Yom Hashoah is the Israeli Holocaust Memorial Day established by law in 1951 when Ben Gurion was Prime Minister. It is marked on 27 Nisan which falls around April or May.

113. 'IsraCast: Darfur and the Holocaust', Sunday 22 April 2007, www.isracast.com/article.aspx?id=546, accessed 15 December 2009.

114. Oona King, 'With fragile optimism' in the *Guardian*, 19 April 2006.

115. Simon Round, interview with James Smith, *Jewish Chronicle*, 2 September 2009.

116. Rabbi Hugo Gryn, *Chasing Shadows: Memories of a Vanished World* (London: Viking, 2000), p. 258.

117. Tara McCartney, 'I kept saying, "Help me, help me." But no one did', the *Guardian*, 4 August 2005.

118. Peter Walker, 'Police errors contributed to suicide of tormented mother Fiona Pilkington', the *Guardian*, 28 September 2009.

119. Edmund Burke, *Thoughts on the Cause of the Present Discontents* (1770), p. 71.

120. Elie Wiesel and Richard D. Heffner, *Conversations with Elie Wiesel* (New York: Schocken Books, 2001), p. 14.

121. Eugene Heimler, *Resistance Against Tyranny* (London: Routledge & Kegan Paul, 1966), p. xi.

122. Zygmunt Bauman, *Modernity and the Holocaust* (Cambridge: Polity Press, 1993), p. 151.

123. Stanley Milgram, *Obedience to Authority: An Experimental View* (Tavistock Publications, 1974).

124. Since the famous Genovese case was reported in the *New York Times* in 1964, several articles have suggested the case was largely misrepresented because of inaccuracies in the article.

125. J.M. Darley & B. Latané, 'Bystander Apathy' in *American Scientist*, 1969, No 57, pp. 244–68.

126. Kristen Renwick Monroe, 'John Donne's People' in *Journal of Politics*, Vol. 53, No 2, May 1991, pp. 394–433.

127. Yehuda Bauer, *The Holocaust in Historical Perspective*, pp. 91–2.

POSTSCRIPT TO THE PAPERBACK EDITION

1. Tiny van Rijswijk and her son Ed, Skype conversation with the author, 17 November 2010.

2. Klara Aardewerk, unpublished memoir (1979), p. 4.

3. Ibid., p. 5.

4. Arleen Kennedy, e-mail to the author, 10 January 2011.

5. Klara Aardewerk, unpublished memoir, p. 7.

6. Ibid., p. 9.

7. Ibid., pp. 10–18.

8. Ibid., p. 21.

9. David Clark, e-mail to the author, 13 February 2011.

10. Siegmund Weltlinger, 'Men Record their Experiences of the Holocaust' for HEART, www.holocaustresearchproject.org/survivor/men.html, accessed 12 February 2011.

11. David Clark, e-mail to the author, 13 February 2011.

12. Clark, e-mail to the author, 13 February 2011.

13. Dr J. Tuchel, address at unveiling of plaque in memory of Dorothy and George Möhring, 16 September 2010. I am grateful to David Clark for his translation from the German on p. 1.

14. Tuchel, p. 3.
15. Barbara Schieb, e-mail to the author, 28 February 2011.
16. Tuchel, p. 3.
17. Ibid., p. 4.
18. Lilian Black, e-mail to the author, 11 February 2011. I am grateful to Lilian, who chairs the Holocaust Survivors Friendship Association based in Leeds, for the information about her father Eugene Black.
19. Doris Stiefel, e-mail to the author, 1 April 2010.
20. Miloslawa Borzyskowska, *Jewish Footsteps Across Kashubia: A Guide Book* (2006). This book is a joint Polish, Kashubian, German and Israeli project by the Kaszubski Institute in Gdansk and the Baltic Academy in Lübeck. There is also a later edition in 2010. These books are only available in Polish/German.
21. Doris Stiefel, *Notes on Max Pintus* (February 2011). Sent to the author 11 February 2011. The US spellings are kept.
22. Dr Borzyskowska, e-mail to the author, 7 December 2011.
23. Stiefel, *Notes on Max Pintus*.
24. Stiefel, e-mail to the author, 27 February 2011.
25. Stiefel, e-mail to the author, 14 February 2011.
26. Martin Gilbert, *Dent Atlas of the Holocaust* (London: J.M. Dent Ltd, 1993), p. 34, Map 30.
27. Jeremy Godden, *The Steinhardts and the Cedar Boys*, unpublished memoir (2004), p. 2. See also, www.scribd.com/doc/24545683/The-Steinhardt-family-and-the-Cedar-Boys.
28. Ibid., pp. 2, 8.
29. Ibid., pp. 17–18.

APPENDIX I

1. Avner Shapiro, 'Beisky's court of the righteous', www.haaretz.com, 17 April 2007.
2. Mordecai Paldiel, Haaretz, Talkback, 17 April 2007.
3. Moshe Bejski in the Italian Parliament, Gardens of the Righteous Worldwide, GARIWO website: www.forestadeigiusti.net/attivita.

BIBLIOGRAPHY

Arendt, Hannah, *Eichmann in Jerusalem* (London: Penguin, 1994)

Bailey, Brenda, *A Quaker Couple in Nazi Germany: Leonard Friedrich Survives Buchenwald* (York: Ebor Press, 1994)

Baker, Leonard, *Days of Sorrow and Pain; Leo Baeck and the Berlin Jews* (New York: OUP, 1981)

Barnett, Victoria J., *Bystanders, Conscience and Complicity During the Holocaust* (Westport: Greenwood Press, 1999)

Batzdorff, Susanne M., *Edith Stein: Selected Writings* (Illinois: 1990)

Bauer, Yehuda, *The Holocaust in Historical Perspective* (London: Sheldon Press, 1978)

———, *Jews for Sale? Nazi-Jewish Negotiations, 1939–1945* (Yale: Yale UP, 1994)

Bauman, Zygmunt, *Modernity and the Holocaust* (Cambridge: Polity Press, 1991)

Bejski, Dr Moshe, 'The Righteous among the Nations', *Rescue Attempts During the Holocaust* (eds) Y. Gutman and E. Zuroff (Jerusalem: 1977), Proceedings of the Second Yad Vashem International Historical Conference, April 1974

———, *Solution in Poland* (New York: HarperCollins, 1992)

Cornwell, John, *Hitler's Pope: The Secret History of Pius XII* (London: Viking, 1999)

Dawidowicz, Lucy S., *The War Against the Jews 1933–45* (London: Penguin, 1990)

Devonshire, Andrew, *Accidents of Fortune* (Norwich: Michael Russell Ltd, 2004)

Donne, John, *Devotions upon Emergent Occasions (1624) Mediation XVII*

Dwork, Debórah, *Children with a Star: Jewish Youth in Nazi Europe* (New Haven: Yale UP, 1991)

Dying We Live: The final messages and records of some Germans who defied Hitler (London: Fontana, 1960)

Eliot, George, *Middlemarch* (London: Penguin, 1994)

Erenburg, Mikhail and Sakaitè, Viktorija, *Hands Bringing Life and Bread* (Vilnius: Vilna Gaon Jewish State Museum, 1997), 2 vols

'Ethics of the Fathers', the *Authorised Daily Prayer Book*, Chapter II, Verses 20–21 (London: Eyre and Spottiswood, 1962)

Fensch, Thomas (ed.) *Oskar Schindler and His List* (Vermont: Eriksson, 1995)

Fogelman, Eva, *Conscience & Courage: Rescuers of Jews During the Holocaust* (London: Cassell, 1995)

Fralon, José-Alain, *A Good Man in Evil Times* (London: Viking, 2000)

Fry, Varian, *Surrender on Demand* (Boulder: Johnson Books, 1997)

Gilbert, Martin, *The Boys* (London: Orion, 1996)

Glowinski, Michal, *Czarne Sezony*, trans. Marci Shore

———, 'A Quarter-Hour Passed in a Pastry Shop', cited in Jan T. Gross, *Neighbors: The Destruction of the Jewish Community in Jedwabne, Poland* (Princeton: PUP, 2001)

Gold, Mary Jayne, *Crossroads Marseilles 1940* (New York: Doubleday, 1980)

Gottlieb, Amy, *Men of Vision: Anglo-Jewry's Aid to Victims of the Nazi Regime 1933–1945* (London: Weidenfeld & Nicolson, 1998)

Gryn, Rabbi Hugo, *Chasing Shadows: Memories of a Vanished World* (London: Viking, 2000)

Grynberg, Michal (ed.) *Words to Outlive Us: Eyewitness Accounts from the Warsaw Ghetto* (London: Granta, 2003)

Gutteridge, Richard, *Open the Mouth for the Dumb! The German Evangelical Church and the Jews 1879–1950* (Oxford: Blackwell, 1976)

Hahn-Beer, Edith, *The Nazi Officer's Wife* (London: Little Brown, 2000)

Harris & Oppenheimer, *Into the Arms of Strangers* (London: Bloomsbury, 2000)

Henson, Hensley, Introduction to the *Yellow Book* (London: Victor Gollancz Ltd, 1936)

Hilberg, Raul, *Perpetrators, Victims, Bystanders: The Jewish Catastrophe 1933–1945* (London: Lime Tree, 1993)

Hughes, Robert, *Frank Auerbach* (London: Thames and Hudson, 1990)

Isenberg, Sheila, *A Hero of Our Own: The Story of Varian Fry* (Random House, 2001)

Jasper, Ronald C.D., *George Bell: Bishop of Chichester* (London: OUP, 1967)

Kershaw, Ian, *Popular Opinion & Political Dissent in the Third Reich: Bavaria 1933–1945* (Oxford: Clarendon Press, 1988)

King, Christine, 'Jehovah's Witnesses under Nazism' in *A Mosaic of Victims: Non-Jews Persecuted and Murdered by the Nazis* (ed.) Michael Berenbaum (London: Tauris, 1990)

Kohn, Dr Ralph, *Nazi Persecution – Britain's gift* (London: The Royal Society & CARA, 2009)

Kuper, Simon, *Ajax, the Dutch, the War: Football in Europe During the Second World War* (London: Orion, 2003)

Latané, Bibb & Darley, John M., *The Unresponsive Bystander: Why doesn't he help?* (New York: ACC, 1970)

LeBor, Adam & Boyes, Roger, *Surviving Hitler: Choices, Corruption and Compromise in the Third Reich* (London: Simon & Schuster, 2000)

Lee, Carol Ann, *The Hidden Life of Otto Frank* (London: Viking, 2002)

Leuner, H.D., *When Compassion was a Crime: Germany's silent heroes* (London: Wolff, 1966)

Levi, Primo, *If this is a Man* (London: Abacus, 1979)

London, Louise, *Whitehall and the Jews, 1933–1948: British Immigration and the Holocaust* (Cambridge: CUP, 2000)

London, Perry, 'The Rescuers: Motivational Hypotheses About Christians Who Saved Jews from the Nazis' in *Altruism and Helping Behaviour*, (eds) Macauley and Berkowitz (1970)

Lovenheim, Barbara, *Survival in the Shadows: Seven Hidden Jews in Hitler's Berlin* (London: Peter Owen, 2002)

Marino, Andy, *American Pimpernel: The man who saved the artists on Hitler's death list* (London: Hutchinson, 1999)

Marks, Jane, *The Hidden Children: The Secret Survivors of the Holocaust* (London: Bantam, 1997)

Martin, Josie Levy, *Never Tell Your Name* (First Books, 2002)

Marton, Dr Judah, *The Diary of Eva Heyman* (New York: Shapolsky, 1998)

Medawar, Jean & Pyke, David, *Hitler's Gift: Scientists Who Fled Nazi Germany* (London: Piatkus, 2002)

Moorehead, Caroline, *Iris Origo: Marchesa of Val D'Orcia* (London: Murray, 2000)

Oliner and Oliner, *The Altruistic Personality* (New York: Free Press, 1988)

Opdyke, Irene Gut, *In my Hands: Memories of a Holocaust Rescuer* (New York: Knopf, 1999)

Origo, Iris, *Images and Shadows: Part of a Life* (London: John Murray, 1998)

———, *War in Val d'Orcia: An Italian War Diary, 1943–1944* (London: Allison & Busby, 1999)

Paldiel, Mordecai, *The Face of the Other: Reflections on the Motivations of Gentile Rescuers of Jews*, (RFTF, 2000)

———, *The Path of the Righteous: Gentile Rescuers of Jews During the Holocaust* (New Jersey: KTAV, 1993)

Paris, Erna, *Long Shadows: Truth, Lies and History* (London: Bloomsbury, 2001)

Polonsky, Antony, *My Brother's Keeper: Recent Polish Debates on the Holocaust* (London: Routledge, 1998)

Porter, Monica, *Deadly Carousel: A Singer's Story of the Second World War* (London: Quartet, 1990)

Quakers, *Gathered Stories: Commemorating the Kindertransport* (London: Quakers, 2008)

Rittner, Carol & Myers, Sondra, *The Courage to Care: Rescuers of Jews During the Holocaust* (New York: New York UP, 1986)

Rosenthal, A.M., *Thirty-Eight Witnesses* (Berkeley: University of California Press, 1999)

Salinger, Margaret A., *Dream Catcher: A Memoir* (New York: Washington Square Press. 2000)

Schindler, Emilie, *Where Light and Shadow Meet: A Memoir* (New York: Norton, 1996)

Schmitt, Hans A., *Quakers and Nazis: Inner Light in Outer Darkness* (Columbia: University of Missouri Press, 1997)

Schreiber, Marion, *Silent Rebels* (London: Atlantic Books, 2003)

Sharf, Andrew, 'The British Press and the Holocaust' in *Yad Vashem Studies V* (Jerusalem: Yad Vashem, 1963)

Shepherd, Naomi, *A Refuge from Darkness: Wilfrid Israel and the Rescue of the Jews* (New York: Pantheon, 1984)

Silver, Eric, *The Book of the Just: The Silent Heroes who Saved Jews from Hitler* (London: Weidenfeld & Nicolson, 1992)

Simpson, William W. & Wehl, Ruth, *The Story of the International Council of Christians and Jews* (London: CCJ, 1988)

Slack, Kenneth, *George Bell* (London: SCM Press Ltd, 1971)

Smith, Michael, *Foley: The Spy Who Saved 10,000 Jews* (London: Hodder & Stoughton, 1999)

Spiegel, Paul, Foreword in *Silent Rebels* (London: Atlantic Books, 2003)

Steinhouse, Herbert, 'The Man Who Saved a Thousand Lives' in *Oskar Schindler and His List* (ed.) Thomas Fensch (Forest Dale, Vermont: Eriksson, 1995)

Szwajger, Adina Blady, *I Remember Nothing More* (London: Collins Harvill, 1990)

Tec, Nechama, *When Light Pierced the Darkness: Christian Rescue of Jews in Nazi-Occupied Poland* (Oxford: OUP, 1987)

The Child Survivors' Association of Great Britain, *Zachor* (London: Elliott & Thompson, 2005)

'The Ethics of the Fathers', in the *Authorised Daily Prayer Book*, trans. Rev. S. Singer (London: Eyre and Spottiswood, 1962)

Tschuy, Theo, *Dangerous Diplomacy: The Story of Carl Lutz, rescuer of 62,000 Hungarian Jews* (Grand Rapids: Eerdmans, 2000)

Wasserstein, Bernard, *Britain and the Jews of Europe 1939–1945* (London: Leicester UP, 1999)

Wiesel, Elie & Heffner, Richard D., *Conversations with Elie Wiesel* (New York: Schocken Books, 2001)

Zembsch-Schreve, Guido, *Pierre Lalande: Special Agent* (London: Pen & Sword Books Ltd, 1998)

INDEX